Under the Maastricht Treaty, the countries of the European Union plan to form a monetary union by 1999, with a single currency and a single central bank. This book provides a comprehensive analysis of the plan for European monetary union contained in the treaty. Peter Kenen examines the provisions of the treaty itself, shows how they evolved, asks what must be done to implement them, and explores the problems they will pose. Kenen goes far beyond the treaty, however, to survey and assess recent research by economists on the benefits and costs of monetary unions, the conduct of monetary policy, and the consequences of large public deficits and debts.

The European exchange rate crises of 1992 and 1993 are analyzed, as well as their impact on the prospects for monetary union and the problems they pose for implementation of the Maastricht Treaty. The author makes specific proposals for handling the transition to a single currency, integrating the existing central banks into a single system, and modifying parts of the treaty itself. The implications of European monetary union for the international monetary system are also considered.

Economic and monetary union in Europe

Economic and monetary union in Europe

Moving beyond Maastricht

PETER B. KENEN
Princeton University

CAMBRIDGE
UNIVERSITY PRESS

PUBLISHED BY THE PRESS SYNDICATE OF THE UNIVERSITY OF CAMBRIDGE
The Pitt Building, Trumpington Street, Cambridge CB2 1RP, United Kingdom

CAMBRIDGE UNIVERSITY PRESS
The Edinburgh Building, Cambridge CB2 2RU, United Kingdom
40 West 20th Street, New York, NY 10011-4211, USA
10 Stamford Road, Oakleigh, Melbourne 3166, Australia

First published 1995
Reprinted 1996

Printed in the United States of America

Typeset in Times

A catalogue record for this book is available from the British Library

Library of Congess Cataloguing-in-Publication Data is available

ISBN 0-521-47079-X hardback
ISBN 0-521-55883-2 paperback

Contents

Preface

In September 1992, I began a five-month visit to the Bank of England as a Houblon-Norman Fellow, planning to think and write about international monetary cooperation. My hosts, however, had other plans. They asked if I would like to follow the work of the intergovernmental conference on economic and monetary union in Europe, concentrating on the long-run issues: How might a European central bank formulate and implement a single monetary policy? What role might remain for the national central banks? What are the implications of monetary union for the conduct of national fiscal policies? How would European monetary union affect the functioning of the international monetary system? I was soon fully absorbed by these questions and deeply interested in the negotiations themselves. I drafted several memoranda on those basic issues and a number of short notes on certain provisions of the proposed treaty.

Shortly before the treaty was adopted at the Maastricht Summit, I looked over my work and discovered that it could be converted into a comprehensive critique of the plan for economic and monetary union (EMU) embodied in the treaty, and my hosts at the Bank of England encouraged me to do that. I began work right after the Maastricht Summit and finished the first draft of a monograph six weeks later, just before leaving London. I presented portions of that draft to a conference at the London School of Economics (LSE) and to a seminar at the International Monetary Fund (IMF), where I was a visiting scholar in the spring of 1992. Comments made at those meetings and by readers of the draft led me to revise the monograph during my stay at the Fund, and the Group of Thirty published it as *EMU after Maastricht* in May 1992.

Thereafter, I received detailed comments from many readers, including some of the participants in the drafting of the Maastricht Treaty, and I began to think about revising my monograph to take account of them, as well as the flow of papers on EMU that had begun to cross my desk. A number of events, however, caused me to postpone the project – the June 1992 referendum, in which Denmark rejected the treaty; uncertainty about the outcome of the French referendum scheduled for September 1992; the outbreak of the first exchange rate crisis just before that referendum, and so on. The time seemed ripe in November 1993, when all twelve members of the European Community had ratified the treaty and it entered into force. By that time, however, my desk was piled high with new books and papers on EMU, and I had to read them. I began working on this book in February 1994.

Shortly after the publication of *EMU after Maastricht*, an Australian bookstore wrote to the Group of Thirty asking whether it was a work of fiction or dealt with the care and feeding of emus. When I told this story to one of my Princeton colleagues, he suggested slyly that any book about the Maastricht Treaty had become a work of fiction, which led me to wonder whether I should continue to work on it. Three reasons made me do so. First, the plan for EMU in the treaty deserves careful study, whether or not it is implemented in its original form. If it is implemented in that form, many hard problems will have to be solved. If it is set aside, any subsequent plan will have to answer the same basic questions that faced those who drafted the Maastricht Treaty. Second, another inter-governmental conference is scheduled for 1996, and although it is meant to focus on those parts of the Maastricht Treaty that deal with political cooperation, nothing can prevent the conference from reopening those parts that deal with EMU. Third, events since the Maastricht Summit have shed new light on some of the issues raised by the treaty and have made me change my views on a number of those issues.

This book has the same purposes as *EMU after Maastricht*. It focuses sharply on the Maastricht Treaty, calling attention to gaps and flaws and suggesting ways to deal with them. It is longer than *EMU after Maastricht* because it examines events after the Maastricht Summit and reviews the large body of literature that has appeared since then. It also fills a gap in my earlier work by offering a general cost–benefit assessment of EMU.

I have had much help with this project. I am grateful to the Houblon-Norman Foundation, the Bank of England, and the International Monetary Fund for their hospitality and financial support. I am indebted to participants in seminars at the LSE, the IMF, Columbia University, and Princeton University for posing helpful questions. I owe much to the busy people who read *EMU after Maastricht,* this book, or both, and took time to make comments and suggestions: John Arrowsmith, Roger Clews, Andrew Crockett, Michael Foot, Merwyn King, Ian Plenderleith, and Chris Taylor of the Bank of England and Huw Evans of the U.K. Treasury; Alexander Italianer of the EC Commission; Erik Hoffmeyer of the Danish National Bank; Jacques de Larosière of the Banque de France; Tommaso Padoa-Schioppa and Francesco Papadia of the Banca d'Italia; Helmut Schlesinger and Wolfgang Rieke of the Bundesbank; Günter Baer and his colleagues in the Economics Unit of the Committee of

Governors of the EC Central Banks; David Folkerts-Landau and Donald Mathieson at the IMF; Barry Eichengreen at the University of California at Berkeley; Daniel Gros at the Centre for European Policy Studies; Charles Goodhart at the LSE; Bennett McCallum at Carnegie-Mellon University; Joanne Gowa and Kathleen McNamara at Princeton University; C. Randall Henning at the Institute of International Economics; and students in my workshop on EMU at Princeton's Woodrow Wilson School, especially Jonathan Portes and Jenny Wilkinson. None of them bears any responsibility for the views expressed, and all of the remaining errors are due to ambiguities in the Maastricht Treaty.

CHAPTER 1

The origins of EMU

Introduction

On December 10, 1991, at the Maastricht Summit, the member states of the European Communities (EC) adopted the Treaty on European Union, usually called the Maastricht Treaty. It amends and extends the 1957 Treaty of Rome, which established the European Economic Community (EEC). The ratification of the new treaty took much longer than expected, because of vigorous opposition in some member countries, including Denmark, France, Germany, and the United Kingdom, but the treaty took effect in November 1993. The Maastricht Treaty extends the domain of the EC in many directions. This book deals with those parts that pertain to economic and monetary union (EMU). These provide for the creation of the European System of Central Banks (ESCB), with the European Central Bank (ECB) at its center, and the creation of a new currency, the ECU, to replace the national currencies of the EC countries.[1]

1. These provisions are contained in Title VI of the Treaty on European Union (cited here as TEU) and certain protocols appended to it, including one on the Statute of the European System of Central Banks and of the European Central Bank (cited here as the ESCB Statute) and one on the Statute of the European Monetary Institute (cited here as the EMI Statute). Two other documents are cited below: the draft of the ESCB Statute prepared by the Committee of Central Bank Governors and dated November 27, 1990 (cited as the Governors' Draft), and the draft of the treaty prepared by the Netherlands presidency and dated October 28, 1991 (cited here as the Netherlands Draft). The Governors' Draft was not published but was quoted and distributed widely; the Netherlands Draft of October 28 was published. Another Netherlands draft appeared on the eve of the Maastricht Summit but is not cited here. There were other drafts of these documents, including one prepared in June 1991 by the Luxembourg presidency, and they were cited in the press, but they were not published and are not cited here. Some of those drafts and other documents are cited by Gros and Thygesen (1992) and Bini-Smaghi, Padoa-Schioppa, and Papadia (1994); see also Italianer (1993), who tracks the key issues through successive drafts. After the treaty was ratified, many authors began to refer to the European Union (EU) rather than the European Communities (EC), but the treaty itself says: "The Union shall be founded on the European Communities, supplemented by . . . this Treaty" (Article A). The EU does not supplant the EC. For this reason and because of the need to use EC when discussing events before the ratification of the treaty, I use EC throughout this book.

Figure 1-1 *EMU and the Institutions of the Community*

Members of the *Commission* are appointed by their national governments but do not represent them; they serve as individuals. The Commission is the executive body of the EC but also initiates legislation by proposals and recommendations to the *Council of Ministers,* which represents the member states. The Council must act unanimously on certain matters, including decisions to amend proposals made by the Commission, but it can act on other matters by qualified (weighted) majority voting. A few decisions pertaining to EMU will require unanimity, and some of them are mentioned below. When Council meetings comprise ministers of economics or finance, the Council is known as Ecofin. The Council of Ministers is not the same as the *European Council,* which is the proper name for the EC Summit. The European Council is attended by heads of state or government and the president of the Commission. It acts by "common accord" instead of formal voting. I will usually refer to meetings of the European Council by the cities in which they were held; e.g., the Maastricht Summit. The ECB will have two councils of its own, a General Council and a Governing Council, and I will refer to them by their full names to avoid confusion; hence, references to the Council, without a qualifying adjective, pertain to the Council of Ministers.

The Maastricht Treaty increased the powers of the *European Parliament,* whose members are elected directly in each member country, but its role in EMU will be quite limited. The Council of Ministers will have to "consult" the Parliament on many matters and will have to act in "cooperation" with the Parliament on some other matters. (Where "cooperation" is required, the Parliament can reject or amend a Council decision, but a unanimous vote of the Council can override an objection or amendment made by the Parliament.) The main change in the powers of the Parliament made by the Maastricht Treaty – the requirement that the Parliament "assent" to certain decisions – crops up only rarely in the parts of the treaty that deal with EMU. Certain provisions of the ESCB Statute, for example, can be amended by the Council after receiving the assent of the Parliament.

Much has been written about this subject, and much more will be written in the years ahead, even if the Maastricht Treaty is not implemented fully. This book does not cover every issue raised in that large literature or dwell on the many opportunities and options rejected or ignored on the way to Maastricht. It examines the plan adopted at Maastricht, the implications for the structure and functioning of EMU, the problems of transition, and the possible effects of EMU on the international monetary system.

Chapter 1 looks back at the origins of EMU and the start of the process that led to the Maastricht Treaty. Chapter 2 examines the main decisions that had to be taken during that process and the design of EMU adopted at Maastricht. Chapter 3 looks ahead to the conduct of monetary policy by the ECB and the problems it must face. Chapter 4 deals with the role of fiscal policy in EMU and the relevant provisions of the treaty. And Chapter 5 examines the implications of EMU for the international monetary system.

Chapter 6 looks more closely at the transitional arrangements embodied in the treaty, including the so-called convergence criteria and the tasks of the European Monetary Institute (EMI); it also considers the problems that will have to be resolved if, as now seems likely, some EC countries will not be ready to enter the final stage of EMU.[2] Chapter 7 reexamines the transitional arrangements in the light of events that followed the Maastricht Summit; it pays particular attention to the lessons taught by the crises that beset the European Monetary System (EMS) in 1992 and 1993. Chapter 8 assesses the benefits and costs of EMU and asks whether the present plan for EMU should be revised in 1996, when an intergovernmental conference will be convened to reconsider other parts of the Maastricht Treaty. (Figure 1–1 provides a brief description of the EC institutions involved in developing and managing EMU.)

The Werner Report

The monetary history of the EC has two dimensions. Monetary cooperation began shortly after the Second World War and was intensified thereafter. From time to time, however, proposals were made to move beyond mere cooperation to full-fledged monetary unification – sometimes by officials and sometimes by academics.[3]

Monetary cooperation in Western Europe began long before the creation of the EC, with the establishment of the European Payments Union (EPU) in 1950. The EPU was designed to multilateralize trade and payments within Western Europe and provide a framework for achieving currency convertibility, which was reached at the end of 1958.

2. Countries will not be able to participate unless they meet the convergence criteria. Denmark and the United Kingdom may not be willing to participate, and they can invoke the protocols that let them "opt out" of the final stage.
3. Gros and Thygesen (1992) provide a detailed history; see also Papadia and Saccomani (1994). Ungerer et al. (1990) supply a useful chronology, on which I draw heavily here. Note that I will not distinguish between the European Economic Community (EEC), established by the Treaty of Rome, and the group of communities that now make up the European Communities (EC), with their single Commission and single Council of Ministers.

Figure 1-2 *A brief chronology of EMU*

October 1970	Final report by Werner Committee
March 1971	Council endorses achievement of economic and monetary union by 1980
March 1972	European "snake" established, surrounding bilateral EC exchange rates by narrow band
April 1973	European Monetary Cooperation Fund established
July 1978	Bremen meeting of European Council endorses plan for European Monetary System
March 1979	European Monetary System begins to operate
February 1986	Signing of Single European Act aimed at completing internal market by 1992
June 1988	Hanover meeting of European Council establishes Delors Committee
April 1989	Delors Committee publishes report
June 1989	Madrid meeting of European Council agrees that Stage One of EMU will start on July 1, 1990
December 1989	Strasbourg meeting of European Council calls for intergovernmental conference to design subsequent stages
October 1990	Rome meeting of European Council, with U.K. dissenting, agrees that Stage Two will start on January 1, 1994
December 1990	Beginning of intergovernmental conferences on EMU and political union
December 1991	Maastricht meeting of European Council adopts Treaty on European Union
June 1992	First Danish referendum rejects Maastricht Treaty
September 1992	French referendum approves Maastricht Treaty
May 1993	Second Danish referendum approves Maastricht Treaty
November 1993	Maastricht Treaty enters into force

Earlier in 1958, moreover, the EC had established the Monetary Committee to review economic and financial conditions, and in 1964 it created the Committee of Central Bank Governors, the only operational result of a more ambitious plan proposed by the EC Commission in 1962, which looked to full-fledged monetary union by 1971.

At the Hague Summit in 1969, however, the EC governments agreed to the gradual formation of an economic and monetary union, and they appointed Pierre Werner, prime minister and finance minister of Luxembourg, to chair a group of experts who would draw up a plan.

The Werner Report was completed in 1970 and called for the completion of monetary union by 1980. (See Figure 1–2 for a brief chronology of EMU.) The report made detailed recommendations for the first two stages of the process and described in more general terms the far-reaching reforms that would have to occur in the third stage. The first stage would take about three years and would focus on the coordination and convergence of monetary and fiscal policies; governments would formulate their national policies in the light of Community guidelines, and policy convergence would take place fast enough to obviate the need for exchange rate changes in the second stage. Exchange rate fluctuations would be narrowed, and a fund for monetary cooperation would be established to provide short-term balance of payments credit to individual EC countries. Eventually, exchange rates would be fixed irreversibly, capital controls would be abolished, and an EC system of central banks, modeled on the U.S. Federal Reserve System, would take over the conduct of monetary policy and of intervention on the foreign exchange market. By that time, the size and financing of national budgets would be decided at the EC level by a body responsible to the European Parliament.[4]

In March 1971, the EC Council of Ministers endorsed the strategy proposed by the Werner Report and took steps to implement some of its recommendations. In March 1972, exchange rate fluctuations were reduced by limiting the swings in bilateral exchange rates to a 2¼ percent band; this arrangement was known as the "snake in the tunnel" because it made the participating currencies move up and down together within the wider 4½ percent band established for the dollar by the Smithsonian Agreement of 1971. But the worldwide shift to floating exchange rates in March 1973 abolished the tunnel, allowing the snake to undulate freely and making it more costly for some countries to participate. They began to drop away, letting their currencies float independently.

In April 1973, the Council established the European Monetary Cooperation Fund (EMCF), adopting another recommendation made by the Werner Report. And in February 1974, the Council agreed to promulgate annual policy guidelines of the sort proposed by the Werner Report to foster policy coordination and convergence.

But divergence, not convergence, was occurring everywhere, as economies and governments were adapting differently to the oil shock of 1973–74. Inflation rates were rising, but at different speeds, as were unemployment rates. Indeed, for the next few years the concerns and energies of

---

4. Gros and Thygesen (1992) provide a critique of the Werner Report; see also Baer and Padoa-Schioppa (1989) and Giovannini (1990a).

the EC governments were focused on pressing economic problems rather than long-term institutional reform. And when they returned to the challenge of monetary integration, they abandoned the agenda of the Werner Report. They responded instead to a call by Chancellor Helmut Schmidt of the Federal Republic of Germany and President Valéry Giscard D'Estaing of France to form a "zone of monetary stability" in Europe by establishing the European Monetary System (EMS). The two leaders' motives were different but were mutually compatible. Schmidt was openly critical of the Carter administration in the United States, especially its failure to combat inflation, and was concerned that the resulting weakness of the dollar would cause the deutsche mark to appreciate, not only against the dollar but also against other European currencies. Giscard d'Estaing shared the familiar French predilection for fixed exchange rates but did not want France to rejoin the snake, because it had not functioned symmetrically.[5]

The Schmidt-Giscard initiative was endorsed by the Bremen Summit in July 1978, the main features of the EMS were defined by the Council in December, and an agreement among the EC central banks brought the EMS into being in March 1979.

The European Monetary System

The EMS was designed to be a more flexible, symmetrical version of the Bretton Woods System, which had governed global exchange rate arrangements from the end of the Second World War until the move to floating exchange rates in 1973. Each country participating in the exchange rate mechanism (ERM) of the EMS is required to keep the exchange rate for its currency within a band defined by a grid of central rates for the various pairs of currencies. When an exchange rate reaches the edge of its band, both countries concerned must intervene on the foreign exchange market to keep the exchange rate from moving further. But they have unlimited access to the short-term credit facilities of

---

5. See Ludlow (1982) on the two leaders' views and the ensuing negotiations; also Gros and Thygesen (1992) and Fratianni and von Hagen (1992). Both of those books argue convincingly that the EMS was designed to function symmetrically and serve as a framework for rule-based policy coordination, not as an asymmetrical system centered on the deutsche mark. They also point out that central banks were wary of the plan. The Bundesbank, in particular, insisted on changes in the design of the system, which had the effect of making it less symmetrical. It also feared that the intervention rules of the EMS could conflict with its obligation to pursue price stability and sought assurances from the German government that the Bundesbank would not be bound by the rules if such a conflict arose. Its reservations on this score played a crucial role in the EMS crisis of 1992; they are discussed in Chapter 7.

the EMCF when they require a partner country's currency for this sort of intervention.[6] The central rates can be revised with the consent of all concerned, and there were twelve such realignments before 1992, some involving several currencies at once.

Eight EC countries joined the ERM initially, but one of them, Italy, was allowed to adopt a wide 6 percent band for its currency instead of the narrow 2¼ percent band carried over from the snake. Spain joined the ERM in June 1989, the United Kingdom in October 1990, and Portugal in April 1992, each of them with a 6 percent band. Italy moved to the narrow band in January 1990, but it left the ERM entirely, along with the United Kingdom, during the exchange rate crisis of September 1992. Greece has not yet joined.

The European currency unit (ECU) was meant to play a major role in the EMS. It is defined as a basket of EC currencies and is the accounting unit of the EMS.[7] But the ECU has played a larger role in international financial markets than in the EMS itself. National governments, EC institutions, and corporations borrow in the ECU; banks accept ECU deposits; and a transnational clearing system has been developed to settle ECU-denominated claims. Under the Maastricht Treaty, the ECU will become a true currency – the single currency of the monetary union.

There were several exchange rate realignments in the early years of the EMS, as the participants sought by trial and error to offset inherited cost and price disparities, as well as the new disparities produced by differences in its members' policies, most notably the different ways in which they responded to the oil shock of 1979. These early realignments, moreover, "were generally agreed without much critical introspection and were not accompanied by comprehensive domestic stabilization measures" (Ungerer et al., 1990, p. 2).

This first phase ended abruptly in March 1983, however, when the Mitterrand government in France abandoned domestic expansion in favor of rigorous stabilization. There was a realignment at that point, but

6. In practice, EC central banks have intervened more frequently *within* the bands than at the limits, and they cannot count on using EMCF credit to finance intramarginal intervention. On the design and evolution of the EMS, see Giavazzi and Giovannini (1989), Gros and Thygesen (1992), Fratianni and von Hagen (1992), or Ungerer et al. (1990). Recent developments are reviewed in Chapter 7.
7. An ECU consists of 0.624 deutsche marks, 1.33 French francs, 152 lire, 0.0878 pounds, and so on. Article 109g of the Maastricht Treaty fixes its currency composition until the final stage of EMU, when the ECU as a basket will give way to the ECU as a currency. Under the Council's 1978 resolution establishing the EMS, the ECU was to be the reserve asset of a European Monetary Fund (EMF), which was to replace the EMCF and serve as the institutional home of the EMS. But that plan died quietly.

very few of them thereafter. In fact, the EMS was transformed into a virtually fixed-rate regime, as France, Italy, and other EC countries sought to "borrow credibility" from the Bundesbank by committing themselves firmly to fixed exchange rates and using that commitment as the rationale for pursuing domestic policies aimed at combating inflation.[8] This change in the nature of the EMS was ratified tacitly by the Basle–Nyborg Agreement of September 1987, in which the central banks of the EMS countries agreed "to the use of interest-rate differentials to defend the stability of the EMS parity grid" and thus tied their own interest rate policies to those of the Bundesbank.[9]

Although there is widespread agreement with this characterization of the transformation in the EMS, research on the EMS has not shown decisively that it is a deutsche mark zone, with the Bundesbank setting monetary policy for the other EMS countries, nor has it shown that Germany's partners acquired a great deal of credibility from the Bundesbank.[10] Some economists have even questioned the underlying premise that a commitment to a fixed exchange rate is intrinsically more credible than a direct, explicit commitment to price stability.[11] Nevertheless, governments and others began to view the EMS as a fixed-rate regime, and

8. Giavazzi and Pagano (1988) are often cited as the authors of this metaphor, but Begg and Wyplosz (1993) note that Fischer (1987) used it first.

9. For its part, the Bundesbank agreed to the more liberal use of EMCF credit lines for intramarginal intervention, in exchange for a commitment by the other central banks to avoid "prolonged bouts" of intramarginal intervention by making fuller use of the exchange rate bands. The phrases quoted here and in the text come from the Council's communiqué of September 12, 1987.

10. On a strict interpretation of the leader–follower model, German monetary policy should affect the monetary policies of other EC countries but should not be affected by them. Yet Fratianni and von Hagen (1992) find that the policy reactions run in both directions, although they are not symmetrical. Similar results are reported by Wyplosz (1989), Weber (1991a), and Gardner and Perraudin (1993). The leader–follower model likewise implies that the Bundesbank should sterilize fully the monetary effects of intervention on the foreign exchange market, but its partners should not, and this has not been true (see Mastropasqua, Micossi, and Rinaldi, 1988). Finally, there is disagreement on the extent to which participation in the EMS has fostered the pursuit of price stability, directly or by altering wage-setting behavior and thus reducing the cost of disinflation. Collins (1988), De Grauwe (1990, 1991), Egebo and Englander (1992), Gros and Thygesen (1992), and Fratianni and von Hagen (1992) find little evidence to this effect, whereas Ungerer et al. (1986), Giavazzi and Giovannini (1988, 1989), Artis and Nachane (1990), and Revenga (1993) find discernible EMS effects. These effects cannot be expected to occur, however, without credible pegging to the deutsche mark, and the evidence suggests that the required credibility was not earned soon enough to affect the speed or cost of disinflation in the 1980s (see Weber, 1991b; Frankel, Phillips, and Chinn, 1993; and Rose and Svensson, 1993). For more on these issues, see the surveys by Haldane (1991), Gros and Thygesen (1992), and Begg and Wyplosz (1993).

11. See, e.g., Corden (1991), Edwards (1992), Fratianni and von Hagen (1992), Svensson (1993), and Kenen (1994a).

some began to think about going all the way to EMU. The case for taking that big step was supported by two considerations, both linked to the signing of the Single European Act in 1986 and the commitment by the Community to completing the internal market by the end of 1992.

- The decision to complete the internal market lent strength to the belief long held by many Europeans that closely integrated national economies like those at the core of the EC have more to gain from exchange rate stability than from occasional realignments. It was argued that the EC countries could not reap the full gains from the internal market unless they banished the exchange rate risks and conversion costs arising from the use of separate national currencies. The strongest statement of this view was made later on, in the Commission's statement of the case for EMU, aptly titled "One Market, One Money" (Commission, 1990).
- Among the first steps taken to complete the internal market was the 1988 decision to require the lifting of all capital controls by July 1990. Once those controls were gone, doubts about the fixity of EMS exchange rates might generate speculative capital movements large enough to force an exchange rate realignment or, at least, to interfere with the normal conduct of monetary policy. This concern was put most vividly by Tommaso Padoa-Schioppa, who warned against trying to pursue an "inconsistent quartet" of policy objectives: free trade, full capital mobility, fixed exchange rates, and independent national monetary policies. "In the long run," he argued, "the only solution to the inconsistency is to complement the internal market with a monetary union" (Padoa-Schioppa, 1988, p. 376).

These two arguments were challenged when they were first made, and they are still controversial. Fixed exchange rates may not be required to capture the gains from the single market. The economies of Canada and the United States are closely integrated, and they will be more tightly linked by the North American Free Trade Agreement (NAFTA), but this is rarely offered as an adequate reason for fixing the exchange rate between the Canadian and U.S. dollars, let alone forming a monetary union.[12] The argument concerning capital controls was likewise put too

12. The governor of Mexico's central bank has rejected the notion that NAFTA will or should lead to a monetary union: "Mexico's possible participation in one or more free trade zones does not imply that we anticipate the formation of monetary unions in these zones. Furthermore, currency areas are not necessarily essential to a free trade zone's good performance, nor are the benefits from the formation of such areas self-evident" (Mancera, 1991, p. 95).

strongly. Capital controls did not prevent speculative crises in the early 1980s, although they probably limited the volume of capital flows associated with them. It has been argued, moreover, that the open-ended credit facilities of the EMCF were more important than capital controls in curbing speculative pressures and that monetary union was not the only way to resolve the dilemma posed by Padoa-Schioppa.[13]

Nevertheless, these two considerations were cited frequently, and they were invoked in an appealing way. It is fine to follow the Bundesbank when fighting inflation is a country's chief concern, but can it afford to follow the Bundesbank over the longer run, when new jobs must be created for a growing labor force? If Europe is to have a common monetary policy, whether by choice or necessity, should that policy be designed by the Bundesbank or by a European institution responsive to the needs of all EC countries?

At first, this argument was taken to mean that the common concern with fighting inflation in the 1980s had concealed temporarily a basic difference between the policy preferences of Germany and those of other EC countries. Therefore, it did not appeal to those who believed that monetary policy should seek price stability and no other goal.

After the unification of Germany, however, the argument was modified. It came to stress the difference between the *domain* of the Bundesbank and that of a truly European institution, rather than possible differences in their policy preferences. As the German budget deficit began to grow and German wage rates rose, the Bundesbank tightened its monetary policy. Its partners, however, did not face those problems; in fact, they faced a recession. Hence, even those who held that monetary policy should aim primarily at price stability began to acknowledge that the policy domain of the Bundesbank may be too narrow to serve the needs of Europe as a whole.[14]

13. On the contribution of the EMCF credit lines to the credibility of the EMS, see Kenen (1988a). On other ways to resolve the Padoa-Schioppa dilemma, see Driffill (1988), Kenen (1988a), and Russo and Tullio (1988), who recommended the use of small exchange rate changes, rather than large realignments, to reduce the gain and raise the risk of speculation. According to Thygesen (1993a), Padoa-Schioppa's view was not widely held by economists or officials; most of them thought that the ending of capital controls would actually foster exchange rate stability by making it possible for EC countries to use small interest rate differences to attract capital inflows and thus finance current account deficits. Most of the issues raised above are discussed at length in subsequent chapters.

14. The problem of policy domains is apt to arise in any asymmetrical pegged-rate system; De Grauwe (1992a) argues that such a system will become asymmetrical precisely because one participant has been able to achieve price stability at home. But the problem of domains is not the inevitable consequence of asymmetry per se. A leader could conceivably formulate its policies to satisfy the needs of all its partners. This

The Delors Report

Although France has been a staunch proponent of firmly fixed exchange rates within the EMS, French officials have never been content with the asymmetrical nature of fixed-rate regimes. There is no clear limit on a country's ability to run a balance of payments surplus; it can acquire reserves indefinitely if it is willing to accept – or able to offset – the domestic monetary consequences. There is a clear limit on a country's ability to a run a deficit; it can run out of reserves, and this is true even in the EMS, with its open-ended credit facilities, because EMCF credits have to be repaid.

These concerns were set forth in a memorandum that the French finance minister, Edouard Balladur, addressed to his EC counterparts early in 1988. He deplored the asymmetric features of the EMS, argued that "the rapid pursuit of the monetary construction of Europe is the only possible solution," and asked his colleagues to contemplate far-reaching reforms, including the formation of a monetary union.[15] The next major step was taken by the Hanover Summit in June 1988. Reaffirming the Community's commitment to the "progressive realization of economic and monetary union," it established a committee to propose "concrete stages" that would lead to EMU.[16] The committee was chaired by the president of the EC Commission, Jacques Delors, and was asked to report to the Madrid Summit in June 1989.

The Worlds of the Werner and Delors reports

Before reviewing the recommendations of the Delors Report, it is worth stressing four major differences between the world of 1969–70, in which the Werner Committee worked, and the world of 1988–90, in which the

point was recognized by economists who used simulations to compare the EMS with EMU. They modeled the EMS as a system in which the Bundesbank stabilized German prices, and they modeled EMU as a system in which it stabilized EC prices. See, e.g., Commission (1990), Hughes Hallett and Vines (1991), Currie (1992a, 1992b), and Fratianni and von Hagen (1992). The less technical literature was slower to focus on the problem of policy domains. I have found few references to it before my own guest column in the *Financial Times* (Kenen, 1992a), where I noted that the Federal Reserve System is concerned with economic conditions in the United States as a whole, not in any single region.

15. The Balladur memorandum and the responses to it are quoted at length by Gros and Thygesen (1992), pp. 312–15.
16. The Committee comprised the twelve central bank governors and five other experts, all of them acting as individuals, and all of them signed its report. The Committee is sometimes accused of focusing narrowly on methods for achieving EMU, without making an adequate case for EMU, but that was its mandate.

Delors Committee worked. These help to explain the differences between the committees' reports and, perhaps, the difference in their subsequent impact.[17]

In 1969–70, faith in fixed exchange rates was declining, especially in Europe, and the collapse of the Bretton Woods System was not far away. Although the Werner Report had recommended a narrowing of exchange rate fluctuations, governments were starting to question their ability to keep exchange rates fixed over long periods of time.[18] In 1988–89, after nearly a decade of experience with the EMS, which was looking more and more like a fixed-rate system, many Europeans had begun to believe that exchange rate changes within Europe were no longer necessary or desirable.

In 1969–70, most EC countries were still using capital controls and were not yet ready to abandon them. Britain was among the first to end them, but it did not do so until 1979. Hence, the Werner Report did not insist on eliminating capital controls and integrating European capital markets early in the process leading to EMU. By 1988–89, most of the controls were gone, and there was a deadline for removing the rest. Furthermore, the Commission was already working on legislation, including the Second Banking Directive, to unify European capital markets. Thus, much of the work needed for economic union was already under way, and the Delors Committee could focus more narrowly on the actual design of a monetary union. Equally important, the Delors Committee could argue with some confidence that capital movements – and even labor movements – would contribute to balance of payments adjustment among the EC countries and thus help to compensate them for giving up control over their own interest rates and exchange rates. The Werner Report could claim that factor mobility would contribute to adjustment in the distant future, not early on in EMU.

In 1969–70, Europe had less settled views about the appropriate division of powers between the Community and its members. France, for example, still strongly opposed any transfer of sovereignty to EC institutions. Hence, the Werner Report provoked opposition when it called for strict limits on national autonomy in monetary and fiscal matters. There is disagreement today, of course, about the appropriate division of responsibilities. But much of the current debate in most countries relates

17. Giovannini (1990a), Gros and Thygesen (1992), and Jacquet (1993) make some of these same points.
18. Although the world was much further from full capital mobility in 1969–70, there was enough to generate large speculative flows, and Padoa-Schioppa's warning about the "inconsistent quartet" could have been uttered even then. Cooper (1968) said much the same thing.

to the new areas – foreign, defense, and social policies – not to the old area of economic policy. The principle of *subsidiarity* has been defined more clearly and is broadly accepted; the Community should not take on tasks that national or local governments can perform with equal or greater effectiveness. This principle may have kept the Delors Committee from proposing more effective fiscal policy arrangements, as explained in Chapter 4, but also protected it from being too ambitious.[19]

Finally, the Phillips Curve was alive and well in 1969–70, and "fine tuning" was a goal, not a term of ridicule. Most economists still believed that a government could choose between unemployment and inflation and could make its choice effective by adjusting its monetary and fiscal policies.[20] These views were reflected in the Werner Report:

> The procedures for policy coordination detailed in the Report implied a very high degree of confidence in the ability of policy instruments to affect policy goals in a known and predictable way. This overoptimistic view of the efficacy of economic management gave rise to a rather mechanistic and relatively rigid approach to policy coordination. (Baer and Padoa-Schioppa, 1989, p. 57)

While many economists continue to believe that monetary and fiscal policies have important roles to play in improving economic performance and stability, few are willing to predict precisely the size and speed of the response to a particular policy change. There is wide agreement in Europe, moreover, on the importance of price stability, the need to dedicate monetary policy to that aim, and the need to insulate central banks from political interference with the pursuit of price stability. It was thus fairly easy for the Delors Committee to agree on the mandate and structure of a central banking system for the final stage of EMU.

What EMU would mean

Echoing the Werner Report, the Delors Report listed three necessary conditions for a monetary union: the total convertibility of currencies,

---

19. As the roles of the Community and its members came to be defined more clearly, there was growing support for the view that the Community should "speak with one voice" on matters of common concern, especially on international monetary issues – a view that led naturally to the belief that it should have a single currency. See Chapter 5.
20. See Corden (1972), whose critique of the case for European monetary union was based in part on the belief that countries have different Phillips curves and different policy preferences. Such differences, he argued, would raise the costs of sacrificing monetary independence.

the complete liberalization of capital flows and full integration of financial markets, and an irrevocable locking of exchange rates. The first and second requirements, it noted, had already been met in Europe. By meeting the third requirement, the EC would become a single currency area but would probably need to go further:[21]

> The adoption of a *single currency*, while not strictly necessary for the creation of a monetary union, might be seen – for economic as well as psychological and political reasons – as a natural and desirable further development of the monetary union. A single currency would clearly demonstrate the irreversibility of the . . . union, considerably facilitate the monetary management of the Community and avoid the transactions costs of converting currencies. . . . The replacement of national currencies by a single currency should therefore take place as soon as possible after the locking of parities. [23]

The formation of a monetary union, however, would have far-reaching implications for monetary policy:

> Once permanently fixed exchange rates had been adopted, there would be a *need for a common monetary policy*, which would be carried out through new operating procedures. The coordination of . . . national monetary policies . . . would not be sufficient. The responsibility for the single monetary policy would have to be vested in a new institution, in which centralized and collective decisions would be taken on the supply of money and credit as well as on other instruments of monetary policy, including interest rates.
>
> This shift from national monetary policies to a single monetary policy is an inescapable consequence of monetary union and constitutes one of the principal institutional changes. [24]

But steps must be taken in three domains to avoid or correct economic imbalances: competition policy and other measures must strengthen market mechanisms; common policies should be devised to enhance the process of resource allocation where market forces are not adequate; and macroeconomic policies should be coordinated, particularly through binding rules in the budgetary field.

The Committee's recommendations on competition and resource allocation lie beyond the scope of this book, but its comments on fiscal policies merit close attention. The Committee began by stressing the need for mutually consistent and sound behavior:

> In particular, uncoordinated and divergent national budgetary policies would undermine monetary stability and generate imbalances in the

---

21. The quotations in this and the next subsection come from the Delors Report (1989). The numbers in brackets refer to the paragraphs of the report, and all italics appear in the original.

real and financial sectors of the Community. Moreover, the fact that the centrally managed Community budget is likely to remain a very small part of total public-sector spending and that much of this budget will not be available for cyclical adjustments will mean that the task of setting a Community-wide fiscal policy stance will have to be performed through the coordination of national budgetary policies. Without such coordination it would be impossible for the Community as a whole to establish a fiscal/monetary policy mix appropriate for the preservation of internal balance, or for the Community to play its part in the international adjustment process. [30]

The Committee went on to argue that markets can discipline governments to some extent but tend to operate erratically; they lend too freely, then shut down abruptly. Accordingly, the Committee made two sets of recommendations:

In the general macroeconomic field, a common overall assessment of . . . economic developments in the Community would need to be agreed periodically and would constitute the framework for a better coordination of national economic policies. The Community would need to monitor its overall economic situation, to assess the consistency of developments in individual countries with regard to common objectives and formulate guidelines for policy. [30]

And then these stronger recommendations:

In the budgetary field, binding rules are required that would: firstly, impose effective upper limits on budget deficits of individual member countries of the Community, although . . . the situation of each member country might have to be taken into consideration; secondly, exclude access to direct central bank credit and other forms of monetary financing while, however, permitting open market operations in government securities; thirdly, limit recourse to external borrowing in non-Community currencies. [30]

Most of these recommendations found their way to Maastricht, apart from the óne about external borrowing. But the weak ones got weaker, and the strong ones got stronger.

Returning to the need for a single monetary policy, the Committee made its most important recommendation:

A new monetary institution would be needed because a single monetary policy cannot result from independent decisions and actions by different central banks. Moreover, day-to-day monetary policy operations cannot respond quickly to changing market conditions unless they are decided centrally. Considering the political structure of the Community and the advantages of making existing central banks part of a new system, the . . . monetary policy-making of the Community should be organized in a federal form, in what might be called a *European System of Central Banks* (ESCB). . . . [It] could consist of a central institution (with its own balance sheet) and the national central banks. At the final stage the ESCB – acting through its Council – would be responsible for formulating and implementing monetary policy as well as managing the Community's exchange rate policy *vis-à-vis* third currencies. The national central banks would be entrusted with the implementation of policies in conformity with guidelines established by the Council of the ESCB and in accordance with instructions from the central institution. [32]

The European System of Central Banks would have a fourfold mandate:

- The System would be committed to the objective of price stability;
- Subject to the foregoing, the System should support the general economic policy set at the Community level by the competent bodies;
- The System would be responsible for the formulation and implementation of monetary policy, exchange rate and reserve management, and the maintenance of a properly functioning payment system;
- The System would participate in the coordination of banking supervision policies of the supervisory authorities. [32]

Most of these recommendations also found their way to Maastricht, along with the Committee's recommendations about the organization, powers, and independence of the ESCB. (There is no need to recite them here, as they will be examined later in their final form.)

How to get to EMU

Like the Werner Committee before it, the Delors Committee proposed a three-stage process for reaching EMU, but it was more specific about each stage and the links between them. After some general observations and rather tentative comments about the role of the ECU, the Committee set out its timetable.

The first stage would initiate the EMU process by taking a number of preparatory steps. On the economic front, the internal market would be completed, the Community's structural funds would be reformed and enlarged in order to reduce regional disparities within the EC, and a comprehensive framework would be introduced for policy surveillance and coordination, using agreed indicators. For fiscal policies, in particular, coordination would employ "precise quantitative guidelines" and "provide for concerted budgetary action by the member countries" [51]. On the monetary side, all obstacles to financial integration would be removed and monetary coordination intensified.[22] All of the EC curren-

22. The report went on to recommend specific changes in the mandate of the Committee of Central Bank Governors. It would be consulted in advance on national decisions about monetary policies, such as the setting of monetary targets; it could address

cies would enter the exchange rate mechanism of the EMS, and EC governments would remove any remaining impediments to the private use of the ECU. "Realignments of exchange rates would still be possible, but an effort would be made by every country to make the functioning of other adjustment mechanisms more effective" [52].[23]

The second stage would usher in several important innovations. The surveillance of economic policy would be strengthened, and precise rules would be used to limit national budget deficits. (The Commission would bring instances of noncompliance to the attention of the Council, which would propose remedial action when necessary, but the rules would not be binding until the third stage.) Furthermore, the Community as a single entity would take part in international discussions on exchange rate matters and policy coordination. But the largest innovations would occur on the monetary front. The ESCB would be established, take over the tasks of the EMCF and the Committee of Central Bank Governors, and begin to move from coordinating national monetary policies to designing and implementing a common monetary policy. The Delors Committee recognized the problems involved in making this gradual transition, but it did not propose a detailed blueprint. Instead, it tried to identify some of the steps that might be taken:

> . . . general monetary orientations would be set for the Community as a whole, with an understanding that national monetary policy would be executed in accordance with these global guidelines. Moreover, while the ultimate responsibility for monetary policy decisions would remain with national authorities, the operational framework necessary for deciding and implementing a common monetary policy would be created and experimented with. Also, a certain amount of exchange reserves would be pooled and would be used to conduct exchange market interventions in accordance with guidelines established by the ESCB Council. Finally, regulatory functions would be exercised by the ESCB in the monetary and banking field in order to achieve a minimum harmonization of provisions (such as reserve requirements or payment

opinions to individual governments on matters of Community-wide concern; and its chairman could decide to make its opinions public. The report also suggested "extending the scope of central banks' autonomy" [52]. It was agreed at Maastricht, however, that no action on this matter would have to be taken until the second stage.

23. Some members of the Delors Committee wanted to create a European reserve fund, which would foreshadow the future ESCB by managing some of the reserves of the EC countries and, possibly, intervening on the foreign exchange market; other members objected, however, that an institution concerned mainly with foreign exchange operations would not foreshadow the ESCB. (What was really foreshadowed at this point was the debate in the weeks before Maastricht about the functions and powers of the EMI.)

arrangements) necessary for the future conduct of a common monetary policy. [57]

The EMS exchange rate band might be narrowed in the second stage, and realignments would be made only in exceptional circumstances.

The third stage of EMU would begin with the irrevocable locking of exchange rates, and the ESCB would assume full control over monetary policy. Eventually, a single currency would be issued to replace the members' national currencies. Foreign exchange reserves would be transferred to the ESCB, which would conduct intervention vis-à-vis third currencies "in accordance with Community exchange rate policy" [60]. Finally, the fiscal rules would take full effect and be enforced by the Council, in cooperation with the European Parliament [59].

The road to Maastricht

In June 1989, the Madrid Summit received the Delors Report and took the first step toward Maastricht. It decided that Stage One of EMU would begin in July 1990. In December 1989, the Strasbourg Summit took the second step. It decided to convene an intergovernmental conference in December 1990 to work on the subsequent stages of EMU. In the months that followed, moreover, the case for EMU gathered support, as the EC governments began to contemplate the long-run implications of events in Eastern Europe. The sudden collapse of the Soviet bloc and the impending unification of Germany forced them to ask whether the further development of the Community (the "deepening" of the EC) should take place before the admission of new members (the "widening" of the EC).

In June 1990, the Dublin Summit chose deepening before widening. It decided to convene *two* intergovernmental conferences – one on EMU and another on political union – and asked them to finish their work by the end of 1992, the deadline for completing the internal market. It also asked the Committee of Central Bank Governors to draft a statute for the ESCB in preparation for the intergovernmental conference on EMU.

CHAPTER 2

The design of EMU

The decisions taken at and after the Madrid Summit reflected strong support for EMU – more than was expected by some members of the Delors Committee. From the start of the subsequent negotiations, however, it was clear to all participants that the actual design of EMU would have to satisfy German concerns. The ECB would have to resemble the Bundesbank; it would have to be protected from political interference and dedicated to pursuing price stability.[1] It was equally clear that there would be no "dash" to EMU. A long transition would be needed, as certain conditions would have to be met before the move to monetary union.[2] These conditions came to be known as the convergence criteria (see Chapter 6).

Some economists criticized this gradual approach. They conceded that time would be needed to make technical preparations but not to await convergence. Their views echoed those of the so-called monetarists in the debates of the 1970s, who had argued that a quick move to monetary union would be a major regime change and would thus induce the changes in economic behavior required for convergence.[3] Some critics

1. Histories of the EMU negotiations, such as those provided by Bini-Smaghi, Padoa-Schioppa, and Papadia (1994), Garrett (1993), Jacquet (1993), and Thygesen (1993b), do not stress this point sufficiently, because they are concerned with the compromises made along the way; but see Begg and Wyplosz (1993).
2. It was even suggested that certain conditions should be met before the move from the first preliminary stage to the second transitional stage (see Thygesen, 1993b). De Grauwe (1993a) says that Germany insisted on convergence because it wanted to limit the number of participants in EMU. In contrast, Jacquet (1993) says that Germany favored a long transition because it wanted to wait until all of its partners were ready; it did not want EMU to divide the EC. Bini-Smaghi, Padoa-Schioppa, and Papadia (1994) note that some other EC countries also wanted a long transition, fearing that EMU would be "unbalanced" (i.e., dominated by Germany) if many countries were excluded because they were not granted enough time to achieve convergence. These concerns and possibilities should not divert attention from the basic issue – that EMU is risky for Germany, which must trade the proven performance of the Bundesbank for the mere promise of equivalent performance by the ECB (see, e.g., De Grauwe, 1992a).
3. On the debate between the monetarists and their antagonists, the so-called economists, see Giovannini (1990a), Gros and Thygesen (1992), and Jacquet (1993). Dornbusch

also warned that a long transition could be hazardous, because shocks and accidents might disrupt the process. Those close to the negotiations tried to answer these objections. They argued, for example, that confidence in the permanence of EMU might be impaired if the economies of the participating countries did not converge sufficiently before their exchange rates were locked. Their arguments, however, had less impact on the outcome than the need for German consent. Germany insisted on convergence, for reasons discussed later, and there would be no EMU without Germany.

The German position was not completely rigid, however, as Germany had other important objectives. It was determined to achieve closer political integration within the EC and was thus willing to make concessions on EMU. At times, in fact, German negotiators argued that political integration was vital for EMU itself, although their reasons were not very persuasive.[4] At Maastricht, Helmut Kohl, the German chancellor, made a crucial concession on EMU by accepting a proposal by François Mitterrand, the French president, for moving automatically to Stage Three in 1999. Some wondered at the time about the quid pro quo. When examining the process that led to the Maastricht Treaty, however, it is wrong to look for finely balanced bargains. The process involved significant concessions on all sides, aimed at making sure that no country would reject the treaty as a whole.[5]

(1990) was one of those who warned against waiting for convergence, but for a different reason. Convergence, he said, had already peaked among an inner core of EC countries, and delay would make matters worse. Therefore, the core countries should move immediately to monetary union.

4. They argued, for example, that a political union is needed to protect the ECB against pressures coming from national governments (see Jacquet, 1993). But a political union might actually transmit and amplify such pressures. Fratianni and von Hagen (1992) suggest that the ECB will enjoy more independence than the Federal Reserve System precisely because it will face twelve separate national governments, whereas the Federal Reserve System faces one unified government. The Bundesbank has also argued that monetary and political union must go together, because the performance of a monetary union "will be crucially influenced by the economic and fiscal policies of and by the behavior of management and labor in all the participating countries" and because a monetary union requires "a more far-reaching association, in the form of a comprehensive political union, if it is to prove durable" (quoted in Gros and Thygesen, 1992, p. 463).

5. Another reason has been offered for the crucial German concession mentioned above. A reader of my earlier monograph (Kenen, 1992b) has suggested that Kohl may have been bound by commitments he made when he sought support from other EC countries, especially France, for German unification. The German negotiators may also have feared that an indefinite postponement of Stage Three would lead to a gradual erosion of national monetary sovereignty (i.e., a de facto transfer of monetary authority to the EMI before the de jure transfer to the ECB). Whatever the reason for Kohl's

The issues

Much of the actual debate about EMU pertained to issues on which the Delors Committee failed to make specific proposals. It favored the creation of the ECB at the start of Stage Two and a gradual transfer of responsibility for monetary policy before the beginning of Stage Three, but it did not provide a plan for making that gradual transfer.[6] Furthermore, it declined to recommend deadlines or propose procedures for passing from one stage of EMU to the next, saying that these were political decisions. Disagreements emerged on other issues as well, including the role of the ECB in prudential supervision and the extent to which the external exchange rate policy of the Community should be determined by governments rather than the ECB.

The governments most firmly committed to EMU, including those of Italy and France, wanted to establish the ECB at the start of Stage Two. They may not have known how best to transfer responsibility to it but believed that rapid institutional change would accelerate the necessary changes in national policies and private sector behavior. Furthermore, an ECB in being would be an active advocate of EMU, which would help to sustain political momentum. Those that favored strict convergence before any move to EMU, such as Germany and the Netherlands, wanted to postpone the creation of the ECB until the beginning of Stage Three. They opposed any gradual transfer of responsibility during Stage Two, because the involvement of the ECB in the making of monetary policy might interfere with the pursuit of price stability in individual countries. They pointed out, moreover, that the Delors Report was inconsistent; while favoring the gradual transfer of

concession, it was deeply resented by the Bundesbank, which was not consulted in advance (see Nölling, 1993).
6. Gros and Thygesen (1992) deplore this omission, saying that the Maastricht Treaty might have been better if the Delors Committee had been able to show how to achieve a gradual transfer. Drawing on earlier proposals by Ciampi (1989), Thygesen (1989), and Gros (1991), they suggest and compare ways in which the ECB could have shared in formulating and implementing monetary policy during Stage Two. Under Ciampi's proposal, the ECB would have imposed reserve requirements on the national central banks, which would have had to meet them by holding ECU deposits with the ECB. Under Gros's proposal, the ECB would have imposed reserve requirements directly on commercial banks. In both cases, the ECB could have influenced the money supply in the EC as a whole by altering the supply of ECU-denominated deposits available for meeting the relevant reserve requirement. A proposal similar to the one made by Ciampi is discussed and criticized in Chapter 3. (Gros and Thygesen criticize Ciampi's proposal because a devaluation of an EC currency would have reduced the ECU value of its money supply, allowing it to expand its money supply without encountering a reserve constraint. They are right, but the same objection applies to Gros's proposal.)

operational authority, it acknowledged the indivisibility of operational responsibility (Crockett, 1991a).

The United Kingdom had grave doubts about the plan for EMU outlined by the Delors Report. It did not oppose the decision of the Madrid Summit to start Stage One of EMU in January 1990, but it favored an "evolutionary approach" thereafter (U.K. Treasury, 1989). In fact, it introduced its own plan for EMU, which involved the creation of a European monetary fund to issue a "hard ECU" in exchange for national currencies. The hard ECU could never be devalued against any EC currency, and it would compete with them in the private sector. If successful in this Darwinian competition, it would gradually become the common currency of the Community and might become the single currency in the longer run.[7]

These issues were debated at the Rome Summit in October 1990, when eleven of the twelve EC governments agreed to start Stage Two of EMU in January 1994 and went on to list the main features of Stage Three. Exchange rates would be locked irrevocably at the outset of that stage, a single currency would be introduced thereafter, and "a new monetary institution" would take full responsibility for the conduct of monetary policy, with price stability as its main aim. The new institution would be independent, although it would report to other "politically responsible" institutions. Nevertheless, the governments refrained from endorsing any gradual transfer of responsibility. In Stage Two, the new institution would coordinate national monetary policies, develop the instruments needed to conduct a single monetary policy in Stage Three, and oversee development of the ECU.[8] Finally, the date for starting

7. See U.K. Treasury (1991) and Crockett (1991b). This was not the first plan to rely on a "parallel currency" as a device for moving gradually to EMU. Several economists made a similar proposal, less fully articulated, in the "All Saints' Day Manifesto for European Monetary Union" published in the *Economist* on November 1, 1975. On parallel currencies in general and the U.K. proposal in particular, see Gros and Thygesen (1992), who stress the obstacles facing a parallel currency when competing with established national currencies; for shorter analyses of the U.K. proposal, see Masson and Taylor (1992) and Fratianni and von Hagen (1992).

8. On the Rome debate, see Bini-Smaghi, Padoa-Schioppa, and Papadia (1994), who note that the Rome Communiqué seems to be referring to the same institution when discussing the second and third stages. (It speaks of "the" institution when referring to the work that must be done in Stage Two.) Accordingly, they argue that the Rome Summit had agreed to create the ECB at the beginning of Stage Two and that the subsequent decision of the intergovernmental conference to create another institution, the EMI, to handle the transition, violated the Rome agreement. See also Gros and Thygesen (1992), who note that the conference debated creating the ECB at the start of Stage Two, and Thygesen (1993b), who reviews the debate about the "indivisibility" of monetary policy.

Stage Three should depend on the extent of the convergence achieved in previous stages. In short, more points for German and Dutch views than for Italian and French views, and fewer points for the United Kingdom, whose dissent was appended to the Rome Communiqué.

While endorsing many of the basic objectives set forth in that document, the United Kingdom was unable to accept the other governments' approach to EMU. It was willing to move beyond Stage One by establishing a new monetary institution and a common currency, but the use of "common" rather than "single" was meant to distinguish its own plan for a hard ECU from the plan contained in the Delors Report. Thereafter, the United Kingdom worked hard to obtain an "opt out" from EMU, with the aim of avoiding civil war within the Conservative party. Writing just after Maastricht, one British journalist put the matter this way:

> The [opt out] will never be used because every sane policy-maker knows that we could not afford for more than a waking hour to stand outside a currency area which included France and Germany. So we have invested our entire political capital in a device which merely delays the ultimate showdown with the Tory right. (Huhne, 1991)

In the event, moreover, the opt out did not serve its purpose. The showdown was not postponed until Britain would have to decide whether to stay out of EMU; it began right after Maastricht, over the ratification of the treaty itself.

When the intergovernmental conference convened, a few weeks after the Rome Summit, many questions had still to be settled. Four of them pertained to Stage Three and the design of EMU itself: To what extent should the Council of Ministers and thus governments control the exchange rate policy of the Community, and how much autonomy should the ECB enjoy in the execution of that policy? To what extent should the ECB be involved in the prudential supervision of the banking system? Should excessive budget deficits be prohibited, and if so, what sanctions would be most effective? Where should the ECB have its home?

The first three questions were answered by the intergovernmental conference before it reported to the Maastricht Summit, but the fourth was not even decided at Maastricht. In early drafts of the ESCB Statute, Article 37 read in full: "The seat of the ECB shall be established at (. . .)." But the Netherlands Draft of October 28 made a small change: "The seat of the ECB shall be established at (. . . . .)," which led to much counting of letters on fingers: Amsterdam or Frankfurt? Edinburgh perhaps? The Maastricht Summit could not settle the issue and decided that the seats of the EMI and ECB should be chosen before the end of 1992 – which did not happen. The matter was not resolved until

November 1993, when the Brussels Summit decided that the EMI and ECB would both go to Frankfurt.

Difficult decisions had likewise to be made concerning Stage Two and the transition to Stage Three: When should the ECB be created? How should the EC decide to start Stage Three, and how should that decision affect individual EC countries? Should a country be barred from entering Stage Three for failing to achieve sufficient convergence, or should the convergence criteria be used merely to determine when Stage Three should start? Should all eligible countries be obliged to enter Stage Three, or should an individual country be able to opt out? Some of these questions were decided by the intergovernmental conference, but two of them had to wait for Maastricht – how to decide when Stage Three should start and whether any country should be able to opt out.

When and how Stage Three should start

Early in its work, the intergovernmental conference decided to create *two* institutions. The first would be established at the start of Stage Two, in January 1994, to coordinate national monetary policies and manage the transition to monetary union. It would be known as the European Monetary Institute. It was created on schedule (its tasks are examined in Chapter 6). The other institution is the ECB itself, which is to be established just before Stage Three begins. Furthermore, the conference adopted strict convergence criteria, not merely to decide if and when Stage Three should start, but also to decide which countries could participate.

These decisions were embodied in a draft of the new treaty prepared by the Netherlands presidency of the intergovernmental conference, which also included a general opt-out clause of the sort favored by the United Kingdom. Although the draft was not fully acceptable to any EC government, it indicated the direction in which the conference was heading six weeks before the Maastricht Summit.

The Netherlands Draft

Under the transitional provisions of the Netherlands Draft, the Commission and the EMI were instructed to report to the Council of Ministers by the end of 1996 on progress made by member states in meeting their obligations with regard to EMU and in achieving "a high degree of sustainable convergence" as measured by specific quantitative criteria. The Commission and EMI were also told to report on the development of the ECU, the integration of markets, the state of current account balances, and the evolution of unit labor costs and other price indexes.[9] The Council would then decide which countries "fulfil the necessary conditions for the adoption of a single currency" and recommend its findings to the European Council. Taking account of these findings and the opinion of the European Parliament, the European Council would then decide whether it would be appropriate to begin Stage Three and, if so, on what date. If it could not agree on a date, the whole process would be repeated periodically thereafter.

An affirmative finding by the European Council would trigger formal action by the Council of Ministers, which would fix the date for starting Stage Three and decide which countries were ready to participate. Those that were not ready, because they had failed to meet the convergence criteria, would be granted "derogations" from their obligations under various provisions of the treaty. But the Council could not compel any country to participate in Stage Three if that country's parliament did not "feel free to approve of the irrevocable fixing of its currency" at the beginning of Stage Three. Such a country would be granted an "exemption" with effects similar to those of a derogation. (A country with a derogation or exemption would be barred from voting in the Council of Ministers or Governing Council of the ECB on matters pertaining to monetary policy or the Community's exchange rate policy for the single currency. Biennially, if not more often, the Council of Ministers would decide whether countries with derogations were ready to participate, and countries with exemptions could ask at any time for their exemptions to be ended.) If the number of countries without derogations or exemptions was sufficiently large, the Council would confirm the starting date for Stage Three.

These procedures were endorsed initially by Germany and other countries wanting to make sure that Stage Three would not start unless there was enough convergence, and they were acceptable to the United Kingdom – the country most likely to seek an exemption. But France and Italy were not happy with them.[10] A French friend put their view this way:

9. The same list appears in Article 109j of the text actually adopted at Maastricht.
10. The other countries of the Southern Tier – Spain, Portugal, and Greece – were likewise unhappy, as they did not want to be excluded from Stage Three for failing to meet the convergence criteria, and their concerns were not fully met by the procedure actually adopted at Maastricht. But Spain succeeded in obtaining an agreement to reform the EC budget, provide more regional assistance, and set up a new "cohesion fund" to finance environmental projects and trans-European transport networks. On the view of individual countries during the debates in the intergovernmental conference, see Bini-Smaghi, Padoa-Schioppa, and Papadia (1994).

> We began with a plan for monetary union – the Delors Report. We wound up with a set of rules for deciding in the future whether to establish a monetary union. Instead of charting a pathway to EMU, the conference has laid out an obstacle course. Worse yet, the finish line may not stand still. It can drift freely into the next century.

Pessimists also warned that Britain might not be the only country to seek an exemption. Germany might want one too, which would scuttle EMU.[11]

The French proposal

In an effort to make sure that Stage Three would start before the end of the century and not be postponed indefinitely, France made a new proposal in the final hours of the intergovernmental conference, and it was accepted at Maastricht. Stage Three will begin automatically in January 1999 if there is no agreement to start it earlier, and Germany will not be able to opt out.[12]

Under the transitional provisions adopted at Maastricht, contained in Article 109j of the treaty and summarized in Figure 2–1, the process will start as before. The Commission and EMI will report to the Council on the state of readiness for Stage Three. The Council will then assess whether each EC country meets the conditions necessary for adopting a single currency and whether a majority does so, and it will report its findings to an unusual meeting of the Council attended by heads of state or government. Taking account of the reports by the Commission and the EMI, the assessment by the Council, and the opinion of the Parliament, that meeting will decide whether a majority of EC countries is ready to adopt a single currency and whether it is appropriate to start

11. See Thygesen (1993b). This concern may explain why Germany itself backed away from the idea, even before the German press began to attack EMU. On the eve of Maastricht, *Bild Zeitung* ran a banner headline, "Our Wonderful Money – The Mark Will Be Abolished," and went on this way for several days, citing opinion polls lopsidedly opposed to EMU (see Nölling, 1993, pp. 136–8).

12. The French proposal appears to have originated with the Italians but was endorsed and presented by the French (see Thygesen, 1993b). When the Bundestag ratified the Maastricht Treaty, it reserved the right to decide at a later date whether Germany should participate in Stage Three, and this declaration weighed in the decision of the German Constitutional Court that the treaty does not violate German sovereignty. Under the treaty, however, Germany cannot decide for itself whether to participate in Stage Three; there is no general opt-out clause, and all decisions affecting the start of Stage Three will be taken by qualified majority voting. (One decision thereafter, on the fixing of the values of the national currencies in terms of the ECU, requires unanimity, and the German government might thus be able to keep the monetary union from getting under way; TEA, Article 109l.)

Figure 2-1 *Schedule for Stages Two and Three*

January 1, 1994:	Stage Two starts
	EMI established
	Bans on monetary financing and bailouts take effect
	Ban on excessive deficits takes effect (but no sanctions until Stage Three)
December 31, 1996:	EMI specifies framework for ESCB
	EC Council decides if majority of EC countries meets conditions required for adopting single currency and if it is appropriate to start Stage Three
	If so, sets starting date for Stage Three
	If not, Stage Three starts automatically on January 1, 1999
Before Stage Three starts:	ECB Board chosen, ECB established, and EMI liquidated
	EC Council approves enabling legislation for ECSB
	Countries not ready for Stage Three granted derogations
When Stage Three starts:	Exchange rates irrevocably locked
	ECB assumes responsibility for monetary policy

Stage Three. If so, it will set the date. All of the Council's decisions, moreover, will be taken by qualified majority voting; there will be no opportunity for any country to exercise a veto.[13]

This process must be completed by the end of 1996 and resembles the process set out in the Netherlands Draft. But now the crucial innovation: "If by the end of 1997 the date for the beginning of the third stage has not been set, the third stage shall start on 1 January 1999" (TEU, Article 109j). No ifs, buts, or maybes. There will be more reports and recommendations, and another special meeting of the Council. But it cannot stop the process; it has merely to decide which countries are ready to enter Stage Three and grant the others derogations under Article 109k. That article resembles the one in the Netherlands Draft, but it has no general opt-out clause. Instead, two protocols have been attached to the treaty, for Britain and Denmark, allowing them to opt out of Stage Three.[14]

13. Britton and Mayes (1992) point out, however, that it may not be possible to muster the votes required to initiate Stage Three if it has been decided that several countries are not ready to participate; those countries might oppose the starting of Stage Three. De Grauwe (1993a) makes the same point but appears to suggest (incorrectly) that the same thing could happen in 1999.

14. The U.K. protocol recognizes that "the United Kingdom shall not be obliged or committed to move to the third stage of Economic and Monetary Union without a

Thus, the French proposal adopted at Maastricht guarantees the advent of Stage Three by a method far more certain than the one proposed in the Delors Report. Although the ECB will not be established at the beginning of Stage Two to work for the early arrival of Stage Three, the latter will start automatically in 1999 unless the EC countries agree unanimously to amend the treaty.[15]

Starting Stage Three

As soon as the starting date for Stage Three has been set, and no later than July 1998, three steps will be taken:

1. The Executive Board of the ECB will be appointed – the president, vice-president, and four other members. They will be chosen by "common accord" of the EC governments participating in Stage Three, on the recommendation of the Council and after consulting the European Parliament and the Governing Council of the ECB. Their terms will normally last for eight years and will not be renewable (ESCB Statute, Articles 11 and 50).[16]

2. The ECB will be established as soon as the Executive Board has

separate decision to do so by its government and Parliament." It goes on to list those provisions of the treaty and the ESCB Statute that will not apply to the United Kingdom (and allows the U.K. government to maintain its Ways and Means facility with the Bank of England, notwithstanding Article 104 of the treaty, which forbids any form of "monetary financing"). The Danish protocol notes that a referendum may be needed before Denmark can participate in Stage Three and grants Denmark an exemption if it cannot participate.

15. Stage Three cannot start, however, unless two or more countries are found to meet the convergence criteria; it takes two to form a monetary union. Kenen (1992b) and Thygesen (1993b) both note that there is one way to *postpone* Stage Three – by deciding before 1998 to start Stage Three after January 1, 1999.

16. To provide for subsequent rotation, however, the first vice-president will serve for only four years and some of the other members will likewise serve for fewer than eight years. Furthermore, the governments will consult the Council of the EMI, because the Governing Council of the ECB will not yet exist. Directors of the Bundesbank likewise serve for eight-year terms, but these are renewable, and the actual terms of office have averaged from ten to twelve years (Kennedy, 1991, p. 16). Governors of the Federal Reserve System have fourteen-year terms, but actual terms have been shorter because of resignations and because new governors are appointed to fill the unexpired terms of those who resign. In a widely cited paper, Alesina and Grilli (1992) argue that the procedure for choosing the president and other members of the Executive Board can result in the selection of persons whose views on price stability differ from those of the median European voter. Their analysis is flawed, however, because they assume that weighted majority voting will be used when, in fact, the choice will be made by "common accord" (i.e., consensus).

been appointed and will exercise its powers from the first day of Stage Three (TEU, Article 109l). Because the ECB will take over the functions of the EMI, the latter will be liquidated as soon as the ECB is established.

3. The Council will adopt the legislation required by certain articles of the ESCB Statute. These pertain to the terms on which the ECB may impose reserve requirements, its right to call up foreign exchange reserves from the national central banks, the issuance of regulations by the ECB, the scope of its advisory functions, and some other matters (TEA, Articles 106 and 109l).[17]

On the first day of Stage Three, moreover, the Council, acting unanimously on a proposal from the Commission and after consulting the ECB, will choose the conversion rates at which the participating countries' currencies will be locked and the rates at which the ECU will replace them, "and the ECU will become a currency in its own right." This decision, however, must not modify the external value of the ECU.[18] The Council will also take the measures needed to introduce the ECU as the single currency of the Community.[19]

It will take a long time to plan and complete the substitution of the ECU for the participants' national currencies, and the task will be expensive. New banknotes will have to be designed and printed and new coins minted. Every coin-using machine will have to be modified and all sorts of menus rewritten, from simple lists of retail prices to stock exchange quotations. Thousands of computer programs will have to be amended.[20] It

17. The Council will act by qualified majority and consult the Parliament, but may follow either of two procedures; it may act on a proposal from the Commission and consult the ECB, or act on a recommendation from the ECB and consult the Commission. There is an apparent anomaly here. If a country does not participate in Stage Three, it cannot vote in the Council on most matters involving the ECB, but it can vote on this legislation; Article 109k of the treaty, which limits the voting rights of nonparticipants, does not cite Article 109l. This legislation will affect them, however, when they are ready to participate.

18. Because this provision refers to the external value of the ECU, it does not formally preclude an exchange rate realignment just before the locking of exchange rates, although it constrains the form of any such realignment (see Chapter 6).

19. All of these steps are listed in Article 109l of the treaty. It should perhaps be noted that the treaty does not address the legal status of privately issued financial instruments denominated in ECU but issued before Stage Three. It is commonly assumed, however, that instruments based on the ECU as a basket will be treated as though they had been based on the ECU as currency.

20. The substitution of the ECU will be made harder by the fact that no EC currency is equal in value to a convenient multiple or fraction of an ECU, and it is impossible to round up or down without a significant change in exchange rates. The problem is

would be comparatively easy, however, to make the change at the "wholesale" level. The ECB could do all of its business in ECU from the start of Stage Three, and the national central banks could also shift to the ECU. Commercial banks would then have to use the ECU in their transactions with the central banks and with one another, but not in transactions with the general public. Chapter 3 shows why it would be wise to make the "wholesale" change quickly.

The mandate of the ECB

A draft of the ESCB Statute was prepared by the Committee of Central Bank Governors, whose members had served on the Delors Committee. The principal participants in the intergovernmental conference came from ministries of finance and had rather different interests and concerns, yet the draft submitted to the Maastricht Summit was remarkably similar to the Governors' Draft. The principal differences are noted below.[21]

The mandate of the ESCB is defined clearly in Article 2 of its statute. Its "primary objective" will be to maintain price stability. Without prejudice to that primary objective, however, the ESCB "shall support the general economic policies in the Community" so as to contribute to the realization of the Community's objectives, laid down in the treaty.[22]

complicated by Article 109g of the treaty, which fixes the currency composition of the ECU basket. Giovannini (1990b, 1991) and Goodhart (1992a, 1995) discuss these problems. A study by Burridge and Mayes (1994), based on a survey of EC firms, concludes that it will take three years for firms to prepare for converting to the ECU and will not begin to prepare until they know when the conversion will occur; the costs will range from ECU 2.25 million for a large multinational firm to ECU 10 million for a large commercial bank, but the costs will be larger if the lead time is shorter. See also the discussion in Nölling (1993). For a proposal similar to the one in the text, see Commission (1995).

21. Portions of the ESCB Statute are replicated in Articles 105–8 of the treaty; for brevity, however, I cite the statute without also citing the treaty. (All such references in this section pertain to the ESCB Statute, not the EMI Statute.) Elsewhere in this book, I follow common practice and refer to the ECB when discussing monetary policy in Stage Three. In the rest of this chapter, however, I refer to the ESCB whenever the statute does so.

22. This wording differs slightly from that of the governors, who referred to the economic policy "of" the Community. Apparently, "of" was seen to invite the ESCB to disregard the policies of the individual EC countries and seemed also to invite the Community to adopt a wide range of common policies. The invitation to set common policies was even stronger in the Delors Report, which said that the ESCB should "support the general economic policies set at the Community level" and that the Community should develop such policies and should set guidelines for national policies; see the quotations in Chapter 1 and the discussion of policy coordination in Chapter 4.

These include: ". . . balanced development of economic activities, sustainable and non-inflationary growth respecting the environment, a high degree of convergence of economic performance, a high level of employment and of social protection, the raising of the standard of living and quality of life, and economic and social cohesion" (TEU, Article 2). These objectives may seem trite but should not be taken lightly. They are cited explicitly at the start of the statute, and the ESCB cannot ignore them. It must pay attention to employment, growth, and other goals insofar as it can do so without jeopardizing price stability. Finally, the ESCB shall "act in accordance with the principle of an open market economy with free competition, favouring an efficient allocation of resources" (ESCB Statute, Article 2).

The tasks of the ESCB are set out in Article 3 of the statute:

— to define and implement the monetary policy of the Community;
— to conduct foreign exchange operations consistent with the provisions of Article 109 of this Treaty;
— to hold and manage the official foreign reserves of the Member States;
— to promote the smooth operation of payment systems.

In addition, the ESCB "shall contribute to the smooth conduct of policies pursued by the competent authorities relating to the prudential supervision of credit institutions and the stability of the financial system."

There are two important differences between this list and the list in the Governors' Draft – one half-hidden and the other all too clear.

Exchange rate policy

First, Article 109 of the treaty divides responsibility for exchange rate policy between the Council of Ministers and the ECB. The full text is quoted in Chapter 5, because it figures importantly in the discussion of exchange rate management and policy coordination at the global level. But its main provisions can be summarized briefly:

1. The Council, acting unanimously, may decide to conclude formal agreements linking the ECU to non-Community currencies. It must consult the ECB in an effort to achieve a "consensus" consistent with price stability, but once the Council has made an agreement, the ECB will be bound by it, even if the ECB must then intervene on the foreign exchange market in a way that jeopardizes price stability.

2. In the absence of any formal agreement, the Council, acting by qualified majority, may adopt "general orientations" for ex-

change rate policy relative to non-Community currencies. But these guidelines must not conflict with price stability.

These provisions have raised doubts about the ability of the ECB to pursue price stability. A binding exchange rate agreement might force it to intervene on the foreign exchange market in a way that could greatly increase the money supply and thus fuel inflation. These concerns were heightened by developments during the EMS crises of 1992 and 1993, when the Bundesbank was obliged to engage in massive intervention and to lend large sums to other EMS countries.

A careful reading of Article 109, however, will show that it cannot greatly impair the ability of the ECB to pursue price stability. A "formal agreement" of the type that would be binding on the ECB is one that would peg the ECU to some other currency, such as the U.S. dollar, and there is little likelihood of any such agreement.[23] The Council might choose to promulgate "general orientations" for exchange rate policy – on its own or in conjunction with informal agreements among the key-currency countries, such as those embodied in the 1985 Plaza Agreement and 1987 Louvre Accord. These guidelines, however, would not be binding on the ECB. Admittedly, Article 109 does not indicate who will decide whether such "general orientations" conflict with price stability. It is widely agreed, however, that the ECB will decide this matter for itself. (It was proposed at one point that the European Court of Justice be asked to rule on the question, which is much like asking the U.S. Supreme Court to decide when a foetus is viable. As the analogy suggests, however, strange things can happen. This idea was dropped.)

Prudential supervision

The Governors' Draft gave the ECB more to say and do about the prudential supervision of the banking system. It would "participate as necessary in the formulation, co-ordination and execution of policies relating to prudential supervision and the stability of the financial system." It would not merely "contribute to the smooth conduct" of policies designed and pursued by others. The Governors' Draft also said that the ECB would be "entitled to offer advice and to be consulted" on the interpretation and implementation of EC legislation concerning prudential supervision and would "formulate, interpret and implement policies

23. Sarcinelli (1992) and Thygesen (1993a) take the same view. Furthermore, Fratianni, von Hagen, and Waller (1992) note that the Council can enter into a formal agreement only on a proposal from the Commission or the ECB.

relating to the prudential supervision of credit and other financial institutions for which it is designated as competent supervisory authority."

The governors, however, did not explain how the ECB would be so designated, and the intergovernmental conference made this difficult. In fact, it weakened the Governors' Draft in two ways. Under Article 25 of the ESCB Statute, the ECB "may" offer advice and be consulted, which is weaker than the phrase "is entitled to" used in the Governors' Draft. Under Article 105 of the treaty,

> . . . the Council may, acting unanimously on a proposal from the Commission and after consulting the ECB and after receiving the assent of the European Parliament, confer upon the ECB specific tasks concerning policies relating to the prudential supervision of credit institutions and other financial institutions with the exception of insurance undertakings.

No one could have built a higher set of hurdles.[24]

The Community's Second Banking Directive aims at creating a single market for banking services; a bank in any EC country may establish subsidiaries and branches in all other EC countries. Under the principle of "mutual recognition," the bank will be subject to home-country (consolidated) supervision, although it will have to conform to a common capital-adequacy standard.[25] These arrangements, however, may be inadequate. First, reliance on mutual recognition, without a comprehensive agreement on minimum standards, invites competitive deregulation, and it can occur even in respect of the rules adopted by each country for applying the common capital-adequacy standard; this point is stressed by Eichengreen (1993a) and Giovannini (1993). Second, the integration of EC financial markets is bound to amplify old externalities and generate new ones:

> In a system of segmented financial markets, differences in bank regulation can be tolerated; in integrated markets they cannot. There are four important "externalities" that cause investors in one country to be affected by regulation in others.

> First, not all customers of banks are domestic residents. Some of the effects of financial failure are felt by depositors overseas . . . or by those who are required to pay deposit insurance.

24. The reduction of the role of the ECB in prudential matters took place late in the intergovernmental conference. The Netherlands Draft, distributed six weeks before Maastricht, was closer to the Governors' Draft than to the final version. Furthermore, the hurdles in the treaty were fewer and lower; the Council would act by qualified majority, not unanimity, and the assent of the Parliament was not required.
25. These standards were adopted by the Basle Committee on Banking Supervision under the auspices of the Bank for International Settlements (BIS); they took effect in 1993 and apply to Canadian, Japanese, and U.S. banks, as well as EC banks. They are embodied with minor modifications in EC directives.

Second, failure may not be restricted to individual banks, and the failure of one bank may cast doubt on the ability of other banks in a country to survive. . . .

Third, a failure in one country could spread contagiously across Europe as well as within countries. More seriously, as markets become integrated, the exposure of banks in one country to those in another increases. . . .

Fourth, with the emergence of the single European currency, banking failures may have repercussions not only through the interbank market . . . but also through the payments system. (Chiappori et al., 1991, pp. 72–4)

These considerations do not necessarily imply that the ECB should take charge of prudential supervision. They do warn that supervision cannot be left safely to national governments, under the principle of subsidiarity. Supervision requires coordination and may require centralization at the Community level.

Yet the strength of the case for centralization may have persuaded some governments of the need to keep the ECB from taking on that task. Monticelli and Viñals (1993) report that certain governments were reluctant to grant so much power to the ECB, partly because it would have political independence. Others may have feared that making the ECB responsible for the integrity of the banking system could induce it to become an overly generous lender of last resort and thus divert it from pursuing price stability.

This last concern, however, can be turned around. When a central bank is obliged to serve as a lender of last resort to individual banks, it must have detailed information about them that may not be readily available to it unless it is involved in prudential supervision.[26] Eichengreen (1992a) suggests that this point has not attracted attention in Europe, because certain central banks do not ordinarily act as lenders of last resort; in Germany, for example, the Liquidity Consortium Bank, not the Bundesbank, is the main lender of last resort. Furthermore, lending by the central bank is fully collateralized in some EC countries, so that the central bank has less need for detailed knowledge about individual banks. Finally, Begg et al. (1991) argue that central banks can always use open-market operations to offset the monetary effects of their lending to individual banks.

All of these considerations, however, reflect rather narrow notions

26. See Giovannini (1993). The same point was made by Alan Greenspan (1993), chairman of the Board of Governors of the Federal Reserve System, when objecting to the plan by the U.S. Treasury to transfer responsibility for prudential supervision to a new and separate agency.

about the role and nature of a lender of last resort – that it intervenes to deal with "runs" on individual banks before those banks must shut their doors and thus impair the liquidity of other banks, as well as the liquidity of their depositors. But central banks are assuming additional obligations. First, they operate the large-value payment systems, a task that can make them provide large amounts of short-term credit to individual banks. Second, they are taking responsibility for the liquidity and stability of the whole financial system, which is why the Federal Reserve System made large amounts of credit available during the stock market crash in 1987.[27]

If the problem of systemic stability looms large in the 1990s and the risk of inflation recedes, the language of the ESCB Statute may become anachronistic before it takes effect. If the ESCB is not given responsibility for prudential supervision, it must at least have access to the information gathered by those who have that responsibility, and it must be consulted by them whenever they expect to act in ways that might affect the banking system or the financial system as a whole.[28]

The organization of the ESCB

The European System of Central Banks will consist of the national central banks and the European Central Bank. It will be governed by the decision-making bodies of the ECB. The national central banks will be the only shareholders in the ECB, and their subscriptions to its capital will depend on a key whose weights will reflect their countries'

27. These points are emphasized by Chiappori et al. (1991) and by Folkerts-Landau and Garber (1992a); see also Folkerts-Landau (1991). Sarcinelli (1992) asks whether the ECB would be able to do what the Federal Reserve did during the stock market crisis. In Chapter 3, I argue that the unification or linking of the large-value payment systems must have high priority in planning for Stage Three.

28. A central banker who wrote to me about my earlier monograph (Kenen, 1992b) expressed optimism on this score: "I doubt that what has been agreed really excludes the ECB from involvement in supervision . . . and in the closing or restructuring of major institutions in difficulty. If there are systemic implications, the ECB is bound to be involved; it is surely inconceivable that the Governing Council will not discuss such operational questions if and when they arise; and although the Council does not have specific powers to instruct individual governors on such occasions, its general powers and responsibilities . . . will surely give it the necessary authority to exercise behind-the-scenes influence." Whether information about individual banks should be supplied routinely to the ECB or to the national central banks will, of course, depend on the division of responsibility within the ESCB. If the national central banks take responsibility for managing the payment system and for direct lending to individual banks, they are the ones that will need the information. The allocation of responsibilities between the ECB and the national central banks is discussed in Chapter 3.

Figure 2-2 *The European System of Central Banks*

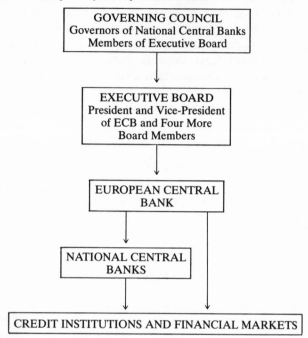

shares in the population and gross national product (GNP) of the whole Community.[29] The structure of the ESCB is shown in Figure 2–2.

The ECB will have an executive board and a governing council.[30] As was indicated earlier, the Executive Board will have a president, vice-president, and four other members, who will be appointed by the "common accord" of the heads of state or government for nonrenewable terms. The six members of the Executive Board will be voting members of the Governing Council, along with the governors of the national central banks. Apart from decisions on certain financial matters, which must be made by weighted voting, decisions by the Board and the Governing Council will be taken by simple majority voting, with the president able to cast a tie-breaking vote.

29. Articles 28, 29, 32, and 33 of the ESCB Statute deal with the subscriptions to the capital of the ECB and the disposition of the income earned by the ECB and national central banks.

30. If some countries do not participate in Stage Three, a third body, the General Council, will be established; it will include the president and vice-president of the ECB and the governors of all the EC central banks. Its role is discussed in Chapter 6.

The responsibilities of the Board and Governing Council are defined by Article 12 of the ESCB Statute, which reads in part:

> The Governing Council shall adopt the guidelines and take the decisions necessary to ensure the performance of the tasks entrusted to the ESCB under this Treaty and this Statute. The Governing Council shall formulate the monetary policy of the Community including, as appropriate, decisions relating to intermediate monetary objectives, key interest rates and the supply of reserves in the ESCB, and shall establish the necessary guidelines for their implementation.

> The Executive Board shall implement monetary policy in accordance with the guidelines and decisions laid down by the Governing Council. In doing so the Executive Board shall give the necessary instructions to national central banks. In addition the Executive Board may have certain powers delegated to it where the Governing Council so decides.

> To the extent deemed possible and appropriate and without prejudice to the provisions of this Article, the ECB shall have recourse to the national central banks to carry out operations which form part of the tasks of the ESCB.

In addition, the Board will prepare the meetings of the Governing Council, while the Governing Council will adopt the internal rules of the ECB and exercise its advisory functions vis-à-vis other Community bodies.[31]

Note that the text is silent on one issue. Which body will decide when it is "possible and appropriate" for the ECB to "have recourse to" the national central banks? Will it be the Governing Council, when adopting "guidelines" for implementing monetary policy, or the Executive Board, when giving "instructions" to the national central banks? The answer is important, because the governors of the national central banks will have a voting majority in the Governing Council and can be expected to favor decentralization so as to preserve the roles of their own institutions. When questioned, EC central bankers say that the Governing Council will decide the matter, and accounts of recent official discussions suggest that the national central banks consistently favor decentralization; see Monticelli and Viñals (1993), and von Hagen and Fratianni (1993). This matter will come up again in Chapter 3.

31. The roles of the Executive Board and Governing Council resemble those of the Bundesbank's Directorate and Central Bank Council more closely than those of the Federal Reserve's Board of Governors and Federal Open Market Committee (FOMC). In the United States, the Board of Governors has certain policy-making functions of its own, and its members constitute a permanent majority on the FOMC. The presidents of the Federal Reserve Banks participate in the work of the FOMC, but the right to vote rotates among them; the president of the New York bank is vice-chairman of the FOMC and a voting member, but only four of the other eleven presidents vote at any one time.

The national central banks will be "an integral part of the ESCB" and must follow the guidelines and instructions of the ECB.[32] But they may perform tasks other than those specified in the ESCB Statute, unless the Governing Council decides that these activities interfere with the work of the ESCB.

The powers of the ESCB

Although the ECB must make use of the national central banks when "possible and appropriate," it may conduct open-market and credit operations for its own account. And the ESCB as a whole has broad powers in the monetary field.

The Governing Council will have the exclusive right to authorize the issue of bank notes in ESCB countries, although the notes themselves may be issued by the ECB or by the national central banks. These will be the only notes to have the status of legal tender in the ESCB countries.[33]

The ECB and national central banks may buy and sell securities and other claims (spot or forward, outright or for repurchase, and in Community or foreign currencies), and it may borrow and lend securities; it may also deal in precious metals. There are no restrictions whatsoever on eligibility. The ECB and national central banks can also conduct credit operations with banks and other financial institutions, but lending must be based on adequate collateral. The ECB will establish "general principles" for the conduct of these operations and announce the conditions under which the ECB and the national central banks stand ready to engage in them.

The ECB may require banks to hold minimum reserves in accounts with the ECB and the national central banks and to levy penalties for noncompliance. But the Council of Ministers must first adopt enabling legislation defining the basis for holding those reserves (i.e., the deposit base), the highest permissible reserve ratio, and the appropriate penalties.

32. The situation of the ECB thus differs from that of the Federal Reserve System in its early years, when there was a power struggle between the Federal Reserve Board and the Federal Reserve Banks (see Eichengreen, 1992b).

33. This provision posed a problem for the United Kingdom, as Scottish banks issue their own bank notes. Hence, a sentence was added to Article 16 of the ESCB Statute: "The ECB shall respect as far as possible existing practices regarding the issue and design of bank notes." Under Article 105a of the treaty, national governments may issue coins in amounts subject to ECB approval, but the Community may adopt legislation standardizing denominations and technical specifications. At the Maastricht Summit, Queen Beatrix of the Netherlands made a gracious concession to EMU. "On my part," she said, "I assure you that I am prepared to make a contribution by sacrificing my head on our coinage to the ECU."

Finally, the Governing Council may decide by a two-thirds vote to use "other operational methods of monetary control" as it sees fit but must meet the general requirement in Article 2 of the ESCB Statute, that the ESCB "shall act in accordance with the principle of an open market economy."

The ECB and national central banks may act as fiscal agents for public entities but may not grant them credit facilities or buy their debt instruments directly from them.[34] They may also provide facilities – and the ECB may issue regulations – to "ensure efficient and sound clearing and payment systems within the Community and with other countries."

At the start of Stage Three, participating governments must shift some of their international reserves to their central banks, and the central banks, in turn, must transfer some reserves to the ECB.[35] Its use of those reserves will, of course, be governed by Article 109 of the treaty, which gives the Council of Ministers the power to issue "general orientations" for exchange rate policy. The use of reserves retained by the national central banks may be regulated by the ECB to protect the exchange rate and monetary policies of the Community.

Independence and accountability

Much has been written about the need for central banks to be independent. Independence is required for credibility, which is in turn required for price stability. The need for independence has even been cited as one of the main advantages of EMU. National governments, it is said, have

34. This prohibition also appears as Article 104 of the treaty and will be discussed in the next section of this chapter. Goodhart (1992a) points out that Article 104 may force governments to replace their central bank credit lines with commercial bank credit lines, which may lead them to transfer other functions to private sector institutions. Hence, the national central banks may cease to serve as fiscal agents for their governments.

35. Governments can continue to hold working balances, and the reserve assets transferred to the ECB may not include EC currencies, ECU balances, IMF reserve positions, or special drawing rights (SDRs), which cannot be readily used for intervention on the foreign exchange market. Nevertheless, the ECB is authorized to hold and manage IMF reserve positions and SDRs and to provide for the pooling of those assets. The initial transfer to the ECB may not exceed ECU 50 billion, and each central bank's share in the total will be proportional to its share in the capital of the ECB (see Article 30 of the ESCB Statute). These arrangements suggest that the ECB is expected to conduct exchange market intervention on its own, rather than use the national central banks, but there is some dispute on this matter. Monticelli and Viñals (1993) take my view, but others disagree.

refused to grant independence to their own central banks. With EMU, they will have no choice.[36]

Several provisions of the treaty and statute bear on the independence of the ESCB. The most important is Article 107 of the treaty, which applies to the ECB and to the national central banks:[37]

> When exercising the powers and carrying out the tasks and duties conferred upon them by this Treaty and the Statute of the ESCB, neither the ECB, nor a national central bank, nor any member of their decision-making bodies shall seek or take instructions from Community institutions or bodies, from any Government of a Member State or from any other body. The Community institutions and bodies and the governments of the Member States undertake to respect this principle and not to seek to influence the members of the decision-making bodies of the ECB or of the national central banks in the performance of their tasks.

The president of the Council of Ministers and a member of the EC Commission may participate in the deliberations of the Governing Council of the ECB, and the president of the Council of Ministers may submit motions for consideration. But they cannot vote.[38]

These provisions are reinforced by the prohibition cited earlier. Because members of the Executive Board cannot be reappointed, they should not feel the need to please politicians – not those of member states nor of the Community.[39] Under Article 14 of the ESCB Statute,

36. On the general argument for independence cast in the context of EMU, see Fratianni and von Hagen (1992) and Monticelli and Viñals (1993). An interesting variant is offered by Pisani-Ferry et al. (1993) and Thygesen (1993b), who argue that the ESCB had to be given independence because the policy-making institutions of the EC are not capable of making monetary policy, and that an independent ESCB had then to be given a simple mandate, the pursuit of price stability, because an independent ESCB could not be given discretion to interpret and implement a more complicated mandate (see also Gros and Thygesen, 1992). On EMU as a way to stop politicians from interfering with monetary policy, see Burdekin, Wihlborg, and Willett (1992). Gros and Thygesen (1992) find it odd, however, that certain EC governments were more willing to grant independence to the ESCB than to their own central banks.
37. It appears with slight modifications as Article 8 of the EMI Statute.
38. Article 109b of the treaty, which also provides that the president of the ECB shall be invited to participate in meetings of the Council of Ministers when it discusses matters relating to the work of the ESCB. Although the language of Article 107 is utterly unambiguous and covers Community institutions as well as other bodies, President Mitterrand assured French voters that there would be political supervision of the ECB, because monetary policy is part of economic policy, which will be decided by the Council of Ministers (cited in Jacquet, 1993). The same view was expressed earlier by a working group on EMU established by the Commissariat Général du Plan (see Pisani-Ferry et al., 1993).
39. Eichengreen (1992a) points out, however, that Board members may try to please politicians precisely because their terms are nonrenewable; they will need jobs after leaving the Board. For more on this issue and additional references, see Neumann (1991).

moreover, the terms of office of national central bank governors cannot be shorter than five years (but reappointments are not ruled out).[40]

The fiscal provisions of the treaty, discussed in Chapter 4, are meant in large measure to protect the independence of the ESCB. But these may not be very effective from that standpoint. Recall the rule cited above against the "monetary financing" of official entities. The ECB and national central banks cannot grant them credit or buy securities directly from them. This prohibition will prevent any government from requiring the ECB or its own national central bank to print high-powered money. Suppose, however, that a large EC country runs a large budget deficit. Even if not "excessive" under the criteria discussed in Chapter 4, the deficit may be large enough to confront the ECB with a difficult problem, much like the problem faced by the Federal Reserve System in the early 1980s, when the United States began to run large budget deficits. If the ECB does not alter its monetary policy, EC interest rates may rise, "crowding out" domestic investment, and an inflow of foreign capital may cause the ECU to appreciate on the foreign exchange market, "crowding out" the domestic production of tradable goods. The ECB may then have to engage in indirect "monetary financing" by intervening on domestic financial markets to keep domestic interest rates from rising or by intervening on the foreign exchange market to keep the ECU from rising.[41]

In what ways will the ESCB be accountable for its actions? The proceedings of the Governing Board will be confidential, but the ECB will publish a quarterly report on the activities of the ESCB, and it will give an annual report to the Council, Commission, European Council, and

40. Other articles protect the Executive Board and governors of national central banks from being dismissed arbitrarily. Under Article 11 of the statute, a member of the Executive Board who no longer meets the conditions required for performing his duties or is guilty of serious misconduct can be compulsorily retired, but only by the European Court of Justice on an application by the Governing Council or Executive Board. Under Article 14, a central bank governor may be removed from office under the same conditions, but any such decision may be referred to the Court of Justice by the governor concerned or by the Governing Council. Finally, under Article 108 of the treaty, participating countries must make their national legislation compatible with these and other provisions of the treaty and of the ESCB Statute before Stage Three begins. Several EC countries – including France, Italy, and Spain – have already taken steps to meet this requirement. The status of the Bank of England, however, will not be altered unless and until the United Kingdom decides to participate in Stage Three.

41. This point has been made many times (see, e.g., Buiter and Kletzer, 1991; and Giovannini and Spaventa, 1991). The problem is not solved by forbidding the ECB to make open-market purchases of government securities, as proposed by Neumann (1991); the ECB could still buy private debt to keep interest rates from rising.

European Parliament. Furthermore, the president of the ECB will present the report to the Council and Parliament, which may then debate it. Finally, the president of the ECB and other members of the Executive Board may appear before the appropriate committees of the Parliament, at the request of the Parliament or on their own initiative.

In one basic sense, however, the ESCB will be more independent than any existing central bank – even the Bundesbank – and thus less accountable. The power of the European Parliament over the ESCB is far less than that of the German Parliament over the Bundesbank or of the U.S. Congress over the Federal Reserve System. Those two national legislatures can amend the laws defining the powers and duties of their central banks and can even abolish the central banks by rescinding the relevant laws. The ESCB Statute, however, is a protocol to the Maastricht Treaty, and any amendment to the treaty or protocols must be ratified by every EC country.[42]

Therefore, the ESCB will not be accountable in the same fundamental sense that the Bundesbank and Federal Reserve are accountable. Those who render an accounting should, presumably, conduct themselves so as to earn the approval of those to whom they render the accounting. To make the ESCB accountable in this larger sense, the Community should do more to close the "democratic deficit." The European Parliament might be given the right to initiate amendments to the ESCB Statute and even the right to enact them.

Several authors – including Cooper (1992a), Lastra (1992), and Eichengreen (1994) – share this view, and Williamson (1993) goes further, saying that the "democratic deficit" helps to explain the decline in political support for EMU. But others insist that accountability should be interpreted narrowly, in the sense of giving an account, not submitting to judgment. Fratianni and von Hagen (1992) take this view, because they believe that the ability of the U.S. Congress to amend the Federal Reserve Act has caused the Federal Reserve to bow to political pressure.[43] Even Thygesen (1993a), who is concerned about the

42. Under Article 106 of the treaty, the Council can amend some articles of the statute, acting by a qualified majority on a recommendation from the ECB, after consulting the Commission and receiving the assent of the Parliament. (Alternatively, it can act unanimously on a proposal from the Commission, but must then consult the ECB and still have the assent of the Parliament.) But the articles in question relate mainly to administrative and financial matters and the scope of ECB operations – the conduct of open-market and credit operations and the imposition of reserve requirements. The Council cannot alter the objectives or tasks of the ESCB or the provisions protecting its independence.

43. Gros and Thygesen (1992) believe that the ESCB needs more independence than, say, the Bundesbank, because the latter enjoys so much popular support. The ESCB, they

difficulty of amending the ESCB Statute, notes that no participant in the negotiations was prepared to suggest that the European Parliament be allowed to amend the statute, because the Parliament is too "remote" from policy making in the Community.

argue, may be uniquely exposed to political meddling because "neither the . . . Council [of Ministers] nor any of its individual members would be faced with the threat of parliamentary crisis in case there is open disagreement with the Governing Council of the ECB" (p. 421). Goodhart (1992a) raises a different concern, that price stability is not defined in the treaty or statute, inviting the ESCB to say that it has done all it could under the circumstances. He favors an arrangement like that adopted in New Zealand, where the government has made a formal contract with the governor of the Reserve Bank, under which the governor will not be reappointed unless he has met an explicit quantitative target. Neumann (1991) and Giovannini (1993) take similar positions.

CHAPTER 3

Monetary policy in Stage Three

This chapter examines the monetary mechanics of EMU and the conduct of monetary policy by the ECB. It concentrates on problems stemming from the use of national currencies early in Stage Three, after exchange rates have been locked but before the ECU has replaced the national currencies.

The first topic is the future role of the ESCB in clearing transactions between EC residents. The analysis shows that national payment systems need not be merged into a single system but may be linked in various ways. Nevertheless, large institutional changes will be required to underwrite the locking of exchange rates and integrate the banking systems of the ESCB countries into a single monetary system. An analogy is drawn with the experience of the United States, where the clearing of transactions between banks in different Federal Reserve Districts results in transactions between the Federal Reserve Banks themselves.

The chapter then turns to the techniques of monetary management currently used by EC central banks and the changes that might be needed in Stage Three of EMU. It also considers the targeting of monetary policy. Should the ECB focus entirely on managing interest rates or be concerned with monetary aggregates as well? Monetary aggregates may matter more after the ECB is established, because the ECB will have tighter control over the total money supply of the ESCB countries than most EC central banks currently have over their own national money supplies.

The last part of the chapter asks how the ECB might use the national central banks to carry out its policies and whether the ECB should deliberately distribute its open-market operations across the securities issued by the various EC governments. Reserve requirements are also discussed. Although they are not truly necessary to manage the money supply, they are used by several EC central banks and may be helpful to the ECB, especially if it concerns itself with managing the quantity of credit, not merely managing interest rates.

Monetary mechanics in a federal system

Before proposing institutional changes to facilitate cross-border payments in Stage Three and integrate the banking systems of the ESCB countries, it is helpful to consider how payments are made between Federal Reserve Districts in the United States and how they are made between EC countries under existing arrangements, with separate national currencies.

A payment between U.S. Federal Reserve Districts

How does Peter, who lives in San Francisco, pay $1 million to Paul, who lives in Chicago? Suppose that Peter has an account with the Pacific Bank and Trust (PB&T), which holds a cash balance with the Federal Reserve Bank of San Francisco (FRBSF), and Paul has an account with the Midwest National Bank (MNB), which holds a cash balance with the Federal Reserve Bank of Chicago (FRBC). Peter will instruct the PB&T to debit his bank account and issue the orders required to credit Paul's account at the MNB.[1] The effects of those orders are shown at Step A of Example I. Peter's bank balance at the PB&T falls by $1 million, along with the cash balance of the PB&T at the Federal Reserve Bank of San Francisco. Paul's balance at the MNB rises by $1 million, along with that bank's balance at the Federal Reserve Bank of Chicago. The Federal Reserve Bank of San Francisco owes $1 million to the Federal Reserve Bank of Chicago.

Two possibilities arise at this point. (1) The PB&T may decide to rebuild its cash balance at the Federal Reserve Bank of San Francisco by borrowing $1 million in the interbank market, known in the United States as the Federal Funds market because it deals in cash balances held with the Federal Reserve Banks, and the MNB may decide to run down its balance at the Federal Reserve Bank of Chicago by lending $1 million in the Federal Funds market. If, by chance, the PB&T borrows directly from the MNB, the previous entries on the books of the Federal Reserve Banks will be reversed completely, and the effects on the books of the

1. The nature of those orders and sequence in which they are executed will vary with the form of Peter's instructions to the PB&T. If he writes an ordinary check and sends it to Paul, the sequence will start when Paul deposits the check in his account at the MNB, run back through the Federal Reserve Bank of Chicago to the Federal Reserve Bank of San Francisco, and conclude when the PB&T receives Peter's check and debits his account. If Paul requires same-day payment, Peter will instruct the PB&T to debit his account immediately. The sequence will run rapidly through the Federal Reserve Bank of San Francisco to the Federal Reserve Bank of Chicago and end when the MNB credits Paul's account.

Example I *A payment between U.S. Federal Reserve Districts (amounts are changes in millions of dollars)*

Step A Making and Clearing the Payment

FEDERAL RESERVE BANK OF SAN FRANCISCO

Assets	*Liabilities*	
	Balance owed to PB&T	−1
	Balance owed to FRBC	+1

FEDERAL RESERVE BANK OF CHICAGO

Assets		*Liabilities*	
Balance owed by FRBSF	+1	Balance owed to MNB	+1

PACIFIC BANK AND TRUST

Assets		*Liabilities*	
Balance at FRBSF	−1	Deposit owed to Peter	−1

MIDWEST NATIONAL BANK

Assets		*Liabilities*	
Balance at FRBC	+1	Deposit owed to Paul	+1

Step B.1 Interbank Borrowing to Restore Banks' Cash Balances

PACIFIC BANK AND TRUST

Assets	*Liabilities*	
	Deposit owed to Peter	−1
	Loan from MNB	+1

MIDWEST NATIONAL BANK

Assets		*Liabilities*	
Loan to PB&T	+1	Deposit owed to Paul	+1

Step B.2 Settlement Between Federal Reserve Banks

FEDERAL RESERVE BANK OF SAN FRANCISCO

Assets		*Liabilities*	
U.S. Government Securities	−1	Balance owed to PB&T	−1

FEDERAL RESERVE BANK OF CHICAGO

Assets		*Liabilities*	
U.S. Government Securities	+1	Balance owed to MNB	+1

PB&T and the MNB are shown at Step B.1 of Example I. (2) The two banks may decide not to adjust their cash balances, in which case the initial entries on the books of the Federal Reserve Banks will not be reversed, and they must then settle the imbalance between them. They do this by transferring U.S. government securities from the Federal Reserve Bank of San Francisco to the Federal Reserve Bank of Chicago, and the final effects on their books are shown at Step B.2 of Example I. The transfer of securities takes place on the books of the Interdistrict Settlement Fund, an obscure institution established precisely for this purpose.

A payment between EC countries with separate national currencies

Suppose that Jean, who lives in Paris, must pay the deutsche mark (DM) equivalent of ECU 1 million to Karl, who lives in Berlin. Jean has a French franc (FF) account with the Banque Nationale de Paris (BNP), which holds a cash balance with the Banque de France but also holds a DM account with the Commerzbank (CB). Karl has a DM account with the Commerzbank, which holds a cash balance with the Bundesbank (BB). Jean will buy marks from the BNP, which will debit his account and issue a DM draft drawn on its account at the Commerzbank. Peter will send the draft to Karl, who will deposit it in his account at the Commerzbank, and the Commerzbank will then debit the BNP's correspondent account. The effects are shown at Step A of Example II. Jean's account at the BNP falls by the equivalent of ECU 1 million, along with the BNP's account at the Commerzbank, and Karl's account at the Commerzbank rises by the equivalent of ECU 1 million.

If the BNP does not want to rebuild its balance at the Commerzbank, there is nothing to be added. If instead it does want to rebuild its balance, it must buy marks with francs, and that is where the fixing of exchange rates starts to matter. Under existing arrangements, the BNP must buy marks with francs in the foreign exchange market, paying the market-determined exchange rate. Its purchase and others like it, however, may cause the franc to depreciate, and the Banque de France may intervene to prevent that from happening. It must then sell marks to the BNP and draw down its balance at the Bundesbank to do so. The effects of this transaction appear at Step B of Example II. The initial reduction in the BNP's balance at the Commerzbank has been reversed and thus drops out. But new entries appear on the banks' books and on those of the Banque de France and Bundesbank. When the Banque de France sells marks to the BNP, the BNP pays in francs by drawing down its balance with the Banque de France, and the Banque de France pays in

Example II *A payment between EC countries with separate national currencies (amounts are changes in millions of ECU equivalents)*

Step A Making and Clearing the Payment

BANQUE NATIONALE DE PARIS

Assets		*Liabilities*	
DM Deposit at CB	−1	FF Deposit owed to Jean	−1

COMMERZBANK

Assets		*Liabilities*	
		DM Deposit owed to Karl	+1
		DM Deposit owed to BNP	−1

Step B Intervention by the Banque de France

BANQUE DE FRANCE

Assets		*Liabilities*	
DM Deposit at BB	−1	FF Balance owed to BNP	−1

BUNDESBANK

Assets		*Liabilities*	
		DM Balance owed to CB	+1
		DM Deposit owed to BF	−1

BANQUE NATIONALE DE PARIS

Assets		*Liabilities*	
FF Balance at BF	−1	FF Deposit owed to Jean	−1

COMMERZBANK

Assets		*Liabilities*	
DM Balance at BB	+1	DM Deposit owed to Karl	+1

Abbreviations Used in EC & ESCB Balance Sheets
BF	Banque de France
BB	Bundesbank
BNP	Banque Nationale de Paris
CB	Commerzbank
DM	Deutsche mark
ECB	European Central Bank
EE	ECU-Endorsed
FF	French franc
IBL	Interbank (ECB Funds) loan

marks by instructing the Bundesbank to debit the account of the Banque de France and credit the balance of the Commerzbank, which then credits the correspondent account of the BNP.

In this example, the payment from Jean to Karl has been cleared by reducing French foreign exchange reserves and German foreign exchange liabilities, and this change in the two countries' reserve positions cannot be offset by any transaction analogous to the transfer of U.S. government securities that occurred at the end of the previous example. Accordingly, the Banque de France may view the outcome with concern and may even tighten its monetary policy in an attempt to rebuild its reserves. By contrast, the Federal Reserve Bank of San Francisco had no cause for concern about the effects of the payment from Peter to Paul, and the reason for this difference is obvious. The assets available to the Banque de France for clearing international payments at a fixed exchange rate are smaller than its monetary liabilities, but the assets available to a Federal Reserve Bank for clearing domestic payments include its holdings of government securities and are thus roughly equal to its monetary liabilities.

Adaptations to facilitate payments in Stage Three

With this basic difference in mind, consider the situation at the start of Stage Three, when the market-determined exchange rate between the mark and franc will be replaced by a conversion rate fixed exactly at the cross rate defined by the ECU values of the franc and mark, and the ESCB will be required to keep the conversion rate from changing. Some discussions of EMU suggest that this will be done in the usual way – official intervention on the foreign exchange market.[2] But the ESCB can do it differently. Each national central bank can stand ready to swap its own national currency for ECU or for the national currencies of other ESCB countries, and it can make those swaps at par. Commercial banks might still be allowed to charge commissions for swapping national bank notes, to reward them for holding the requisite inventories of those notes. Under the arrangements proposed below, however, there would be no justification for charging commissions on conversions involved in cross-border payments that pass through the banking system.

Several institutional changes will be required to facilitate cross-border

2. De Grauwe (1992a), for example, assumes that foreign exchange trading in the ESCB currencies will not end until the ECU replaces the national currencies; in that case, the central banks would have to keep the conversion rates fixed by intervening on the foreign exchange market. Fratianni and von Hagen (1992) appear to make the same assumption.

payments at par and integrate the banking systems of the ESCB countries at the beginning of Stage Three. They will achieve the result described in Chapter 2 – an immediate move to the ECU at the "wholesale" level even when national currencies are still being used at the "retail" level. Suppose that Stage Three has just started, and that the following conditions obtain:[3]

1. The balance sheets of the ECB and the national central banks are denominated in ECU.
2. Commercial banks hold ECU balances with their national central banks. They may or may not be *required* to hold them; the examples given below are valid in both cases (although the subsequent paths of the monetary aggregates will depend on the presence or absence of reserve requirements).
3. There is an ECB Funds market, where commercial banks can make or take interbank loans and can thus lend or borrow ECU cash balances held at the national central banks.
4. Governments have attached "ECU endorsements" to all of their marketable obligations, guaranteeing to redeem them in ECU, and ECU endorsements have also been attached to all of the other securities, such as commercial bills, bought or sold by the national central banks.[4]
5. There are unified markets for all securities bearing these ECU endorsements, where interest rates on individual securities differ only insofar as the securities themselves differ in default risk, liquidity, or taxability.
6. Firms and individuals still use their own national currencies, but they also hold securities with ECU endorsements.
7. The payment systems of the ESCB countries have been made fully compatible and sufficiently accessible to all commercial banks in the ESCB countries, which does not necessarily mean that the systems have been completely unified.

3. Item 7 in the following list did not appear in Kenen (1992b), which paid too little attention to the integration of payment systems. Some of these items are listed by Pisani-Ferry et al. (1993) and by Monticelli and Viñals (1993), who stress the importance of creating an ECB Funds market and of linking the national payment systems in order to make that market operate efficiently; see also Melitz (1993) and Sardelis (1993).
4. Most of the arrangements examined below would work quite well without ECU endorsements. The endorsements, however, would underscore the irrevocability of the move to Stage Three and locking of exchange rates, help to unify the national securities markets, and make the securities themselves more readily transferable between the ECB and national central banks. (Instruments other than government securities could be endorsed by the original issuers or by institutions selling the securities to the ESCB.)

The meaning of "sufficient" access will be clarified shortly, in the discussion of cross-border payments under the arrangements described above.[5] The schematic balance sheets in Example III reflect these arrangements. The ESCB is represented by the ECB, the Banque de France, and the Bundesbank; the French and German banking systems are represented by the Banque Nationale de Paris and the Commerzbank; the private sector is represented by Jean in France and Karl in Germany. As the ECU has not replaced the national currencies at the "retail" level, Jean continues to do business in francs, using the BNP, and Karl continues to do business in marks, using the Commerzbank.

The liabilities of the central banking institutions are denominated in ECU, but some of their assets are not. Their foreign exchange reserves are, of course, denominated in third-country currencies, and their holdings of securities are still denominated in francs and marks, although they bear ECU endorsements (EE). The deposit liabilities of the banking systems are still denominated in national currencies, but those of the central banks have been redenominated in ECU. The assets of the banking system include ECU-denominated balances held with the national central banks, securities denominated in francs and marks but bearing ECU endorsements, and national-currency loans to Jean and Karl.[6]

5. The payment systems of the EC countries differ in many ways, even in their operating hours. The differences are narrowing, however, as more EC countries shift to real-time gross-settlement systems. For descriptions of the existing systems, see Committee of Governors Ad Hoc Working Group (1992a, 1992b); on recommendations for standardization, see Committee of Governors Ad Hoc Working Group (1992b, 1993). The notion of "sufficient" accessibility used in the text goes beyond the recommendation of the Working Group that, under the EC's Second Banking Directive, commercial banks having branches or subsidiaries in other EC countries should have full access to the payment systems of those countries (and, by implication, to intraday credit from their central banks) on the same terms as banks headquartered in those countries. The working group was concerned with the ability of a branch or subsidiary to compete with local banks and, therefore, its ability to make and receive large-value payments within the country in which it operates; it was not addressing the character of the access required to make cross-border payments in Stage Three of EMU. (In the absence of reforms needed to facilitate such access, a multinational bank could use its branches in other ESCB countries to make cross-border payments through those countries' payment systems; if this were the only means of access, however, banks might have then to use their branches to operate in the interbank market, and this would reduce the efficiency of that market, as well as discriminate against those banks that did not have branch networks.) Nevertheless, the approach adopted in this chapter conforms to the main recommendation of the Ad Hoc Working Group, which invoked the principle of subsidiarity to argue that payment systems should be linked, not unified fully, and that they should be managed by the national central banks.

6. They will also include securities without ECU endorsements. Certain other items are also omitted from the banks' balance sheets, although they will appear in subsequent exhibits illustrating the effects of particular transactions.

Example III *Schematic balance sheets at the beginning of Stage Three*

EUROPEAN CENTRAL BANK	
Assets	*Liabilities*
FF Securities (EE)	ECU Balances owed to BF and BB
DM Securities (EE)	
Foreign Exchange Reserves	

BANQUE DE FRANCE	
Assets	*Liabilities*
ECU Balance at ECB	ECU Balance owed to BNP
FF Securities (EE)	
ECU Credit extended to BNP	
Foreign Exchange Reserves	

BUNDESBANK	
Assets	*Liabilities*
ECU Balance at ECB	ECU Balance owed to CB
DM Securities (EE)	
ECU Credit extended to CB	
Foreign Exchange Reserves	

BANQUE NATIONALE DE PARIS	
Assets	*Liabilities*
ECU Balance at BF	FF Deposit owed to Jean
FF Securities (EE)	ECU Credit extended by BF
FF Loans to Jean	

COMMERZBANK	
Assets	*Liabilities*
ECU Balance at BB	DM Deposit owed to Karl
DM Securities (EE)	ECU Credit extended by BB
DM Loans to Karl	

When the ECU replaces the national currencies at the retail level, all of these items will be redenominated in ECU, apart from foreign exchange holdings. It is therefore easy to see that statements made below about transactions in national currencies will continue to hold later in Stage Three, after the switch to the ECU.

A payment between EC countries in Stage Three

Suppose again that Jean must pay Karl the DM equivalent of ECU 1 million. Jean will acquire the marks in the usual way – by drawing down his account at the BNP. But the transfer of marks will not involve an ordinary foreign exchange transaction or the use of a correspondent account, as it did before Stage Three. The BNP will instruct the Banque de France to debit the BNP's ECU-denominated balance and instruct the Bundesbank to credit the Commerzbank's ECU-denominated balance, in order for the Commerzbank to credit Karl's DM balance. Finally, the transfer between the two central banks will take place on the books of the ECB. The balance of the Banque de France will fall, and the Bundesbank's balance will rise. (The ECB might ask the Banque de France to restore its balance, but the Banque de France could do that merely by transferring ECU-endorsed securities to the ECB, which could then transfer them to the Bundesbank to reduce its balance. In this case, the ECB would play a role like that of the Interdistrict Settlement Fund in the United States.)

The effects of these transactions are shown at Step A of Example IV, which resembles its counterpart in Example I, illustrating the effects of interregional payments in the United States. They also bear a resemblance to those at Step B of Example II, illustrating intervention by the Banque de France. But the Banque de France has not run down its foreign exchange reserves; it has instead run down its cash balance with the ECB (and the Bundesbank has built up its cash balance). Furthermore, these transactions with the ECB do not reflect liquidity or balance of payments support. They are mere entries on the books of the ESCB (and would in fact vanish completely from a consolidated balance sheet for the ESCB). The two central banks should not worry about them, nor can they do much about them when they belong to a monetary union. That is why one must be wary of analogies between central bank transactions within a monetary union and seemingly similar reserve movements between independent central banks.[7]

7. This point seems obvious, yet central bankers and others in Europe find it hard to believe that the national central banks should be indifferent to their net positions vis-à-vis the ECB and that the ECB should be indifferent to them too. Responding to my treatment of this issue in Kenen (1992b), one official wrote: "Persistent balance of payments problems, of a kind that ultimately cannot be financed by private sector non-bank borrowing, will tend to show up as accumulations of country X debt in the hands of the ECB; there will not be the random rotation of transfers normally seen within a national banking system. If in due course the ECB's balance sheet is dominated by country X debt, . . . other governments must surely object eventually, especially if the solvency of country X's government begins to be questioned. The problem of official balance of payments financing [is] bound to end up on the ECB's plate." This objection raises interesting issues. Interdistrict settlements in the United States are made by transferring government securities, but no such securities are available for transfer within the ESCB; there will have thus to be transfers of German, French, or Italian securities, and the ECB may find itself holding large quantities of bonds issued by countries whose residents have chronic deficits in their net payments to the residents of other ESCB countries. These deficits may reflect the governments' own fiscal deficits, but not necessarily. Some of the issues raised in my reader's comment will come up again, when I discuss whether the ECB should be indifferent to the composition of its own portfolio and whether there is a strong case for limiting national budget deficits in a monetary union.

Example IV *A payment between EC countries in Stage Three (amounts are changes in millions of ECU equivalents)*

Step A Making and Clearing the Payment

EUROPEAN CENTRAL BANK

Assets		Liabilities	
		ECU Balance owed to BF	−1
		ECU Balance oweed to BB	+1

BANQUE DE FRANCE

Assets		Liabilities	
ECU Balance at ECB	−1	ECU Balance owed to BNP	−1

BUNDESBANK

Assets		Liabilities	
ECU Balance at ECB	+1	ECU Deposit owed to CB	+1

BANQUE NATIONALE DE PARIS

Assets		Liabilities	
ECU Balance at BF	−1	FF Deposit owed to Jean	−1

COMMERZBANK

Assets		Liabilities	
ECU Balance at BB	+1	DM Deposit owed to Karl	+1

Step B Transactions in Securities to Restore Bank Balances

BANQUE NATIONALE DE PARIS

Assets		Liabilities	
FF Securities (EE)	−1	FF Deposit owed to Jean	−1

COMMERZBANK

Assets		Liabilities	
FF Securities (EE)	+1	DM Deposit owed to Karl	+1

Note that the entries at Step A of Example IV do not require the merging of the French and German payment systems or direct involvement by the ECB in the management of those systems. They require "sufficient" access in the sense that the BNP must be able to send messages through the Banque de France that cause the Bundesbank to credit the account of the Commerzbank and cause the Commerzbank to credit Karl's account. The BNP does not need to be able to issue instructions directly to the Bundesbank (or, for that matter, to the ECB). Furthermore, the responsibility for providing intraday credit to the BNP, if and when required, remains with the Banque de France.

Reserve requirements might matter at the end of Step A, because the BNP has lost reserves and the Commerzbank has gained them. But even if there were reserve requirements and they were binding, there might be no further effect on lending or money supplies. The BNP can acquire reserves from other banks. It can borrow reserves in the ECB Funds market, with results like those shown at Step B.1 of Example I. (The loan would appear as a liability on the books of the BNP, and the clearing of the loan through the central banks would reverse the initial entries on the books of the ECB and the national central banks.) Alternatively, the BNP can sell French franc securities bearing ECU endorsements, and the Commerzbank can buy them, with the results shown at Step B of Example IV. Once again, the initial entries on the books of the central banking system would be reversed (and are thus omitted), and the only remaining effects would be those shown on the books of the BNP and the Commerzbank.[8]

An open-market operation

Suppose that the ECB decides on an open-market purchase of securities bearing ECU endorsements and orders the Banque de France to make the purchase for its own account. Suppose further that the BNP is the seller of the securities, whether because the Banque de France deals only with French banks or because the BNP makes the most competitive offer.[9]

The initial effects of the purchase are shown at Step A of Example V. (The balance sheets of the ECB, the Bundesbank, and Commerzbank are omitted, as they are not yet affected.) The BNP holds fewer securities but more reserves at the Banque de France, and the money supply has not changed. In the normal course of events, however, the BNP can

8. If the Commerzbank wanted to buy DM securities rather than FF securities, the BNP sale would tend to raise interest rates on FF securities, the Commerzbank purchase would tend to reduce interest rates on DM securities, and the two banks would switch from DM securities to FF securities in quantities that would reduce if not eliminate the interest rate changes. The books of the BNP would show net sales of FF *and* DM securities, and the books of the Commerzbank would show net purchases of both securities.

9. These suppositions are discussed in the next part of this chapter, along with other ways in which the ECB might conduct its open-market operations.

Example V *An open-market purchase from the BNP via the Banque de France (amounts are changes in millions of ECU equivalents)*

Step A Making the Purchase

	BANQUE DE FRANCE		
Assets		*Liabilities*	
FF Securities (EE)	+1	ECU Balance owed to BNP	+1

	BANQUE NATIONALE DE PARIS	
Assets		*Liabilities*
ECU Balance at BF	+1	
FF Securities (EE)	−1	

Step B Lending the Proceeds to Karl

	EUROPEAN CENTRAL BANK		
Assets		*Liabilities*	
		ECU Balance owed to BF	−1
		ECU Balance owed to BB	+1

	BANQUE DE FRANCE	
Assets		*Liabilities*
ECU Balance at ECB	−1	
FF Securities (EE)	+1	

	BUNDESBANK		
Assets		*Liabilities*	
ECU Balance at ECB	+1	ECU Balance owed to CB	+1

	BANQUE NATIONALE DE PARIS	
Assets		*Liabilities*
FF Securities (EE)	−1	
FF Loan to Karl	+1	

	COMMERZBANK		
Assets		*Liabilities*	
ECU Balance at BB	+1	DM Deposit owed to Karl	+1

---

be expected to invest the increase in its liquid assets, and the money supply will change. If the BNP makes a loan to Jean, the results are straightforward, and they need not be shown separately. There will be the usual cumulative increase in loans and deposits at French banks, with the size of the increase bounded by the "leakage" of liquidity into currency holdings and, with reserve requirements, by the transfer of liquidity from "excess" to "required" reserves resulting from the increase in deposits at French banks.[10]

But there is another possibility. Suppose that the BNP lends to Karl, who is willing to incur franc-denominated debt but wants to transfer the loan proceeds to his mark-denominated account at the Commerzbank. The effects appear at Step B of Example V. The loan itself appears on the BNP's books, replacing the increase in the BNP's ECU deposit at the Banque de France. The loan proceeds appear on the Commerzbank's books as an increase of DM deposits owed to Karl, and this entry is matched by an increase in the Commerzbank's ECU deposit at the Bundesbank. Finally, the transfer between the two banks leads to transfers on the books of the Banque de France, the Bundesbank, and the ECB. Similar results would obtain, of course, if the BNP did not lend to Karl directly but made an interbank loan to the Commerzbank, which then made the loan to Karl.[11]

What would happen if the ECB made the open-market purchase for its own account, instead of using a national central bank? The outcome would depend on the nationality of the counterparty to the transaction. If the BNP supplied the securities bought by the ECB, the entries on its balance sheet would look like those shown at Step A of Example V, but the entries on the central banks' books would be slightly different. They are shown in Example VI, where the open-market purchase appears on the books of the ECB, and the entries on the books of the Banque de France link that purchase with the entries on the books of the BNP. If the Commerzbank supplied the securities, the entries on its books would look like those for the BNP at Step A of Example V, and the corresponding entries on the central banks' books would resemble those in Example VI (but the Bundesbank would replace the Banque de France when the Commerzbank replaced the BNP). In both cases, of course, the ECB's balance sheet would serve as something more

10. But some of the increase in lending and deposits might take place on the books of German banks, because borrowers from French banks might use their loan proceeds to make payments to Germany and thus transfer part of the increase in liquidity from French to German banks.

11. If the Commerzbank supplied the securities bought by the Banque de France, the changes on the books of the Commerzbank would resemble the changes on the books of the BNP at Step A of Example V. But the Commerzbank holds its cash balance at the Bundesbank, so that entries would have to appear on the books of the Bundesbank and ECB to shift the newly created cash from the Banque de France to the Bundesbank. (Those entries would be identical to the ones shown at Step A of Example IV, where Jean's payment to Karl was cleared through the national central banks and the ECB.)

Example VI *An open-market purchase by the ECB from the BNP (amounts are changes in millions of ECU equivalents)*

EUROPEAN CENTRAL BANK			
Assets		*Liabilities*	
FF Securities (EE)	+1	ECU Balance owed to BF	+1

BANQUE DE FRANCE			
Assets		*Liabilities*	
ECU Balance with ECB	+1	ECU Balance owed to BNP	+1

than a settlement fund. It would become the source of the central bank credit provided by the open-market purchase. The credit would then pass through the books of the national central banks on the way to its ultimate destination. But its route would depend on its destination, which would in turn depend on the institution or individual selling the securities to the ECB.

More transactions are examined in the appendix to this chapter. They show how the ECB might intervene on the foreign exchange market and how it might deal with speculation reflecting doubts about the permanence of EMU. But those examples reinforce the general conclusions produced by the transactions already examined:

1. Cross-border settlements early in Stage Three, when national currencies are still used, will not differ greatly from those later in Stage Three, when the ECU has replaced the national currencies.
2. The distributional effects of an open-market operation depend on the identities of the counterparties, not the identity of the particular central bank undertaking the operation.
3. But an ECB Funds market and integrated securities markets will reduce and even neutralize the distributional effects of cross-border payments and open-market operations.
4. If the ECB uses the national central banks to operate in the securities and foreign exchange markets rather than conducting those operations for its own account, its balance sheet will play a role analogous to that of the Interdistrict Settlement Fund in the Federal Reserve System.
5. Even if credit institutions and markets are unwilling or unable to redistribute the liquidity created by the ESCB, the initial distribution can affect the allocation of bank credit only if the

ultimate users of bank credit are unwilling or unable to engage in cross-border borrowing.

It must be stressed, however, that some of these conclusions depend crucially on the rapid development of an ECB Funds market and the speedy integration of the markets for government securities and for other instruments held by commercial banks.[12] Furthermore, those vital adaptations cannot take place without links among the payment systems of the ESCB countries.

Techniques of monetary management in Europe

The ECB is expected to use the national central banks whenever "possible and appropriate" to implement its monetary policy. There are various ways to do that, involving different degrees of centralization, as explained later in this chapter. Nevertheless, the national central banks will have to pursue the same policy targets and will have to adopt similar techniques to conduct open-market and credit operations. Will they have to change their present practices extensively?

Interest rates and monetary aggregates

A decade ago, the major EC central banks pursued rather strict quantitative targets defined in terms of various monetary aggregates. Different countries used different aggregates, and some countries shifted from one to another. Some EC central banks still publish and pursue such targets. With the possible exception of the Bundesbank, however, they appear to attach less importance to those targets. The reasons are well known. The relationships between economic activity and monetary aggregates have not been sufficiently stable to justify their use in formulating monetary policy.

Financial innovation is frequently blamed for loosening the link between the growth rate of aggregate demand and that of the money stock, but it cannot bear all the blame. Artis (1991) shows that the link has been somewhat more stable than might have been expected in the U.S. and U.K. cases, although innovation was extensive in those countries, and somewhat less stable than might have been expected in the German case, where innovation was less extensive.

Other explanations for the looser link focus on the endogeneity of money. When exchange rates are pegged tightly, as in the EMS before

12. The ESCB banking system needs *both* markets to function effectively; they are not perfect substitutes, because borrowed and owned reserves are not perfect substitutes.

1993, the money supply can be affected strongly by official intervention on the foreign exchange market and by changes in the foreign claims and liabilities of the banking system.[13] Furthermore, measures of the money stock commonly omit nonresidents' deposits with domestic banks and residents' deposits with foreign banks in domestic and foreign currencies alike. Corrections for these omissions have been shown to improve econometric estimates of the demand for money in certain EC countries (see Angeloni, Cottarelli, and Levy, 1991).

Whatever the reasons for the recent weakness of the link, the loss of confidence in monetary targeting has led EC central banks to emphasize the influence of interest rates on aggregate demand. Monetary aggregates, they say, continue to provide timely information about the behavior of aggregate demand, because monetary data are available more speedily than price or output data. When it comes to *affecting* aggregate demand, however, interest rates are now the instruments of choice, even in countries that follow German interest rates and thus do not try to set their own rates independently.[14]

Interest rates matter. That much is clear. Furthermore, Artis (1991) has shown that interest rate effects did not weaken in the 1980s. The present emphasis on interest rates, however, revives an old question. Is there any significant difference between a policy aimed at affecting the cost of credit and a policy aimed at affecting the supply of credit?[15]

There can be no difference at all in a simple, partial-equilibrium model of the market for loanable funds. But that model omits two possibilities. On the one hand, a central bank that sets an interest rate and supplies reserves freely at that rate may forgo the use of credit

13. Mastropasqua, Micossi, and Rinaldi (1988) have examined the effects of intervention on the money supplies of the EMS countries.
14. The Bundesbank stresses interest rate policy more strongly than it did some years ago but continues to set monetary targets and pay close attention to them. Hence, the central bank with the greatest freedom to pursue an independent monetary policy uses an interest rate policy to control the money supply, whereas central banks with less independence typically use interest rate policy to follow the Bundesbank and thus stabilize their EMS exchange rates. They may be reluctant to say that, however, and so make a virtue of necessity by describing interest rate policy as a substitute for money-supply policy. (This interpretation may be too simple, however, as the Bank of England shifted from monetary targeting to an interest rate policy even before sterling entered the ERM, forcing the bank to pay close attention to German interest rates; the policy shift occurred even before Nigel Lawson's attempt to "shadow the deutsche mark" in 1987–8.)
15. An analogous question was raised about monetary targeting. Was the aim to regulate the quantity of money, in and of itself, on the implicit supposition that the real-balance effect is large and reliable, or rather to regulate the quantity of credit supplied by the banking system? I take the second view in the next two paragraphs.

rationing by the banking system. By aiming instead at restricting the supply of reserves, it can expect to intensify credit rationing by the banks and thus reduce borrowing and spending by sectors whose demand for credit is interest-inelastic.[16] On the other hand, a monetary policy that focuses primarily on interest rates can have important intramarginal effects on aggregate demand, by affecting old debtors as well as new borrowers, especially those debtors whose obligations must be rolled over frequently or bear floating interest rates. These intramarginal effects may be stronger than they used to be, because many firms and households are heavily in debt.

One wonders, moreover, whether the current emphasis on interest rate policy will survive in Stage Three, after exchange rates are locked. There will be no need for an interest rate policy to defend exchange rates within the EMS. The notion itself will cease to be meaningful. Furthermore, the ECB will not have to peg the ECU by intervening on the foreign exchange markets, and it will thus have more control over the money supply of the ESCB countries as a group than EC central banks now have over their own national money supplies.[17] Therefore, the ECB may pay close attention to the quantity of credit and may want to use an EC monetary aggregate as a proxy for it.

Methods of monetary management in the major EC countries

There are substantial differences in the operating procedures of the EC central banks.[18] But some of them appear to reflect cross-country differences in the structures of national financial systems and in the asset holdings of the commercial banks. Accordingly, the central banks' procedures have tended to converge as those differences have diminished (see Kneeshaw and Van den Bergh, 1989; and Batten et al., 1990). In fact, Table 3–1 shows that the four largest central banks – the Bundesbank, Banque de France, Banca d'Italia, and Bank of England – use very similar methods in their operations.

Each of the first three central banks has established a "corridor" for

16. This effect may not be very strong unless many borrowers are bank-dependent. It is also weakened when banks can mobilize loanable funds by issuing debt of their own, such as negotiable certificates of deposit. For a recent review of these issues, see Bernanke (1993).
17. This point is stressed by Monticelli and Viñals (1993) and by Rey (1993).
18. For detailed accounts, see Padoa-Schioppa and Saccomanni (1992), Strauss-Kahn (1992), on which I draw heavily, and Committee of Governors (1993a), which also reviews recent changes; Bini-Smaghi (1993) provides a good summary. Useful papers on France, Germany, Italy, and the United Kingdom, along with an overall summary, appeared in the *ECU Newsletter* 43–46 (March through December 1993).

Table 3-1 *Principal instruments of monetary policy in EC countries*

Instrument	Belgium	Denmark	Germany	Greece	Spain	France	Ireland	Italy	Nether-lands	Portugal	United Kingdom
Reserve Requirements for Monetary Policy Purpose											
Used	No	No	Yes	Yes	Yes	Yes	Yes	Yes	No	Yes	No
Remunerated	–	–	No	Partly	No	No	Partly[a]	Partly	–	Partly	–
Standing Facilities[b]											
Below market rate	Low	None	Medium	None	None	None	None	Medium	High	None	None
Deposit facility	Low	Low	None	None	None	None	Medium	None	None	None	None
Penalty rate	Low	None	Low	Medium	Low	Low	Medium	Medium	Low	Low	Medium
Open-Market Operations[b]											
Outright	Low	High	Low	Medium	None	Medium	None	Medium	Low	High	High
Repurchase	High	High	High	Low	High	High	High	High	High	Medium	Medium
Forex swaps	Medium	Low	Low	Low	Low	None	High	Medium	Low	Low	None
Frequency[c]	High	Medium	Low	Medium	Medium	Medium	High	Medium	Low	Medium	High
Type of tender[d]	Both	Volume	Both	Rate	Both	Rate	Rate	Rate	Volume	Both	Rate

[a]Below market rate.

[b]Ranked by importance in affecting supply of liquidity to the market.

[c]Low meaning about once a week; medium meaning several times a week; high meaning more than once each day.

[d]Volume or interest-rate tender.

Source: Adapted from Committee of Governors of the Central Banks of the Member States of the European Economic Community, *Annual Report 1992*, 1993, Table 6.

short-term interest rates. The corridor is bounded from below by the interest rate at which the central bank supplies liquidity on its own initiative by open-market operations – the repurchase rate on securities in the German case and the intervention rate in the French case; it is described here as the tender rate. The corridor is bounded from above by the interest rate at which the central bank supplies liquidity at the initiative of the banking system – the Lombard rate in the German case and the repurchase rate in the French case. It is described here as the penalty rate.[19] Yet these and other EC central banks conduct their open-market operations differently, and some of them use more than one technique. In France and Germany, open-market operations take place periodically. In Italy and the United Kingdom, the central banks operate more or less continuously.[20] Furthermore, EC central banks have different ways to limit the banks' use of their credit facilities; there are bank-by-bank limits in Italy but not in France or Germany. And some, including the Bundesbank, have more than one such facility.[21]

The French, German, and Italian central banks deal directly with their banks (although other financial institutions may participate in tenders held by the Banque de France). The Bank of England, by contrast, deals primarily with the London discount houses. Furthermore, the top of the interest rate corridor is not defined as sharply in Britain as in France, Germany, or Italy, because the Bank of England does not have a fixed penalty rate. The interest rate at which it conducts its "2:30 lending" can change from day to day. But these differences are not fundamental. Liquidity supplied by the Bank of England, through open-market operations and lending to the discount houses, flows on to the clearing

19. On the structure of official interest rates in EC countries, see Strauss-Kahn (1992), Table 3.
20. The ECB would find it difficult to maintain tight control over continuous operations conducted simultaneously by a number of national central banks. If it adopted the French or German method, however, the banking system might require large and liberal credit facilities to relieve short-term cash shortages. Note in this connection that EC central banks differ in the extent to which they rely on open-market operations and on direct lending to their banks. Furthermore, they use different assets in their open-market operations; most of them operate in government and commercial paper, but the Danish and Portuguese central banks also issue their own certificates of deposit.
21. The Bundesbank provides substantial amounts of credit through its discount facility, and it uses bank-by-bank limits in this instance; see Deutsche Bundesbank (1989). The discount rate, moreover, is lower than the market rate, a practice that is sometimes defended by noting that the Bundesbank does not pay interest on the banks' reserves. Before Stage Three begins, a decision will have to be made concerning the future of such subsidized facilities.

banks as they call in loans from the discount houses or sell commercial paper to them.

As the ECB will have to use the national central banks to carry out its operations, it is likely to use techniques resembling those used currently by the largest central banks – all the more so because the smaller central banks have been imitating those techniques. Nevertheless, there will have to be changes in the practices and balance sheets of the national central banks, and the nature of those changes will depend on how the ECB interprets the requirement that it use the national central banks. The ECB must also decide whether to use reserve requirements.

Subsidiarity and standardization

There are several ways to use the national central banks for open-market operations. Discussion has focused on three possibilities:

- A *centralized model* in which the terms and size of each tender would be set by the ECB. Bids would be collected by the national central banks from their own financial institutions, and the ECB would make the individual allotments.
- A *distributive model* in which the ECB would set the size and terms of each tender but the global amount would be parceled out to the national central banks, which would conduct their own tenders.
- A *decentralized model* in which each national central bank would conduct its own tenders but work within two bands set by the ECB – one for its interest rate instrument and the other for its balance with the ECB.[22]

Note that all three models assume implicitly that each national central bank will continue to deal with its own commercial banks – that French

22. Ciampi (1989), Thygesen (1989), and Gros (1991) made similar proposals. They were cited in Chapter 2, because they were meant for use in Stage Two, to implement the recommendation of the Delors Report that the ECB should be created at the beginning of that stage and gradually assume responsibility for monetary policy. A band to limit net positions with the ECB is justified by its proponents as a way to prevent the national central banks from offering credit too liberally to their own commercial banks; see Monticelli and Viñals (1993), who do not favor this device but analyze schemes for decentralization using a typology somewhat different from the one used here. (It should be noted that the national central banks would have no incentive to offer credit on excessively liberal terms if, as proposed below, commercial banks from every ESCB country were free to participate in all of the central banks' tenders.)

banks will not be allowed to participate in the Bundesbank's tenders and so on.

Before looking at the problems raised by the first and second models and, a fortiori, an even more centralized model, consider the main problem raised by the third model. The decentralized model appears to assume that there will still be some separation of national financial markets even in Stage Three. If there is instead a single, well-functioning ECB Funds market, arbitrage within that market will eradicate incipient interest rate differences produced by the central banks' open-market operations. In that case, the decentralized model would serve mainly to produce large changes in the central banks' balances with the ECB.[23] Hence, the national central banks would have to fine-tune their open-market operations in order to keep their cash balances within the bands set by the ECB. Those balances will change, moreover, whenever there are net payments from one country to another. That was the lesson taught by Example III, above. Because the decentralized model would force the national central banks to offset such changes by altering the terms of their open-market operations, it could inject unnecessary noise into the financial system, making it more difficult for market participants to read the signals being sent by the ECB.

The same point can be made in terms used earlier. The decentralized model implicitly attaches normative importance to the central banks' balances with the ECB. But changes in those balances should be ignored completely in a monetary union. They are clearing balances, not reserve balances, and no one should pay any attention to them. If the operating rules of the ESCB say that the central banks' balances must not fluctuate widely (or must be balanced at the end of the day), fluctuations should be offset by transferring securities between the ECB and the national central banks, as suggested in connection with Example III. They should not be offset by open-market operations, in the manner in which a central bank normally uses monetary policy to protect its external reserves.

If the decentralized model would take the ECB in the wrong direction, what can be done to take it in the right direction? Should the ECB move directly to the centralized model? Or should it begin by moving to the distributive model and perhaps move later to the centralized model?

---

23. There might still be small cross-country differences in the tender rates obtaining on the different money market instruments used by the various central banks, and this could also be the case under the second proposal listed above. Such differences would have no serious consequence for the conduct or influence of monetary policy. The ECB Funds rate and penalty rate are far more important. With a unified interbank market, moreover, the former cannot differ from country to country and the ECB itself can keep the latter from differing.

Evolutionary standardization

In the early years of the Federal Reserve System, the individual Federal Reserve Banks conducted their own open-market operations, mainly to buy income-earning assets. It took many years to coordinate those operations fully, and many more years before they became the main instrument of monetary policy.[24] The ECB will not face this problem. Its statute gives it full control of monetary policy and of the instruments needed to conduct it. But the governors of the national central banks will have more influence in the ECB than the presidents of the Federal Reserve Banks have in the United States. They will all be voting members of the Governing Council, where they will outnumber the members of the Executive Board, and they are likely to oppose any method of monetary management that could give some central banks more prominence than others or favor the use of some countries' markets.[25] Hence, the ECB is less likely to adopt a centralized model than a distributive model and quite unlikely to adopt a tightly centralized model like that of the United States, where the Federal Reserve Bank of New York acts for the entire Federal Reserve System.

Furthermore, a distributive model may be most appropriate to the situation early in Stage Three, as a centralized model will not work well until several conditions are met. Two such conditions have already been mentioned. First, there must be an ECB Funds market in which commercial banks can lend and borrow ECU-denominated balances held at the national central banks. Second, there must be well-integrated markets in ECU-denominated securities. But a third condition must also be met. Commercial banks in each ESCB country must hold adequate amounts of the securities traded on the integrated markets. Unless these three conditions are fully satisfied, the effects of open-market operations will not spread fast or evenly across the ESCB countries.

The examples given earlier in this chapter showed why the first two conditions are important, but it may be possible to satisfy them quickly by following two more recommendations: the ECB and national central banks should keep their books in ECU as soon as Stage Three starts, and ECU endorsements should be attached to the securities traded by

24. See Eichengreen (1992b). Even after they were coordinated fully, open-market operations did not displace discount-window lending as the main instrument of monetary policy. In fact, that did not really happen until the 1951 accord, which freed the Federal Reserve System from its commitment to support the prices of government securities.

25. It was noted in Chapter 2, however, that the ESCB Statute does not state clearly whether these matters will be decided by the Council or the Board.

the ESCB. It may take more time, however, to satisfy the third condition. Some countries' commercial banks may not hold the bills and bonds most likely to be traded on integrated markets or those most likely to be used by the major central banks in open-market operations. In that case, the national central banks will want to go on using securities and methods best suited to the needs of their own commercial banks, and the ECB will have to parcel out its open-market operations merely to permit differentiation. There may be some convergence in commercial banks' portfolios before Stage Three begins, but not enough to rule out the need for differentiation and thus weaken the case for the distributive model.[26]

How might the ECB tilt the distribution of its operations in favor of centralization? It could give disproportionately large shares to the national central banks in the main financial centers, which would encourage other countries' commercial banks to use those major centers and thus induce them to adapt their portfolios accordingly. To this end, it would have to insist from the outset that all commercial banks in all ESCB countries be allowed to participate in the tenders conducted by each of the national central banks.[27] The ECB might also encourage EC governments to standardize the terms of the securities they issue – a practice that would also benefit the governments by giving them easier access to the most efficient markets.

To carry standardization further, the ECB could encourage competition among the national central banks. If commercial banks were free to participate on equal terms in tenders conducted outside their own countries – if French banks could sell bills directly to the Bundesbank – they would take their business to the most efficient centers, and that would have two consequences. First, the banks would have a strong incentive to adapt their portfolios: to build up their holdings of the securities used in the most efficient financial centers. Second, the banks would make less use of the more expensive tenders. Activity would come to be concentrated on the national central banks having the most attractive methods, and the ECB, in turn, could tilt the distribution of its

26. Monticelli and Viñals (1993) make this same point but favor a different solution – that the ECB use many securities in its open-market operations. That would be cumbersome, however, and might be opposed by the national central banks, which would see it as an artificial way to centralize the operations of the ECB.

27. This rule would also give effect to the requirement that the ECB "act in accordance with the principle of an open market economy with free competition" (TEU, Article 105) and would attack the restrictive practices of some countries' banks. Each national central bank would have to retain the right to judge the creditworthiness of commercial banks seeking to do business with it, but it could not discriminate by nationality.

tenders more sharply in favor of those central banks. It could raise the shares of the central banks whose tenders were, on average, most heavily oversubscribed.[28]

Some central banks that lost out in this competition might be unable to do much about it. Others might alter their methods. If, for example, intermediation by the discount houses made it more expensive for commercial banks to sell bills in London, the Bank of England would lose business to other central banks, and it might then decide to open its tenders directly to banks, rather than conduct them *via* the discount houses. The discount houses would have to adapt – find new work to do – but adaptation induced by competition would be far easier to justify than adaptation forced by fiat of the ECB.

Would this evolutionary process culminate in the complete centralization of ECB operations? Not necessarily. Every national central bank might continue to perform two important tasks.

First, each national central bank might be allowed to initiate open-market operations to offset the effects of its government's financial operations on the liquidity of the banks that hold their cash balances with that central bank. Fluctuations in the governments' payments and receipts are the main source of short-term instability in EC money markets, and they will still be localized in Stage Three.[29] Therefore, the national central banks will probably have the most timely information about them. If given the task of offsetting them, however, the national central banks must be instructed to offset them completely, although they may fall short of doing that in practice. If granted discretion to offset *some* of the governments' cash flows, the national central banks

28. The ECB would have to begin by devising a rule for distributing its open-market operations. Initially, the rule might be based on the key contained in Article 29 of the ESCB Statute for distributing shares in the capital of the ECB. Alternatively, it might be based on the shares of the national central banks in total "monetary assets" (i.e., the shares used in Article 32 of the ESCB Statute to determine the distribution of the "monetary income" of the ESCB); at present those shares are distorted by cross-country differences in reserve requirements, but the distortions would vanish in Stage Three because reserve requirements would have to be standardized, if they were used at all. There would be no need to adjust the distribution of open-market operations for factors affecting liquidity on the various national markets, as proposed in the original descriptions of the distributive model; those factors would be offset by the ECB Funds market. Note that the proposals outlined here assume implicitly that the ECB will focus on the supply of reserves to the banking system and that the national central banks will use volume tenders rather than interest rate tenders.

29. See Strauss-Kahn (1992). Foreign exchange transactions may produce more instability at times, but their impact is easier to predict and offset, because settlements are lagged.

might act in ways that generate uncertainty about the stance of monetary policy.[30]

Second, each national central bank might still engage in direct, short-term lending to its own commercial banks. That is the practice in the United States, where each Federal Reserve Bank makes discount-window loans to those banks that hold reserves at that particular Reserve Bank.[31] This would be quite sensible in Stage Three if, as seems likely, payment systems are not unified completely or managed by the ECB directly but are still managed by the national central banks. Each national central bank, however, would have to charge the same penalty rate and impose the same ceilings, if any, on the quantities of credit available to individual commercial banks. Otherwise, the decentralization of direct lending would confer abnormal profit opportunities on those banks with access to the cheapest central bank facility. There could conceivably be conflict between the decentralization of direct lending and the centralization of responsibility for the stance of monetary policy, but that is unlikely. The uniform penalty rate would be set by the ECB and would continue to serve as the upper bound of the common interest rate corridor. Furthermore, the volume of direct lending, as well as its duration, could be regulated by the ECB. Finally, commercial banks would not borrow heavily from the national central banks unless the ECB drove up market interest rates by reducing its open-market purchases or making open-market sales.

A practical problem may arise, however, if the ECB adopts a distributive approach to the conduct of open-market operations while allowing the national central banks to take charge of direct lending. To parcel out its open-market operations, the ECB will have to use periodic tenders resembling those of the Bundesbank, rather than the frequent tenders employed by the Banca d'Italia or the nearly continuous dealings favored by the Bank of England. If that is the case, however, commercial banks will have to rely on the credit facilities of the national central banks to cope with the cash shortages arising between tenders, and the ECB will have to exercise rather close control over those facilities. Hence, there is a tradeoff between the extent to which the ECB can involve national central banks in the conduct of open-market operations, to satisfy the perceived need for differentiation, and the autonomy it can grant them to manage their own credit facilities.

---

30. There is no comparable case for decentralizing this task in the United States, where there is only one national government, whose cash flows are much larger and fluctuate more sharply than those of the state governments.
31. Mishkin (1993) draws the same analogy; see also Monticelli and Viñals (1993).

Why asset composition should not matter

Under Article 104 of the Maastricht Treaty, the ECB is barred from lending directly to governments or buying securities directly from them. Critics of this rule have argued that it is too narrow. If the rule is meant to protect the ECB from having to engage in "monetary financing" of budget deficits, the ECB should also be barred from buying government securities in the open market.[32] Its open-market operations should be confined to commercial paper and similar instruments.

The validity of this objection depends, of course, on the true purpose of the prohibition, and two interpretations are plausible. First, it may be viewed as an attempt to reinforce the ban on "excessive" budget deficits contained in Article 104c of the treaty and discussed in Chapter 4.[33] Second, it may be viewed as an attempt to reinforce the independence of the ECB by giving it better control over the money supply.

On the first interpretation, Article 104 is too narrow in one sense but too broad in another. It is too narrow because it exempts open-market purchases. It is too broad because it applies to all EC governments, not merely to those that are running excessive budget deficits; in other words, it belongs on the list of sanctions that can be applied when a government fails to correct an excessive deficit.[34] Because the ban on monetary financing is not selective and because it appears in the treaty before the ban on excessive deficits, this interpretation does not stand up well.

On the second interpretation, that the ban on monetary financing is meant to protect the integrity of monetary policy, Article 104 is not too narrow, and it should not be extended to open-market purchases. An open-ended obligation to lend directly to governments or to buy securities directly from them could, of course, interfere with ECB control over the money supply. But the right of the ECB to buy government securities in the open market, exercised at its discretion, cannot interfere with

---

32. Neumann (1991) takes this position; Gros and Thygesen (1992) discuss it but do not endorse it.

33. A variant of this interpretation was suggested by one reader, who argued that the ban would indirectly reinforce the ban on excessive deficits by forcing governments to rely exclusively on market borrowing and thus strengthening the discipline imposed by market forces. This interpretation limits the force of the point made below, that a ban on obligatory monetary financing would have been sufficient.

34. That list includes a recommendation to the European Investment Bank (EIB) that the recalcitrant country be barred from further EIB borrowing. It could have included a recommendation to the ECB that it cease to make open-market purchases of the recalcitrant country's securities. Admittedly, any such recommendation, even if nonbinding, might be seen to infringe on the independence of the ECB.

monetary control. On this interpretation, then, a ban on open-market purchases would unduly limit the independence of the ECB, and the ban on direct purchases is too broad.[35] It could have been confined to obligatory purchases, as was proposed early on (see Italianer, 1993).

These considerations lead to a more general conclusion, that the ECB need not be greatly concerned about the asset composition of its open-market purchases or, for that matter, the composition of its whole portfolio. Three additional considerations support this broad conclusion.

First, the rules for distributing the interest income of the ESCB will not favor a country whose debt instruments bulk large in the whole portfolio of the ESCB. The larger its holdings of Italian debt, the larger will be the interest payments that Italy must make to the ESCB. But the share of the Banca d'Italia in the total income of the ESCB will not be affected; it will be proportional to its share in the capital of the ECB.[36] Hence, open-market purchases of Italian debt will generate flows of interest income from Italy to other ESCB countries, via their national central banks, and there will be no reason to accuse the ECB of favoring Italy if it buys disproportionate amounts of Italian debt.

Second, the composition of open-market operations is not apt to affect the structure of interest rates substantially. Once government securities have been redenominated in ECU, the interest rates on individual securities can differ only insofar as the securities differ in default risk, taxability, and liquidity. They will not be very responsive to transitory changes in demand or supply. The ECB could perhaps affect the structure of interest rates if it conducted the bulk of its business in one country's bills or bonds and was expected to do so regularly. It would deepen the market for them, impart more liquidity to them, and thus reduce interest rates on them. But it would have to concentrate heavily on those securities to make much difference on this score. The interest rate effect would be particularly small if the ECB focused mainly on the short end of the market, where liquidity premia are not very large.[37]

---

35. Article 104b of the treaty, which says that the EC will not "bail out" governments or other public entities by assuming responsibility for their obligations, cannot prevent the ECB from buying those obligations on the open market, and it may have to do that if and when it has to act as lender of last resort in the broad sense suggested in Chapter 2.

36. The allocation of the "monetary income" of the national central banks is governed by Article 32 of the ESCB Statute; the allocation of the net profit or loss of the ECB is governed by Article 33. But the same basic rule will be used to distribute the two types of income.

37. Monticelli and Viñals (1993) appear to be more concerned about this issue, which is one reason for their recommendation, cited earlier, that the ECB should distribute its open-market purchases across a wide variety of securities.

Finally, open-market purchases by the ESCB will be quite small compared with total stocks of debt outstanding. If the total domestic assets of the ESCB were made to grow at 5 percent per year on average, and *all* of the growth reflected open-market purchases of Italian government debt – the unrealistic but limiting case – its annual acquisitions would be smaller than 2 percent of Italy's total debt.[38]

At the start of Stage Three, of course, the composition of open-market purchases will reflect the allocation of those open-market purchases among the national central banks. Recall the rationale for distributing those purchases: the need to accommodate cross-country differences in the asset holdings of the commercial banks. Thereafter, however, the ECB may wish to adopt broad guidelines aiming at some sort of balance in the composition of total ESCB assets. It may want to avoid the appearance of preferential treatment. But that would be the only conceivable reason for giving the matter any attention.

The use and application of reserve requirements

Although the EC central banks use similar techniques to influence money market conditions and short-term interest rates, they differ in their use of reserve requirements. These are used in France, Germany, Italy, and four more countries but not in the United Kingdom, Belgium, Denmark, or the Netherlands.

Those who were taught that the money supply depends on the stock of bank reserves and the deposit multiplier, which depends on the reserve requirement, find it hard to believe that the money supply can behave in a nonexplosive way unless it is constrained by a reserve requirement. Yet the money supply does not behave much differently in Britain than in other EC countries. The existence and stability of a finite money multiplier does not depend on the use of a reserve requirement. It is enough to have a stable relationship between the demand for currency and the total money stock, so that part of any increase in the banks' cash balances will leak into currency held by the public.

In an open economy, moreover, with a pegged exchange rate, large external leakages will limit any increase in the money supply resulting from an increase in the banks' cash balances; an increase in cash balances will stimulate capital outflows, which will in turn induce official intervention on the foreign exchange market. (Alternatively, the risk of inducing a capital outflow, and therefore a reserve loss, may deter the

38. At the end of 1992, the domestic claims of all EC central banks – direct lending plus holdings of securities – amounted to about ECU 420 billion, and the Italian government debt amounted to about ECU 1,070 billion.

central bank from raising the banks' cash balances. The money multiplier may be high, but it will have nothing to multiply.)

It can even be argued that the regime employed by the Bank of England, with no reserve requirements, gives it more control of money market conditions than the regimes employed by some other EC countries. British banks must balance their cash positions on a daily basis; they cannot run cash deficits from one day to the next. In most countries using reserve requirements, by contrast, banks must meet them on average in each accounting period, but they can have deficiencies within each period.

Some central banks acknowledge that reserve requirements are not absolutely necessary for effective short-term monetary management – not even for long-term control over the money supply. They even concede that reserve requirements can weaken their control of the money supply by driving domestic deposits offshore, where they are not subject to reserve requirements. Nevertheless, they appear to believe that reserve requirements give them additional leverage and allow them to control money market conditions without having to intervene as frequently or heavily as some other regime might require. When banks are allowed to have short-term cash deficiencies, the central bank is relieved of the need to intervene on a daily basis; it can provide or withdraw reserves periodically and allow the banks to adjust thereafter.[39] Hence, national central banks that use reserve requirements are apt to press for their adoption by the ECB rather than agree to abandon them.

If the ECB decides to impose reserve requirements, it will have to do so uniformly. It will also have to decide whether to impose them on a host-country (decentralized) basis or a home-country (consolidated) basis. The choice between these two regimes would not matter very much if required reserves earned interest at competitive market rates, but that does not happen in most EC countries; some central banks pay no interest whatsoever, and others pay only partial remuneration (see Table 3–1).

At present, EC central banks typically impose their reserve requirements on home currency deposits at the domestic branches of domestic and foreign banks. They exempt home currency deposits at foreign branches of domestic banks, as well as all foreign currency deposits. This treatment is consistent with the principle embodied in the Basle Concordat and in the Second Banking Directive: that rules relating to bank liquidity should be applied on a host-country basis, whereas rules relating to solvency should be applied on a home-country basis.

39. Recall the point made in an earlier footnote that this is the practice in France and Germany.

The advent of a single currency, however, may require changes in these practices. The distinction between home and foreign currencies will disappear in respect of the ESCB currencies, so that most of the existing foreign currency deposits will be subject automatically to reserve requirements. Furthermore, the requirements themselves will be uniform. But the jurisdictional issue will not disappear. It will merely crop up differently. German banks will have to hold reserves against ECU deposits at their French branches, but should they have to hold them with the Banque de France or with the Bundesbank?

If every major EC country joined the monetary union, it would not make much difference, and administrative convenience might then dictate a shift to home-country (consolidated) reserve accounting. That is the practice in the United States; a bank having branches in two or more Federal Reserve Districts holds its required reserves with the Federal Reserve Bank for the district in which the bank has its head office.[40] But matters will be complicated if some countries do not join the monetary union.

Suppose that the United Kingdom does not join and that reserves do not earn interest. How would the two accounting regimes affect the ability of the ECB to control the volume of ECU deposits?

Under host-country reserve accounting, the banks of the ESCB countries would have an incentive to book ECU deposits in London, because they would not have to hold reserves against those deposits and would not then be handicapped when competing with British banks for those deposits. But British banks would have no incentive to attract ECU deposits by opening branches in the ESCB countries, as deposits at such branches would be subject to reserve requirements. Hence, the ECB's control over the volume of ECU deposits would be impaired by the existence of a large offshore market in London – which would be a significant limitation. But there would be no limitation on its control over the volume of ECU deposits held at banks in the ESCB countries.

Under home-country reserve accounting, the banks of the ESCB countries would have no incentive to book ECU deposits in London, so the off-shore market would be dominated by British and foreign banks, and the market might therefore be smaller. In this case, however, British banks would have an incentive to compete for ECU deposits in the ESCB countries, as they would not have to hold any reserves against them. In fact, they would want to take full advantage of their rights under the Second Banking Directive. This might limit sharply the ECB's

40. A separately incorporated subsidiary, however, holds its reserves with the Federal Reserve Bank for the district in which it has its own head office.

control over the volume of ECU deposits in the ESCB countries, and the limitation could be far more serious than the one produced by a larger off-shore market.

If the ECB decides to impose reserve requirements but not to move to full remuneration, it may be imprudent to switch to home-country accounting, although that system would be less cumbersome.[41]

Appendix: Additional banking transactions

This appendix uses the framework set out in the text to illustrate additional transactions. The relevant abbreviations are reproduced for convenience:

BF	Banque de France
BB	Bundesbank
BNP	Banque Nationale de Paris
CB	Commerzbank
DM	Deutsche mark
ECB	European Central Bank
EE	ECU endorsed
FF	French franc

Four transactions are considered here:

1. Intervention in the foreign exchange market via the Banque de France.
2. Intervention in the foreign exchange market directly by the ECB.
3. A switch by Jean from franc to mark deposits.
4. A switch by Jean from French to German securities.

As in the text, entries are changes in balance-sheet items expressed in millions of ECU equivalents.

Intervention in the foreign exchange market via the Banque de France

Suppose that the ECB decides to buy dollars in the foreign exchange market to prevent appreciation of the ECU and that it instructs the Banque de France to buy the dollars for its own account. As in the case

41. The Maastricht Treaty calls for EC legislation to set the deposit base and the maximum reserve ratio if the ECB decides to use reserve requirements, but it does not require legislation to set a minimum interest rate. That was suggested but rejected.

Example A: *Purchase of dollars by the ECB via the Banque de France (amounts are changes in millions of ECU equivalents)*

		BANQUE DE FRANCE	
Assets		*Liabilities*	
Dollar Reserves	+1	ECU Balance owed to BNP	+1

		BANQUE NATIONALE DE PARIS	
Assets		*Liabilities*	
ECU Balance at BF	+1	FF Deposit owed to Forex Dealer	+1

Example B: *Purchase of dollars by the ECB for its own account (amounts are changes in millions of ECU equivalents)*

		EUROPEAN CENTRAL BANK	
Assets		*Liabilities*	
Dollar Reserves	+1	ECU Balance owed to BF	+1

		BANQUE DE FRANCE	
Assets		*Liabilities*	
ECU Balance at ECB	+1	ECU Balance owed to BNP	+1

		BANQUE NATIONALE DE PARIS	
Assets		*Liabilities*	
ECU Balance at BF	+1	FF Deposit owed to Forex Dealer	+1

of an open-market purchase, the immediate results depend on the identity of the counterparty selling the dollars. If the counterparty is a foreign exchange dealer wanting to buy francs and having an account with the BNP, the results will be those shown in Example A. They resemble the results at Step A of Example V in the text, except that the BNP's books show an increase in deposit liabilities to the dealer rather than a fall in securities held by the BNP.

Intervention in the foreign exchange market directly by the ECB

If the ECB decides to buy dollars for its own account, the results will be those shown in Example B. They resemble the results in Example VI of

Example C: *Currency substitution by Jean (amounts are changes in millions of ECU equivalents)*

EUROPEAN CENTRAL BANK		
Assets		*Liabilities*
DM Securities (EE)	−1	
FF Securities (EE)	+1	

BANQUE DE FRANCE		
Assets		*Liabilities*
FF Securities (EE)	−1	ECU Balance owed to BNP −1

BUNDESBANK		
Assets		*Liabilities*
DM Securities (EE)	+1	ECU Balance owed to CB +1

BANQUE NATIONALE DE PARIS		
Assets		*Liabilities*
ECU Balance at BF	−1	FF Deposit owed to Jean −1

COMMERZBANK		
Assets		*Liabilities*
ECU Balance at BB	+1	DM Deposit owed to Jean +1

the text, where the ECB made an open-market purchase for its own account.

A switch from franc to mark deposits

When exchange rates are fixed irrevocably, there is no reason for anyone to switch from one currency to another, apart from pure convenience. When there are doubts about the irrevocability of the fixing, however, there can be a "run" from one currency into another.

Suppose that Jean distrusts the irrevocability of the fixing and switches from franc deposits at the BNP to mark deposits at the Commerzbank. The immediate effects are shown in Example C, together with the transfers of securities needed to balance the positions of the Banque de France and Bundesbank vis-à-vis the ECB. They resemble closely the effects of a payment from Jean to Karl combined with a corresponding transfer of securities, shown at Step B of Example IV in the text. (The only difference is the ownership of the deposit appearing on the liability side of the Commerzbank balance sheet, which belongs to Jean instead

Example D: *Asset substitution by Jean (amounts are changes in millions of ECU equivalents)*

	EUROPEAN CENTRAL BANK	
Assets		*Liabilities*
DM Securities (EE)	−1	
FF Securities (EE)	+1	

	BANQUE DE FRANCE	
Assets		*Liabilities*
FF Securities (EE)	−1	ECU Balance owed to BNP −1

	BUNDESBANK	
Assets		*Liabilities*
DM Securities (EE)	+1	ECU Balance owed to CB +1

	BANQUE NATIONALE DE PARIS	
Assets		*Liabilities*
ECU Balance at BF	−1	FF Deposit owed to Anne −1

	COMMERZBANK	
Assets		*Liabilities*
ECU Balance at BB	+1	DM Deposit owed to Karl +1

of Karl.) There is no change in the total money supply of the ECB countries, only in its currency composition, and no need for the central banks to take any other steps. They have merely to regard the transfers of securities to and from the ECB as being routine matters, not as liquidity or balance of payments support.

How far can this process go? Under an ordinary fixed-rate system, a central bank cannot defend its currency indefinitely, as it will exhaust its foreign exchange reserves before the "Jeans" have withdrawn all of their deposits. There are no such reserves in the examples studied here. But an analogous problem may arise eventually. The BNP may exhaust its balance at the Banque de France and its ability to borrow in the ECB Funds market. At that point, the Banque de France must start to buy securities from the BNP (or make loans to it) and must transfer securities to the ECB to balance its own account with the ECB. This process can continue for as long as the BNP has assets it can sell (or pledge) to the Banque de France. If the BNP is solvent, of course, its assets will exceed its deposit liabilities. Its problem is to mobilize those assets, and the solution to that problem rests with the Banque de France, which must buy them (or accept them as collateral) to defend the irrevocably fixed exchange rate against speculative pressure.

But doubts about the irrevocability of the fixed exchange rates could cause Jean to sell off other franc-denominated assets (presumably those that do not bear ECU endorsements – although he might have doubts about those, too). This case is examined in the final example.

A switch from franc to mark bonds

To switch from franc to mark bonds, Jean must sell franc bonds for francs, use the francs to buy marks, and use the marks to buy mark bonds. Assume for simplicity that he sells the franc bonds to Anne, another French resident, and buys the mark bonds from Karl. The results are shown in Example D, together with the corresponding transfers of bonds within the ESCB. They differ from those in Example C in only two small ways: (1) the reduction in franc deposits shown on the books of the BNP is the reduction in Anne's deposit, reflecting her purchase of bonds from Jean; and (2) the increase in mark deposits shown on the books of the Commerzbank is the increase in Karl's deposit, reflecting his sale of bonds to Jean.

If Anne becomes increasingly reluctant to buy franc bonds from Jean, the interest rate on those bonds will rise, curbing Jean's appetite for mark bonds. Even if that does not happen and the process of asset substitution continues, it need not jeopardize the fixed-rate system, so long as the Banque de France is willing to replenish the cash reserves of the BNP.

CHAPTER 4

Fiscal policy and EMU

In the 1970s, research and debate on macroeconomic issues focused largely on monetary policy. In the 1980s, the focus shifted to fiscal policy, and much of the recent debate about EMU has thus been concerned with its implications for the conduct, financing, and coordination of national fiscal policies.

The dimensions of fiscal policy

Any analysis of fiscal policy must deal with three macroeconomic issues: the stabilization problem, the coordination problem, and the solvency problem. All three take on special forms in a monetary union.[1]

1. For surveys of the literature on these problems as they relate to EMU, see Commission (1990, 1993) and van der Ploeg (1991a). Two more fiscal problems lie on the boundary between the macro and micro dimensions: (1) the extent to which EMU will distort the financing of public expenditure by preventing governments from making optimal choices between taxation and seigniorage when the costs of collecting taxes differ across countries; and (2) how EMU will affect the size of the public sector itself and thus the supply of public goods. The first problem was raised by Canzoneri and Rogers (1990), but others, including Masson and Taylor (1992), have challenged the main assumption implicit in their analysis – that governments' choices between taxation and seigniorage are made to minimize the distortions involved in financing public expenditure. The second problem was raised by van der Ploeg (1991b), who argued that EMU will reduce revenues from seigniorage below what they have been in some EC countries and that completion of the internal market will reduce tax revenues by raising factor mobility and fostering tax competition. On seigniorage, see Drazen (1989) and Grilli (1989); on tax competition, see Giovannini (1989) and Eichengreen (1991, 1993a). (Both phenomena, however, can lead to more borrowing rather than less spending, and they are thus stressed in the literature on the solvency problem, discussed below.) Casella (1992) provides a model in which governments acting independently supply excessive quantities of public goods, so that fiscal policy coordination is needed for an optimal outcome, and a monetary union can substitute for fiscal coordination. I have shown, however, that Casella's results flow from her assumption that governments are indifferent between taxation and money financing to pay for the production of public goods (see Kenen, 1991). Therefore, I arrive by a different route at van der Ploeg's conclusion. When taxation and money financing are not perfect substitutes, a monetary union does not obviate the need for explicit fiscal policy coordination. In fact, a monetary union by itself can lead governments to produce too few public goods.

The stabilization problem

When a country joins a monetary union, forgoing the use of monetary and exchange rate policies to stabilize its national economy, the independent use of fiscal policy becomes more attractive, despite the political obstacles to fiscal flexibility. It is indeed the only instrument available for dealing with country-specific shocks – disturbances different in nature or timing from those affecting other members of the union, as well as those that are common to all members but affect them differently.

It is easy to devise hypothetical cases in which fiscal policies, used independently, can offset country-specific shocks without harming other members of a monetary union or forcing them to alter their own fiscal policies. It is equally easy, however, to devise cases in which a change in one country's fiscal policy affects other countries adversely and thus leads them to change their own fiscal policies in ways that nullify the intended effects of the initial policy change. The likelihood of this second outcome is increased by "model uncertainty" and the vagaries of the political process, which make it hard to adjust fiscal policies at the right times and by the right amounts.[2]

Much recent research on the stabilization problem in EMU has taken as its point of departure the notion of an "optimum currency area" as defined by Mundell (1961). Two countries may be said to constitute an optimum currency area when the fixing of the nominal exchange rate between their currencies does not impose real costs on their economies. That will be the case, of course, when both countries' prices and wages are perfectly flexible; the *real* exchange rate will be flexible even though the *nominal* exchange rate is fixed. But it will also be the case when labor and capital are perfectly mobile between the two countries. A switch in demand between their exports will reduce the demand for labor and capital in one of the two countries and will raise it in the other, but it will not pose a major problem when labor and capital can move freely from one country to the other. The effects of a switch in demand can be greatly reduced, moreover, if each country can use fiscal policy to stabilize output and employment. In different terms, a currency area is optimal if it does not increase its members' vulnerability to real shocks or reduce their ability to deal with them.

Clearly, there can be no optimum currency area in this strict sense.

2. The notion of "model uncertainty" encompasses all sorts of ignorance about economic behavior and the international transmission process. Its implications for policy coordination have been discussed extensively (see, e.g., Frankel, 1988; Bryant et al., 1988; and Ghosh and Masson, 1994), but it is also relevant to the conduct of a single country's fiscal policy in an open-economy setting.

Prices and wages are not perfectly flexible. Labor and capital are not perfectly mobile. And the EC does not resemble an optimum currency area in this same strict sense, as labor mobility is fairly low. It may rise in the future, with the completion of the single market, but linguistic and cultural barriers will continue to limit it.[3] This conclusion, however, says nothing about the *extent* to which the EC falls short of being an optimum currency area, and it makes no allowance for the benefits of EMU. The final chapter of this book will provide an overall cost–benefit assessment of EMU. Here, the central concern is the extent to which individual EC governments will continue to require fiscal autonomy once they have forsworn monetary autonomy.

When national economies are highly diversified, industry-specific shocks need not show up as country-specific shocks. They may offset each other and thus average out instead of adding up.[4] When national economies are similar, they will experience similar shocks, and when they belong to a monetary union, they can then alter the union's monetary policy or change its external exchange rate to offset the common effects of the shocks. Hence, the greater the degree of diversification or economic similarity, the smaller the cost of joining a monetary union.[5]

From the standpoint of a single country, then, the real cost of entering a monetary union will depend on the size and nature of the shocks to which the country is exposed, given the extent of factor mobility among the members of the union and the degree of price flexibility. If the shocks are small or symmetric, the real cost will be low; if the shocks are large or asymmetric, the real cost will be high. This conclusion has produced a large body of research on the nature of the shocks actually experienced by EC countries, compared with those experienced by regional economies in the United States and in other multiregional countries, which are treated for this purpose as monetary unions.[6]

3. Eichengreen (1990, 1992c) provides evidence suggesting that labor mobility is lower among EC countries than among U.S. or Canadian regions; Eichengreen (1993b) also provides new evidence that the internal mobility of labor is lower in Italy and Great Britain than in the United States. On factor mobility and interregional adjustment in the United States, see Blanchard and Katz (1992).

4. But there must still be mobility within each economy in order to average out the employment effects of industry-specific shocks, even when the economies are thoroughly diversified.

5. The first possibility was raised in Kenen (1969), and both possibilities were cited by the Commission (1990) as reasons for believing that the costs of EMU will not be very high. But recent research discussed below has raised doubts about the Commission's conclusion. Furthermore, Masson and Melitz (1990) stress a point made by Corden (1972), that countries facing the same shock may want to respond to it differently when they have different policy preferences.

6. Eichengreen (1990) inspired much of this research with his early survey of U.S. experience; important contributions have been made by Lamfalussy (1989), Weber (1991a),

One such study (Bini-Smaghi and Vori, 1992) showed that the economies of EC countries tend to be more diversified internally than the economies of U.S. regions. On both sides of the Atlantic, moreover, sector-specific disturbances account for a large part of the variance in total output – larger than the part that can be ascribed to aggregate, country-specific shocks. Taking these findings together and ignoring all other considerations, one would be led to predict that the shocks affecting EC countries have been smaller and more symmetric than the shocks affecting U.S. regions. But that has not been true.

Weber (1991a) conducted a thorough statistical study of the EC countries, using techniques adapted from Cohen and Wyplosz (1989). He found that the shocks to nominal variables, such as inflation rates, have been highly symmetric and that the asymmetric components have been shrinking. He also found that supply shocks have been fairly symmetric – which is what one would expect for diversified national economies. But Weber also found that labor market and demand shocks have been rather asymmetric – so much so, in Weber's view, as to warn the EC governments that they will need fiscal autonomy when they move on to EMU.

Although Weber used sophisticated methods, he treated each change in each variable as being a new exogenous shock. Bayoumi and Eichengreen (1993) tackled the problem differently. They treated each change in each variable as a weighted sum of current and past shocks. Furthermore, they decomposed the shocks into demand and supply shocks by imposing strong restrictions on the long-run behavior of output and price levels.[7] Their approach provides results strikingly different from those obtained when each output and price change is treated as a new exogenous shock.

In the first four columns of Table 4–1, every output and price change is treated as a separate shock. Columns 1 and 3 use standard deviations

Eichengreen (1992c), Bayoumi (1993), Bayoumi and Eichengreen (1993), De Grauwe and Vanhaverbeke (1993), and von Hagen and Neumann (1994). Eichengreen (1992c) points out, however, that some of these studies are flawed, because they use changes in real exchange rates to measure asymmetric shocks. Changes in real exchange rates reflect endogenous responses to shocks, and their sizes will therefore reflect the manner in which countries have adjusted to shocks, not merely the sizes of the shocks themselves. If two countries or regions comprise an optimum currency area in the Mundellian sense, with perfect labor mobility between them, asymmetric shocks cannot affect the real exchange rate between their currencies. As the studies by Weber (1991a) and Bayoumi and Eichengreen (1993) come closest to avoiding this methodological problem, they are the ones featured in the text.

7. Demand shocks were assumed to have transitory output effects but permanent price effects; supply shocks were assumed to have permanent output and price effects. See Minford (1993) for a critique of this methodology.

Table 4-1 *Shocks to economies of EC countries and U.S. regions: Standard deviations and correlations with anchor areas (Germany for EC and Mideast Region for United States)*

| Country or region | Crude measures of shocks | | | | Extracted measures of shocks | | | |
| | Output growth | | Inflation | | Supply shocks | | Demand shocks | |
	St dev (1)	Corr (2)	St dev (3)	Corr (4)	St dev (5)	Corr (6)	St dev (7)	Corr (8)
Belgium	2.2	0.73	2.4	0.57	1.5	0.61	1.6	0.33
Denmark	2.5	0.67	2.3	0.69	1.7	0.59	2.1	0.39
France	1.8	0.74	3.1	0.47	1.2	0.54	1.2	0.35
Germany	2.2	–	1.7	–	1.7	–	1.4	–
Greece	3.5	0.66	6.7	0.00	0.3	0.14	1.6	0.19
Ireland	2.2	0.09	5.0	0.49	2.1	-0.06	3.4	-0.08
Italy	2.3	0.52	5.4	0.33	2.2	0.23	2.0	0.17
Netherlands	2.2	0.79	2.8	0.68	1.7	0.59	1.5	0.17
Portugal	3.4	0.57	7.4	-0.07	2.9	0.21	2.8	0.21
Spain	2.7	0.56	4.4	0.26	2.2	0.31	1.5	-0.07
United Kingdom	2.1	0.54	5.2	0.48	2.6	0.11	1.6	0.16
Average	2.5	0.59	4.2	0.39	1.8	0.33	1.9	0.18

	St dev	Corr	St dev	Corr	St dev	Corr	St dev	Corr
Mideast	2.5	–	2.0	–	1.2	–	1.9	–
New England	3.1	0.94	2.0	0.98	1.4	0.86	2.5	0.79
Great Lakes	4.0	0.88	2.2	0.98	1.3	0.81	3.3	0.60
Plains	2.7	0.85	2.3	0.94	1.6	0.30	2.2	0.51
South East	2.7	0.76	2.2	0.72	1.1	0.66	1.8	0.50
South West	2.2	0.40	3.5	0.89	1.9	-0.12	1.8	0.13
Mountain	2.4	0.27	2.4	0.84	1.8	0.18	1.5	-0.28
Far West	3.3	0.66	1.8	0.96	1.3	0.52	1.7	0.33
Average	2.9	0.68	2.3	0.90	1.5	0.46	2.1	0.37

Note: St dev = standard deviation; Corr = correlation.

Source: Bayoumi and Eichengreen (1993), Tables 7.1, 7.4, and 7.6; computations on year-to-year changes in logarithms of raw data for 1960–1988 (but standard deviations are multiplied here by 100 and thus approximate percentages).

to measure the sizes of the shocks affecting EC countries and U.S. regions. Columns 2 and 4 show how closely the shocks affecting a country or region are correlated with the contemporaneous shocks affecting an "anchor area" (Germany in the EC case, and the Mideast region in the U.S. case); high correlations testify to symmetry between the shocks affecting a particular country or region and the shocks affecting the corresponding anchor area. The numbers suggest that the shocks to real growth have been slightly smaller in EC countries than in U.S. regions, whereas the opposite appears to have been true for shocks to inflation rates. But the shocks affecting EC countries have been less symmetric than those affecting U.S. regions, most clearly in the case of the shocks to inflation rates.[8]

The same basic data on output and inflation were used to obtain the numbers in columns 5 through 8 of Table 4–1, but the numbers themselves pertain to the size and symmetry of the demand and supply shocks extracted from the data by Bayoumi and Eichengreen. Here, it would appear that EC countries have suffered somewhat larger supply shocks than have U.S. regions but that they have suffered slightly smaller demand shocks. This method of measurement also reveals that the shocks have been less symmetric on both sides of the Atlantic (but are, as before, even less symmetric in Europe). As Figure 4–1 makes clear, an additional result is lurking in these numbers: the shocks affecting the "core" countries of the EC have not been markedly less symmetric than those affecting U.S. regions. (The average correlation for the supply shocks affecting Belgium, Denmark, France, and the Netherlands is 0.58, which exceeds the U.S. average; the average correlation for the demand shocks is 0.31, which is not far below the U.S. average.) Hence, Bayoumi and Eichengreen conclude that there is a strong case for a two-speed approach to EMU. The core countries are ready to move faster.

All such conclusions, however, are open to a serious objection. Although numbers like those in Table 4–1 may provide an accurate characterization of the shocks experienced by EC countries, they may not say much about the shocks that lie ahead. The advent of EMU may make demand shocks more symmetric, because individual EC countries will not be able to generate demand shocks of their own by altering their monetary policies differently. The effects of EMU and those of the

---

8. In anticipation of a point made below, note that the average of the correlations for the "core" EC countries (Belgium, Denmark, France, and the Netherlands) are not much higher than those for the EC as a whole. (The average is 0.73 for the shocks to real growth and 0.60 for the shocks to the inflation rate, with the former being about equal to the corresponding U.S. correlation but the latter being far below the U.S. correlation.)

Figure 4-1 *Correlations of EC countries' shocks with German shocks and of U.S. regions' shocks with Mideast Region's shocks*

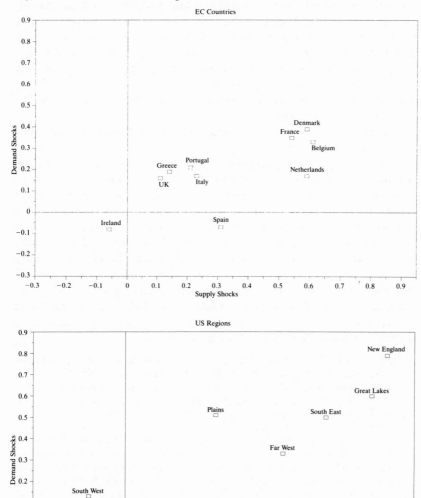

single market on the future supply shocks are more difficult to assess. There are those who maintain that the closer integration of the EC countries will promote intraindustry trade and thus tend to diversify output within individual EC countries. On this view, industry-specific shocks will be more likely to average out rather than add up, and the shocks themselves will become more symmetric, as the national economies become more similar.[9] Yet recent research on geography and trade suggests that tighter integration may lead to more specialization, not diversification. In that case, supply shocks could become larger and less symmetric than they were before.[10]

The numbers in Table 4–1 raise another important issue. Individual regions in the United States appear to experience large, asymmetric shocks, but state governments do not use their fiscal autonomy to stabilize output or employment. Most of them operate under self-imposed rules that force them to balance their budgets. The rules themselves range from the rather weak requirement that the governor submit a balanced budget all the way to limits on actual borrowing (see von Hagen, 1992). Therefore, the states' fiscal systems tend to operate procyclically, not countercyclically; spending must be cut or tax rates raised whenever the states' tax revenues are reduced by a recession.[11] But the federal fiscal system compensates in part for the perversity of the state systems. Whenever economic activity falls in a particular state or region, its citizens' federal tax payments fall, and they receive more transfer payments from the federal government.[12]

9. This was the view taken by the Commission (1990); see also Bini-Smaghi and Vori (1992), Gros and Thygesen (1992), Bofinger (1994), and Viñals (1994).

10. See Krugman (1993). It should be noted, however, that Bayoumi (1993) could not find differences between the shocks experienced by EMS countries in the 1980s and those that they experienced before joining the EMS. (The responses to shocks, however, became more similar across the EMS countries.)

11. Eichengreen and Bayoumi (1994) show that states with tight fiscal rules borrow less than other states (i.e., that the rules are effective). They also make an important point about the behavior of state budgets. Many states must take procyclical budget-cutting measures during recessions, most notably on the expenditure side. Nevertheless, their budgets fluctuate countercyclically. Their fiscal rules do not prevent their budgets from moving from surplus into deficit when the states' economies slip into recession. See also Bayoumi, Goldstein, and Woglom (1993).

12. Note that this flexibility has two parts – an effect on the distribution of federal receipts and payments and an effect on their levels. Suppose that the federal budget is balanced initially. If economic activity falls in one region but rises in another – the case studied by Mundell (1961) and purest of asymmetric disturbances – the redistribution of federal receipts and payments can help to stabilize activity in both regions without producing a surplus or deficit in the federal budget. If activity falls in one region without rising in another, the changes in federal receipts and payments can still help the afflicted region, but they will produce a federal deficit. In effect, the federal government will

This phenomenon was identified initially by Ingram (1959, 1973) and has been studied closely by those seeking to compare fiscal arrangements in the EC with those in the United States and other fiscal federations. The first such study, by Sala-i-Martin and Sachs (1992), found that a region's tax payments to the U.S. federal government fall by about 34 cents when its per capita income falls by a dollar, and federal transfers to the region rise by about 6 cents. The two figures together say that the net change in the federal "take" offsets about 40 cents of every one-dollar fall in a region's income.

The results obtained by Sala-i-Martin and Sachs were criticized by von Hagen (1992) for failing to segregate the cyclical effect from a very different structural effect – the fact that a high-income region normally pays more taxes than a low-income region, regardless of the cyclical situation. When making his own estimates, von Hagen produced a much lower figure for the cyclical change in the federal take.[13] Nevertheless, subsequent studies, although they pay attention to von Hagen's critique and try to impound the structural effect, come somewhat closer to the estimate by Sala-i-Martin and Sachs. Bayoumi and Masson (1994) find that the cyclical change in the federal take offsets about 28 cents of a one-dollar fall in regional income; Goodhart and Smith (1993) find that it offsets about 20 cents; and Pisani-Ferry, Italianer, and Lescure (1993) put the figure at 17 cents.[14]

Clearly, the change in the federal take cannot offset an asymmetric

borrow on behalf of the afflicted region – and the federal government can borrow on less costly terms than the regional authorities would face (see Masson and Taylor, 1992; and Krugman, 1993). Krugman attaches particular importance to this point. Citing Blanchard and Katz (1992), who show that a declining region usually suffers an outflow of capital and labor, he argues that the region's government will not be free to run a large budget deficit because its creditworthiness has been impaired. This may be true, Krugman suggests, even when the shock affecting the region is itself temporary; the outflows of capital and labor induced by the shock will have permanent (hysteretical) effects on output and income, impairing the region's ability to service more debt. But see the comments by Casella (1993) and De Grauwe (1993b).

13. See also Fratianni and von Hagen (1992), who defend von Hagen's estimate against recent criticism. (They also claim that the states' fiscal rules have little effect on their actual budgets and do not appreciably reduce the danger of egregiously extreme fiscal outcomes.)

14. These studies differ in methodology and coverage; von Hagen, for example, focused exclusively on the tax side. A compilation of recent studies, including those for Canada and other countries, will be found in the report of the group of economists prepared for the EC (Commission, 1993). See also Gros and Jones (1994), who examine the methodological issues and take an innovative approach to measuring the structural effect; they argue that earlier studies overestimated the importance of interregional redistribution, compared with the importance of changes in the federal budget itself.

shock completely, but its contribution is not negligible. Recall the point made in the Delors Report (1989), however, that the EC budget is very small and does not have much cyclical flexibility. It cannot help to stabilize output and employment in the EC as a whole or to offset any significant part of an asymmetric shock by making implicit transfers among EC countries. There have been proposals to make it more flexible by transferring more fiscal functions to the EC. This was the line taken by the MacDougall Report (Commission, 1977), which said that any future monetary union would call for a large increase in the budget. More recently, several economists have urged that certain social insurance programs, notably unemployment insurance, be shifted from the national to the EC level,[15] and a study prepared by a group of experts (Commission, 1993) has proposed the creation of an EC fund to make block grants to countries that suffer severe shocks.[16] But none of these recommendations will be adopted soon, and the Delors Report was right: the stabilization problem has to be solved at the national level, albeit with strong safeguards at the EC level to protect the fiscal stance of the EC as a whole.

The coordination problem

Because the EC budget is small, the fiscal stance of the EC will depend mainly on the sum of the national surpluses and deficits. No single

15. See Masson and Melitz (1990), van der Ploeg (1991a), Wyplosz (1991), Eichengreen (1992c), and MacDougall (1992).
16. See also the detailed presentations in Italianer and Vanheukelen (1993) and Italianer and Pisani-Ferry (1994), which show that the experts' proposal could have effects similar in size to those of the implicit transfers made by federal fiscal systems. The group itself concedes that its proposal will not help to stabilize incomes and activity unless the block grants are passed along from governments to households; if they are used merely to reduce the national budget deficits, they will not have the desired effect. The group also concedes that its proposal involves explicit intergovernmental transfers and may therefore meet political resistance. As Masson and Melitz (1990) note, the implicit transfers made through federal fiscal systems are not meant or seen to stabilize regional incomes; they are by-products of the ways in which those systems treat individual citizens. It should also be noted that Article 103a of the Maastricht Treaty already provides for Community assistance to a country experiencing "severe difficulties caused by exceptional occurrences beyond its control." (Such assistance, however, must be approved unanimously by the Council unless the country's difficulties are due to a natural disaster, when assistance can be voted by a qualified majority.) It has sometimes been suggested that the Community's structural funds could be used to cushion the effects of asymmetric shocks. These suggestions confuse stabilization with cohesion and real convergence; the structural funds are meant to reduce basic disparities in levels of economic development, not to deal with cyclical changes in income and activity. On the question of cohesion and the structural funds, see, e.g., Begg and Mayes (1992), de la Dehesa and Krugman (1992), and Commission (1993).

government, however, can be expected to pay much attention to the effects of its own fiscal policy on the fiscal stance of the EC as a whole, although it will have important effects on each and every EC country. When combined with the monetary policy of the ECB, it will define the policy mix, which will, in turn, affect the national economy of every EC country, because of its effect on interest rates and ECU exchange rates.

Recall the example in Chapter 3, in which a large EC country ran a big budget deficit. With no change in ECB monetary policy, EC interest rates will rise and crowd out investment in all EC countries, not just the one running the budget deficit. Furthermore, there will be a capital inflow, which will cause the ECU to appreciate and crowd out the production of tradable goods by reducing exports and raising imports. These effects may not be large enough to reduce output and employment in the country running the budget deficit; the outcome will depend on whether the increase in domestic demand resulting from the deficit exceeds the crowding-out effects on investment and trade flows. But they are apt to reduce output and employment in other EC countries, which cannot expect to enjoy a comparable increase in aggregate demand but are bound to share the crowding-out effects. The net effect on the rest of the world is harder to predict; higher EC interest rates will raise world interest rates, which will reduce investment in the outside world, but the appreciation of the ECU will raise the demand for the tradable goods produced by the rest of the world. Uncertainty about the sign of the net effect, however, does not diminish the importance of the policy mix for capital formation in the EC and the outside world or for the composition of aggregate demand.

The recommendations in the Delors Report (1989) were aimed partly at this problem and its implications for the economic environment in which the ECB will function. It called for fiscal policy coordination as well as binding limits on national budget deficits. Without them, it said, the Community cannot expect to establish a policy mix appropriate for internal balance and will not be able to play its part in the global adjustment process.

The Maastricht Treaty pays scant attention to these considerations. It is concerned with restrictions on the fiscal autonomy of the individual EC countries. Therefore, the debate about the Maastricht Treaty has focused on the reasons for imposing those restrictions and has featured two such reasons: externalities and solvency.[17] The externalities argu-

17. The attention given to these arguments may have less to do with the actual provisions of the treaty than with the current concerns of economists; the microeconomic and intertemporal issues posed by externalities and solvency problems are more intriguing to many economists than the macroeconomic issues raised by the familiar policy-mix

ment was set out most forcefully by Canzoneri and Diba (1991), and is discussed below.[18] The solvency argument is discussed in the next section of this chapter.

The increase in interest rates resulting from a budget deficit will have two effects, apart from curbing aggregate demand by depressing investment and the production of tradable goods. First, it will reduce future output by slowing the growth of the capital stock. Second, it will force the government to raise taxes in the future, not merely to service the new debt created by the budget deficit but also to cover the increase in interest payments on the existing stock of debt. This increase in taxes will reduce future income because taxes are distortionary. A government deciding to run a budget deficit may, of course, take due account of these real costs. An increase in one country's interest rate, however, will raise other countries' rates, imposing some of the costs on those countries' citizens. These are the main externalities of budget deficits.

De Grauwe (1992a) discounts the importance of these externalities because, he says, one country's budget deficit will not affect other countries' interest rates when capital markets function efficiently. It need not even raise the interest rate of the country with the deficit unless it poses a threat to that country's solvency and thus raises the risk premium attached to its debt. He would, of course, be right for the case of a small country – one whose budget deficit would be too small to absorb an appreciable share of total EC saving. If the country is larger than that, its deficit is likely to raise interest rates in every EC country. But De Grauwe (1992b) makes another point that is far more valid. The externalities described above cannot be ascribed to EMU per se unless it can be shown that exchange rate risk is a major barrier to capital mobility, so that EMU will increase capital mobility and thus raise the exposure of the EC countries to the effects of their partners' budget deficits.[19] This possibility cannot be dismissed, but it is not an adequate basis for using EMU to justify stringent restrictions on the fiscal autonomy of the EC countries. If the fiscal externalities are truly large and worrisome, fiscal autonomy should have been restricted by the Single European Act, which was aimed effectively and explicitly at dismantling barriers to capital mobility.

As for the fiscal limits themselves – their form and the context in

problem. (In fact, the exchange rate effect of a large budget deficit is sometimes described in the academic literature as an externality that must be prevented by imposing limits on national autonomy.)
18. See also De Grauwe (1992b), Eichengreen (1992b), Gros and Thygesen (1992), and Aizenman (1994).
19. Goodhart (1992c) and Langfeldt (1992) make the same point.

which they appear – they are meant to deal with the solvency problem rather than the externalities problem.

The solvency problem

A debtor can be said to be solvent if its obligations do not exceed the present value of the future revenues available to service them. But there is a crucial difference between the solvency problem faced by a government and the problem faced by a private debtor. A government can increase taxes to augment its future revenues. No private debtor can.

The basic solvency constraint can be reformulated to say that the growth rate of a government's debt must not exceed the interest rate on that debt.[20] For this purpose, the growth rate of the debt is defined as the ratio of the budget deficit (excluding interest payments) to the stock of debt outstanding. This reformulation of the solvency constraint can then be used to ask whether a government's fiscal stance is sustainable. Calculations of this sort, with numerous refinements, have been made by Corsetti and Roubini (1991). They find that solvency is not a problem for most of the large EC countries but is a problem for Italy and some smaller EC countries, including Greece, Belgium, Ireland, and the Netherlands.[21]

If markets were able to price risk accurately, a government would find it more costly to borrow as its deficits and debt brought it closer to its solvency constraint, and there is some evidence to this effect.[22] Too often, however, markets have been slow to realize that a government is facing a solvency problem, and they have reacted very sharply when forced to contemplate that possibility. This was certainly true in 1982, when Mexico's debt crisis led banks to change their views abruptly about a large number of developing countries, and it was also true in the case of New York City a few years earlier.[23] Many reasons have been offered for this behavior, ranging from misunderstanding of the debtor's situa-

20. On the analytics of the solvency constraint, see Corsetti and Roubini (1993); for a critique of recent empirical applications, including those cited below, see Weber (1993).
21. Other studies reach similar conclusions but are less pessimistic about Belgium and Ireland; see Giovannini and Spaventa (1991) and Buiter, Corsetti, and Roubini (1993).
22. Eichengreen and Bayoumi (1994) study the experience of U.S. states; see also Goldstein and Woglom (1992) and Bayoumi, Goldstein, and Woglom (1993). Edwards (1986) studies the experience of developing countries. But Frenkel and Goldstein (1991) note that we have as yet no firm basis for believing that governments are sensitive to higher borrowing costs; see also Lane (1993).
23. See Begg et al. (1991), Goldstein and Woglom (1992), and Frenkel and Goldstein (1991).

tion to the creditors' belief that some other party will bail them out.[24] Governments publish lots of numbers – far more than private debtors – but those numbers do not reveal much about the long-term fiscal outlook. To assess that outlook properly, moreover, one must forecast politics as well as economics.

Why should the debt problems of an EC government be cause for concern by the whole Community? Might they interfere with the functioning of EMU? Buiter, Corsetti, and Roubini (1993) argue correctly that there can be no justification for EC concern unless a debt problem is likely to have large externalities, and they believe that the externalities are small. Accordingly, they argue that the national debt of each EC country should be the responsibility of that country alone. Furthermore, the "no bail out" clause of the Maastricht Treaty tries to make sure of that:

> The Community shall not be liable for or assume the commitments of central governments, regional, local or other public authorities, other bodies governed by public law, or public undertakings of any Member State. . . . A Member State shall be not liable for or assume the commitments of central governments, regional, local or other public authorities, other bodies governed by public law or public undertakings of another Member State. (TEU, Article 104b)[25]

But the authors of the treaty went further, to deal with two possibilities. The first is the possibility of political pressure from a heavily indebted government wanting the ECB to help it. The second is the possibility of market pressure coming from the threat to financial stability posed by a prospective or actual default.

Economists like to put the first possibility in Machiavellian terms, saying that a heavily indebted government will want the ECB to inflate away its debt by departing from the maintenance of price stability.[26] But

24. Kenen (1992c) describes the uncertainties that attached to the prospects of developing countries just before the 1982 crisis. Guttentag and Herring (1986) suggest that those countries' creditors displayed disaster myopia – the tendency to underestimate the likelihood of a rare calamity. Dooley (1995) argues that the creditors' behavior reflected their belief that their own governments would bail them out. Eaton, Gersovitz, and Stiglitz (1986) survey the large theoretical literature on dealings between sovereign debtors and private creditors.

25. This clause does not cover the ECB directly, but the ECB is more likely to acquire public sector obligations as assets than as liabilities. Fratianni and von Hagen (1992) suggest, in fact, that the "no bail out" clause was not adopted to safeguard the monetary union per se, but rather to discourage heavily indebted EC countries from invoking the solidarity of the Community to extract assistance from their partners; see also Masson and Taylor (1992) and Frankel (1993).

26. See, e.g., Froot and Rogoff (1992), who predict that the heavily indebted governments will deliberately raise their inflation rates just before Stage Three begins; they

Giovannini and Spaventa (1991) point out that such a government will not gain much from generating an inflation. Some of its debt will already be indexed, and much of it will be short term, which means that it must be rolled over at a higher interest rate when the inflation rate rises.[27] Begg et al. (1991) take a similar line, arguing that the political threat could be reduced substantially if heavily indebted EC governments were required to index more of their debts before the beginning of Stage Three. Furthermore, the Machiavellian view misrepresents the problem and is controverted by the evidence. No one has been able to demonstrate clearly that heavily indebted governments deliberately adopt inflationary policies to reduce their real debts (see Grilli, Masciandaro, and Tabellini, 1991).

Pressure from a government is more likely to develop when markets come to believe, rightly or wrongly, that the government faces a solvency problem. Markets will then refuse to roll over the government's debt unless interest rates are raised. The ECB could not be asked to acquire the country's debt directly, but it might be asked to make open-market purchases in order to hold down the interest cost of rolling over the debt. That is how the problem was posed right after World War II, when several central banks, including the Federal Reserve and the Bank of England, had to hold down interest rates by open-market purchases, and in the early 1960s, when the Banca d'Italia had to do the same thing. Buiter, Corsetti, and Roubini (1993) point out, however, that the ECB will enjoy more independence than any of those central banks and should therefore be able to resist such pressure.

The possibility of market pressure is related to this form of the political problem, but it is more serious. Suppose that Italy was to default on its debt or was expected to do so. Holders of Italian debt would suffer large capital losses, the solvency of financial institutions might be threatened, and the ECB might have to intervene.[28] It would not have to buy Italian debt, but it might have to make other open-market purchases to stave off the threat to the financial system. The gravity of the threat, moreover, would not depend on the ownership of the debt at issue. The

will engineer "one final realignment" of the EMS currencies and thus undermine exchange rate stability.

27. Much of the Italian debt is short term, but most of it is not indexed. In 1989, the average maturity was 2.5 years in Italy, compared with 5.0 years in Germany and 9.4 years in the United Kingdom (see Begg et al., 1991).
28. Giovannini and Spaventa (1991) claim that the potential losses would be small, because much of the debt would be short term, but that is not quite true. The prices of short-term bonds do not fall very much when interest rates rise. The prices of all bonds will fall sharply, however, when a default is in prospect.

ECB might not be able to stand aside even if the whole Italian debt were owned by Italian banks and other Italian investors. There will be a single banking system in Stage Three of EMU, and all of its parts will be linked via the interbank market. In fact, localization of the problem could intensify the threat to the whole banking system; the potential losses would be concentrated on a small number of banks and would thus be larger in relation to their capital.

Nevertheless, economists who agree on little else are virtually unanimous in their belief that ex ante limitations on deficits and debt are not the best way to protect the financial system from the effects of prospective or actual defaults.[29] It would be better to rely on prudential supervision and, perhaps, to reconsider the zero-weighting of government debt when assessing the capital adequacy of financial institutions.[30]

Fiscal hopes and fears

There are two views of fiscal policy. Optimists continue to believe that fiscal policy can play a useful role in macroeconomic stabilization, and some of them also believe that the governments of highly open economies can and should coordinate their fiscal policies. In this sense, the Delors Report (1989) was moderately optimistic. Although it called for limits on national budget deficits, it also called for policy coordination.

The fiscal provisions of the treaty reflect more pessimistic views about fiscal policy. Pessimists have various reasons for their views, but they unite in their belief that fiscal policy can do great harm and little good. Some say that budget deficits do not matter, because taxpayers know that a deficit today will have to be offset by a surplus tomorrow, so as to satisfy the solvency constraint; they will therefore reduce their spending whenever their taxes are cut, knowing that their taxes will be raised in the future. Others believe that deficits matter but also believe that democratic politics constrain the use of fiscal policy for countercyclical purposes. Spending and tax changes are delayed by political bickering and

29. See, e.g., Begg et al. (1991), Bovenberg, Kremers, and Masson (1991), van der Ploeg (1991b), Wyplosz (1991), and Goodhart (1992c). Giovannini and Spaventa (1991) are almost alone in favoring ex ante limits to head off possible threats to financial stability.
30. Begg et al. (1991) make the same proposal and also recommend that a high-debt country be required to lengthen the average maturity of its debt. The zero-weighting of government debt, however, could not be adopted by the EC countries alone or with respect to the debts of the EC governments alone. It would have to be done by all of the countries subscribing to the Basle Concordat on capital adequacy and with respect to the debts of all the industrial country governments. Bank supervisors cannot be expected to impose harsher capital requirements on their own countries' banks or to make invidious judgments about the solvency of individual governments.

take effect too late; hence, they may actually amplify economic fluctuations. Furthermore, it is easier to mobilize political support for measures to raise budget deficits than for those to cut them back or turn them into surpluses.

The Maastricht Treaty provides for policy coordination, but it stresses restraints on national policies, not collective policy formation. Furthermore, the budgetary limits in the treaty seem to be aimed chiefly at the solvency problem, not at the stabilization and coordination problems. They pay attention to levels of indebtedness, not exclusively to budget deficits.

Policy coordination in the treaty

Under Article 103 of the treaty, the EC countries must treat their economic policies "as a matter of common concern" and must coordinate them in the Council in order to achieve the Community's objectives. To this end:

> The Council shall, acting by a qualified majority . . . , formulate a draft for the broad guidelines of the economic policies of the Member States and of the Community, and shall report its findings to the European Council.

> The European Council shall, acting on the basis of this report from the Council, discuss a conclusion on the broad guidelines of the economic policies of the Member States and of the Community.

> On the basis of this conclusion, the Council shall, acting by a qualified majority, adopt a recommendation setting out these broad guidelines. (TEU, Article 103)

The Council must report its recommendation to the European Parliament, but the Parliament has no role in designing the guidelines – which is rather odd.

What will be done with the guidelines? Basing its work on reports from the Commission, the Council will monitor economic developments in each EC country and in the EC as a whole. If it finds that a government's policies are inconsistent with the guidelines or may jeopardize the functioning of EMU itself, the Council may make the "necessary recommendations" to that government.

The Council adopted the first set of policy guidelines in December 1993, just before Stage Two began, and adopted a second set in July 1994. It emphasized the need for a "determined commitment" to reduce budget deficits, especially by Greece, Italy, and Spain, and the need for microeconomic measures to reduce unemployment. Even before adopting the first set of guidelines, however, the Council had begun to review the economic policies of individual governments. Governments were asked to report on the policies they will pursue to achieve economic convergence and thus meet the requirements for entering Stage Three. The reports were reviewed by the Monetary Committee, an advisory body comprising two persons from each EC country and two members of the Commission, which reports to the Council and the Commission.[31]

The approach embodied in the treaty, however, does not contemplate full-fledged coordination, which is usually defined as a process involving mutual modifications in the participants' national policies.[32] Furthermore, governments cannot be penalized for failing to comply with the recommendations made under Article 103, although the Council can publish its recommendations to individual governments, exposing them to criticism. But the Council *can* impose sanctions if a government fails to eliminate an excessive budget deficit.

Excessive deficits in the treaty

The Maastricht Treaty sets out an elaborate procedure to define and deal with excessive budget deficits. The procedure is described at some length here because of its intrinsic importance and because an EC country that is found to have an excessive deficit cannot enter Stage Three of EMU.

The process

Article 104c of the treaty begins with a binding commitment and goes on to define criteria for judging compliance with it:

> Member States shall avoid excessive government deficits.

> The Commission shall monitor the development of the budgetary situation and of the stock of government debt in the Member States with a view to identifying gross errors. In particular it shall examine compliance with budgetary discipline on the basis of the following two criteria:

31. The national participants serve as individuals, not as representatives of their countries' governments, and usually come from the ministry of finance or economics and from the national central bank. The Monetary Committee has played a key role in arranging EMS realignments. Under Article 109c of the treaty, the new Economic and Financial Committee will replace it in Stage Three, with a modified mandate and membership. (The reports themselves were solicited under Article 109e of the treaty, on steps to be taken before Stage Three; when necessary, it said, governments should adopt multiyear programs to ensure the convergence required for EMU.)
32. See, e.g., Kenen (1989) or Dobson (1991) and the sources cited there.

(a) whether the ratio of the planned or actual government deficit to gross domestic product exceeds a reference value, unless
— either the ratio has declined substantially and continuously and has reached a level that comes close to the reference value;
— or, alternatively, the excess over the reference value is only exceptional and temporary and the deficit remains close to the reference value;

(b) whether the ratio of government debt to gross domestic product exceeds a reference value, unless the ratio is sufficiently diminishing and approaching the reference value at a satisfactory pace. . . .

If a Member State does not fulfil the requirements under one or both of these criteria, the Commission shall prepare a report. The report . . . shall also take into account whether the government deficit exceeds government investment expenditure and take into account all other relevant factors, including the medium term economic and budgetary position of the Member State.

If the Commission concludes that a particular government is running or may run an excessive deficit, it will address an opinion to the Council, which will decide the question formally. If the Council agrees with the Commission, it will make recommendations to the government with a view to correcting the situation "within a given period."[33] If there is no effective follow-up on the part of the government, the Council may publish its recommendations.

All of these provisions apply from the start of Stage Two.[34] But more can be done in Stage Three. If a government persists in failing to heed the Council's recommendations, the Council may "give notice to the Member State concerned to take, within a specified time limit, measures for the deficit reduction which is judged necessary by the Council in order to remedy the situation." (This rather cumbersome phrasing is meant to distinguish between the size of the reduction and the measures

33. At this initial stage, the Council will act by qualified majority on a recommendation from the Commission and after considering any observations made by the government concerned. All subsequent steps in the process, including a decision that a country no longer has an excessive deficit, will be taken by two-thirds of the weighted votes of the member countries, excluding the votes of the country concerned. (At this initial stage, moreover, the Council may give advice regarding the policy measures required to end an excessive deficit. When taking the next steps, the Council may be quite firm about the size of the requisite reduction in the deficit but may not instruct the country to take particular policy measures. See the quotation and discussion in the next paragraph of the text.)

34. In Stage Two, however, the formal obligation at the beginning of Article 104c is replaced by a promise that governments will "endeavor" to avoid excessive deficits.

needed to achieve it. The Council will judge the need for reduction, not the need for particular policy measures.) Furthermore, the Council may apply one or more of these penalties:

> require that the Member State concerned shall publish additional information, to be specified by the Council, before issuing bonds and securities;
>
> invite the European Investment Bank to reconsider its lending policy toward the Member State concerned;
>
> require that the Member State concerned make a non-interest-bearing deposit of an appropriate size with the Community until the excessive deficit has . . . been corrected;
>
> impose fines of an appropriate size.

And it can "intensify" these penalties when appropriate. When a country has been found to have an excessive deficit, that finding will remain in force until, in the opinion of the Council, the deficit has been corrected.

The provisions of Article 104c are somewhat more flexible than those in earlier drafts of the treaty. In the Netherlands Draft distributed six weeks before Maastricht, the reference value for the budget deficit was described as a "ceiling" and there were no "indents" beneath subparagraph (a), allowing for exceptional or temporary features or for the trend in the deficit.[35] But the reference values themselves are very strict. The one for the planned or actual deficit is 3 percent of gross domestic product; the one for the total debt is 60 percent of GDP; and both are meant to cover the consolidated figures for central, regional, and local governments, including social security funds.[36]

The numbers

Although parts of Article 104c do not apply until Stage Three, the rules and criteria used to define an excessive deficit may be more influential in Stage Two, because a country found to have an excessive deficit will not

35. Bini-Smaghi, Padoa-Schioppa, and Papadia (1994) discuss the evolution of Article 104c.

36. In its own draft of the treaty, Germany had proposed that actual EC-wide averages for deficits and debts be used to identify an excessive deficit; see Italianer (1993). But this proposal raised several problems; it could be too lax at times and too harsh at others. Furthermore, a country that cut its deficit or debt would also reduce the corresponding average and might thus have to intensify its efforts. The reference values actually chosen, however, were based on the EC-wide averages obtaining at the time. It is worth noting that the reference value for debt is far lower than the numbers usually cited in the analytical literature on the solvency problem (see, e.g., Wyplosz, 1991).

be eligible to enter Stage Three.[37] It is thus worth looking at the deficits and debts of the EC countries and the outlook for them.

At the end of 1991, when the Maastricht Treaty was adopted, seven countries had debt ratios higher than 60 percent of GDP (see Table 4–2). Furthermore, three of the other five countries would soon run budget deficits larger than 3 percent of GDP. In other words, most of the EC countries might have been found to have excessive deficits if Article 104c had been applicable early in 1992. Yet the reference values did not look utterly unrealistic. Of the debt ratios higher than 60 percent at the end of 1991, three were below 80 percent. In the previous year, moreover, six countries had run budget deficits smaller than 3 percent.[38]

By 1993, however, a combination of cyclical and other developments had led to a sharp deterioration in the fiscal situation. The same seven countries still had debt ratios above 60 percent of GDP, but five of those ratios had risen. By that time, moreover, four of the five remaining countries were running budget deficits larger than 3 percent of GDP. (Luxembourg was the only exception.) In September 1994, the Commission concluded that ten EC countries were running excessive deficits, and the Council endorsed that conclusion formally. No such finding was made for Luxembourg, and none was made for Ireland; its deficit was below 3 percent, and its debt ratio, though high, had fallen markedly in the late 1980s and was expected to fall further in the 1990s (see Figure 4–2).[39]

The authors of the Maastricht Treaty could not have expected the fiscal situation to deteriorate so sharply. Nevertheless, one must wonder whether the governments of the high-debt countries realized from the start how difficult it would be to bring down their debt ratios. The 60 percent reference value for debt is not wildly inconsistent with the 3 percent reference value for the deficit. If a country's nominal GDP

---

37. That is the view taken by Gros and Thygesen (1992), who point out that exclusion from Stage Three will be more costly and embarrassing than any of the sanctions the Council can impose after Stage Three starts.
38. It should also be noted that the Monetary Committee, which worked on the definition of an excessive deficit, appeared to be thinking primarily about its applicability in Stage Three, several years ahead, not that a country found to have an excessive deficit might be kept from entering Stage Three; see Italianer (1993) and Bini-Smaghi, Padoa-Schioppa, and Papadia (1994).
39. German officials had misgivings about the treatment of Ireland, because they have called for a strict interpretation of Article 104c. But Theo Waigel, the German finance minister, defended the decision after it was taken; only Edmond Alphandéry, his French counterpart, expressed concern about it (*Financial Times*, September 12, 1994).

Table 4-2 Public debts and budget deficits of EC countries as percentages of GDP

Country	Debt						Deficit					
	1991	1992	1993	1994	1995	1996	1991	1992	1993	1994	1995	1996
Belgium[a]	129.5	133.8	138.9	140.1	138.7	136.0	6.8	6.7	6.6	5.5	4.7	4.0
Denmark	64.2	68.8	79.5	78.0	78.0	78.2	2.1	2.5	4.4	4.3	3.0	2.2
France	35.5	39.6	45.8	50.4	53.4	55.6	2.1	3.9	5.8	5.6	4.9	3.9
Germany	42.1	44.8	48.1	51.0	59.4	58.9	3.2	2.6	3.3	2.9	2.4	2.0
Greece[b]	103.9	110.2	115.2	121.3	125.4	128.1	14.4	11.7	13.3	14.1	13.3	12.9
Ireland	97.0	93.4	96.1	89.0	83.7	79.1	2.0	2.2	2.5	2.4	2.0	1.5
Italy	101.4	108.4	118.6	123.7	126.8	128.6	10.2	9.5	9.5	9.6	8.6	7.9
Luxembourg[a,c]	6.2	6.0	7.8	9.2	9.8	9.9	-2.3	-0.3	-1.1	-1.3	-1.6	-2.0
Netherlands	79.0	79.9	81.4	78.8	78.8	78.0	2.5	3.9	3.3	3.8	3.5	2.7
Portugal[d]	69.4	61.7	66.9	70.4	71.7	72.3	6.6	3.3	7.2	6.2	5.8	4.8
Spain	45.2	48.2	59.8	63.5	65.8	66.1	4.9	4.2	7.5	7.0	6.0	4.7
United Kingdom	35.8	42.0	48.6	50.4	52.4	53.1	2.8	6.2	7.8	6.3	4.6	3.4

[a]Excludes social security debt.
[b]Excludes military debt.
[c]Not consolidated; budget data for 1991 not strictly comparable with subsequent data.
[d]Budget data for 1991 not strictly comparable with subsequent data.
Source: EC Commission. Data for 1994, 1995, and 1996 are EC projections, given policies being pursued when the projections were made.

grows steadily at 5 percent per year and the country runs a 3 percent budget deficit, its debt ratio will converge eventually to 60 percent of GDP.[40] But how long will that take? If the country starts with a debt ratio at 100 percent of GDP, two full decades will be needed to reduce it to 75 percent and two more to get close to 60 percent. Even if the country could balance its budget without depressing the growth rate of nominal GDP, it would need a full decade to bring its debt ratio down to 60 percent (see Figure 4–3).[41]

In full-fledged fiscal-policy simulations, the problems of the high-debt countries appear to be even more formidable. Some of the countries' debt ratios already exceed 100 percent of GDP, and most of the high-debt countries have budget deficits larger than 3 percent of GDP. They cannot expect to cut them quickly to 3 percent, let alone balance their budgets, without depressing real economic activity. Having studied several fiscal scenarios, Buiter, Corsetti, and Roubini (1993, p. 72) conclude that "Greece, Italy, Belgium and Ireland need serious fiscal retrenchment, but getting even halfway to the Maastricht debt targets . . . involves dangerous fiscal overkill. A blatantly unrealistic debt target is unhelpful for these countries in designing effective fiscal programs." Retrenchment on the necessary scale, they say, would involve "the economics of the lunatic asylum." Ludlow (1993, p. 14) says the same thing less flamboyantly:

> If the Maastricht targets are adhered to, something significant will have to give in terms of public expenditure in many EC countries, with social consequences which could be highly disruptive. Clawing back public deficits, which are across the Community higher in GDP percentage terms than they have been at any moment since the EC was founded, at a time when more and more "legitimate" demands are made on the public purse, looks increasingly like trying to run up a downward moving escalator.

40. See, e.g., Corsetti and Roubini (1993). De Grauwe (1994) says that the two reference values were chosen for this reason, citing Bini-Smaghi, Padoa-Schioppa, and Papadia (1994) as his source. But they say no such thing. They note that the two numbers are consistent in the long run, when GDP is growing by 5 percent, but do not say they were chosen for that particular reason.

41. Furthermore, the 5 percent growth rate for nominal GDP may not be easy to achieve when inflation rates are low. In 1986–9, the unweighted average of growth rates in nominal GDP was 9.1 percent for the EC countries, and only one country (the Netherlands) had a growth rate below 5 percent. In 1990–3, the average was 6.9 percent, but four countries (Belgium, Denmark, France, and the Netherlands) had growth rates below 5 percent, and three of the countries with growth rates above 5 percent (Greece, Italy, and the United Kingdom) achieved them because they had inflation rates higher than 4 percent (i.e., their growth rates of real GDP were below 1 percent).

Figure 4-2 *Debt ratios of EC countries, 1980–93*

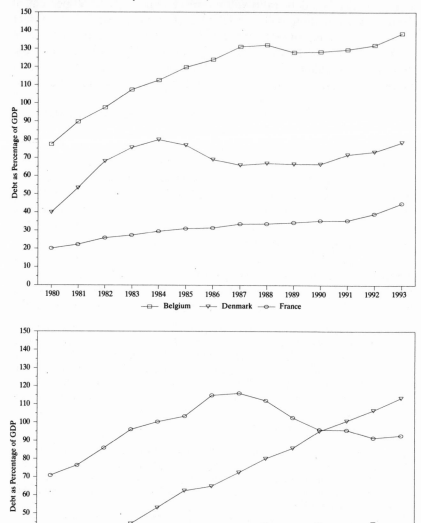

Source: EC Commission. Data for 1991–3 not strictly comparable to those in Table 4–2.

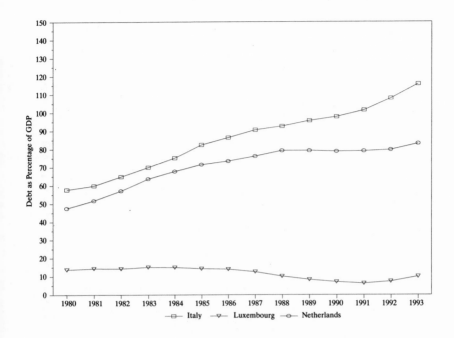

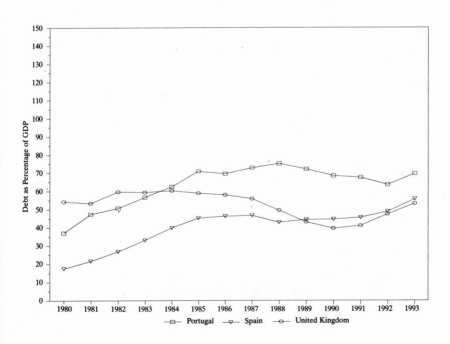

Figure 4-3 *Hypothetical paths for debt ratios with 5 percent GDP growth*

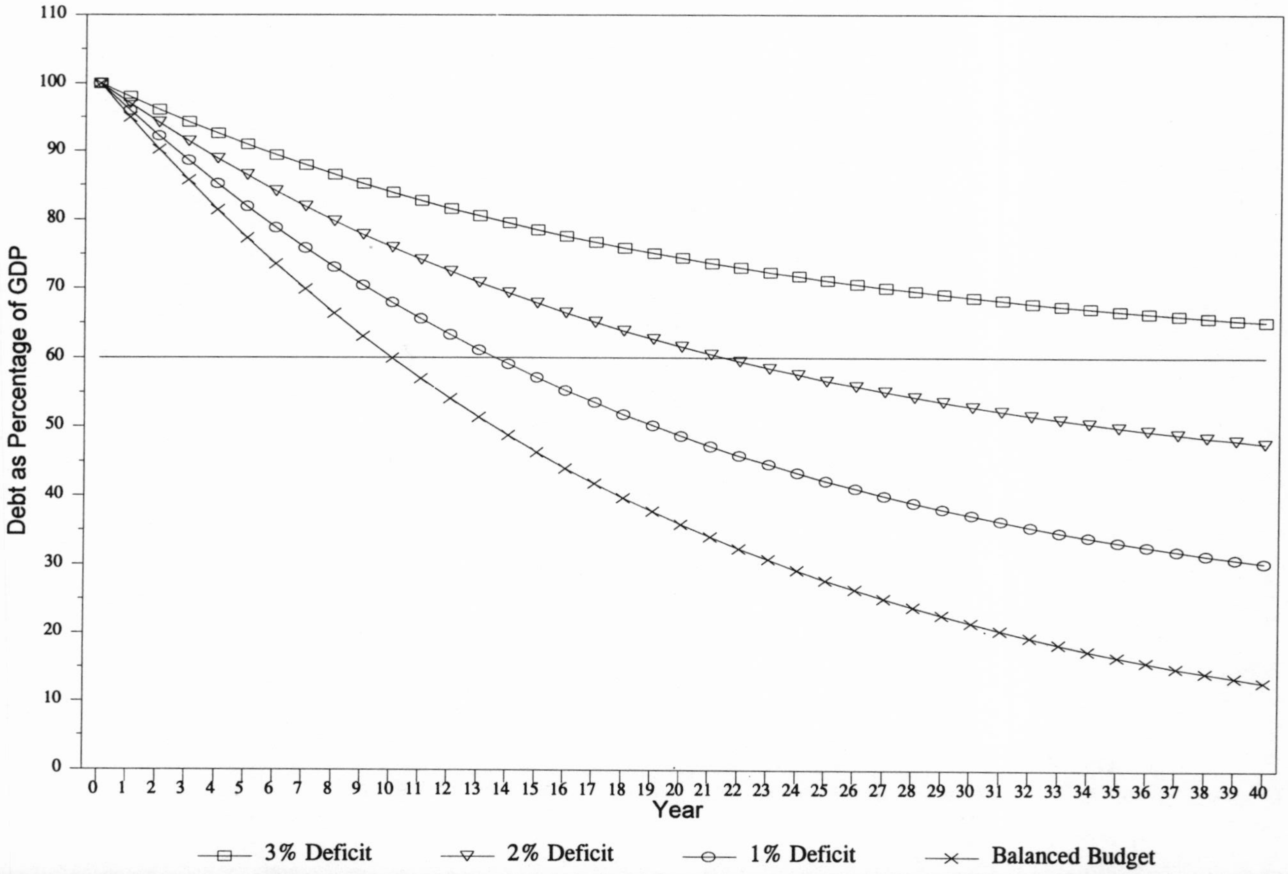

Two long-run concerns

Critics of the fiscal provisions of the treaty have focused on the problem discussed above – whether those provisions will prevent a number of EC countries from entering Stage Three. That matter is discussed in Chapter 6. There are, however, two more reasons for concern.

First, the fiscal provisions of the treaty may prevent the EC countries from using fiscal policy to deal with asymmetric shocks. They may indeed be so strict that they block the workings of the "built-in" stabilizers, let alone the taking of discretionary measures. A budget that is balanced at high levels of activity may move sharply into deficit during a recession – by more than enough to breach the 3 percent reference level. Such a breach should surely be regarded as temporary. If it is not, governments may have to make procyclical adjustments in their fiscal policies. Unlike states and regions in the United States, moreover, they cannot anticipate significant relief from countercyclical fluctuations in the EC budget.[42]

Second, the comprehensive coverage of the fiscal criteria – the inclusion of regional and local governments – may have unintended consequences. Some form of consolidation may be required for cross-country standardization and, more importantly, to discourage creative accounting – the shifting of expenditures, revenues, and obligations from one level of government to another in order to meet the fiscal criteria. But it may also lead some countries to change their internal arrangements; central governments may start to supervise more closely the fiscal affairs of their regional and local governments. The Protocol on the Excessive Deficit Procedure is explicit on this point: "In order to ensure the effectiveness of the excessive deficit procedure, the governments of the Member States shall be responsible under this procedure for the deficits of general government . . . . [They] shall ensure that national procedures in the budgetary area enable them to meet their obligations in this area. . . ." Ironically, the independence of the ECB could conceivably be guaranteed at the cost of sacrificing subsidiarity within individual EC countries.

42. Viñals (1994) suggests that the 3 percent reference value will be applied on average, across the business cycle, but that is not the usual interpretation. It may not be treated as a ceiling, as it was in the Netherlands Draft, but it is not meant to be a permissible average. The group of experts on the EC budget (Commission, 1993) come closer to the usual view when they say that the 3 percent reference value will not force procyclical policy changes because governments will be expected to run budget deficits smaller than 3 percent on average.

CHAPTER 5

EMU and the outside world

Outsiders often complain that discussions of EMU do not pay sufficient attention to the international environment in which EMU will operate and even less attention to the impact of EMU on other countries and the international monetary system.

The first omission is more serious for those who seek to understand how EMU will operate. The performance of the European economy will be affected by the exchange rates connecting the ECU with other major currencies, including the dollar and yen, and the policies of the ECB will influence those exchange rates. This issue is ignored by much of the academic literature, which typically studies the effects of a monetary union in a two-country setting closed to the outside world. The issue was raised by the Delors Report (1989), which stressed the need for the EC as a whole to adopt an appropriate policy mix, and it was discussed in Chapter 4, which criticized the fiscal provisions of the Maastricht Treaty for failing to deal adequately with the issue.

The second omission is easier to understand. Efforts to appraise the benefits and costs of EMU have concentrated on those benefits and costs that Europeans are most likely to experience, because Europeans will have to decide whether to move ahead with EMU and, if so, how rapidly. Nevertheless, EMU will have external benefits and costs that have to be appraised realistically. These have been discussed by the Commission (1990) and others,[1] but some of their findings are questionable, especially those concerned with policy coordination in the Group of Seven (G-7).[2]

Most economists agree that the ECU will eventually become an important international currency, alongside the dollar and yen, but they do not agree completely on the implications. Advocates of EMU sometimes claim that EMU will make the international monetary system more symmetric, by reducing the role of the dollar, and that this will relieve

1. See especially Alogoskoufis and Portes (1991, 1992) and Gros and Thygesen (1992); also Johnson (1994), who weighs the benefits and costs to the United States and finds that they are fairly small.
2. The seven are Canada, France, Germany, Italy, Japan, the United Kingdom, and the United States.

the United States of a heavy burden. Yet some of those who take this view once agreed with Charles de Gaulle that the global role of the dollar conferred an "exorbitant privilege" on the United States. Advocates of EMU also argue that it will facilitate policy coordination among the major industrial countries, because Europe will speak with one voice. Perhaps. But what will it say?

This chapter examines these issues. It starts with the effects of EMU on the functioning of foreign exchange markets and on the official and private demands for the various key currencies. It then asks how EMU is apt to affect the role of the EC in policy coordination and exchange rate management at the global level. Like Chapters 3 and 4, it concentrates mainly on Stage Three.[3]

The ECU as an international currency

A national currency is deemed to be an international currency when it is widely used by the governments and residents of other countries. Governments use foreign currencies to define external values for their own domestic currencies and for intervention on the foreign exchange market. They also hold foreign currency reserves. A single currency is often used in major commodity markets, to price and trade such products as oil and grain; in foreign exchange markets, where time and effort are saved by quoting the prices of many currencies in terms of a single "vehicle" currency; and in securities markets, where borrowers issue bonds and other instruments in currencies other than their own. Finally, many firms and individuals hold foreign currency balances for commercial and financial reasons.

In the 1950s and 1960s, the U.S. dollar was the dominant currency in all of these domains – in the official and private sectors, in commodity and foreign exchange markets, and in financial markets. The situation began to change in the 1970s, with the collapse of the Bretton Woods System and dismantling of exchange controls that had limited the usefulness of most other currencies. Although the dollar remains the most important single currency and the dominant currency in some domains, the deutsche mark and other EC currencies are very widely used, along with the yen.

The pace of change has been uneven. It has been rapid in those domains that permit incremental change; securities are issued in many currencies (and in the basket ECU), and cross-border deposits are held in many currencies. It has been slow in those domains where time and

---

3. The chapter draws on Kenen (1993a), as well as the earlier monograph on which this book is based (Kenen, 1992b).

money are saved by using a single unit of account or medium of exchange, as in commodity and foreign exchange markets. Continued use of the dollar in these domains, moreover, has probably slowed diversification in some other domains; because the dollar is still the main vehicle currency in foreign exchange markets, it remains the most important intervention currency. For that reason, in turn, governments may hold larger dollar reserves than they would choose to hold if foreign exchange trading were differently organized.[4] For that same reason, the international role of the ECU will be affected crucially by the impact of EMU on the foreign exchange market.

EMU and the foreign exchange market

In a lecture given shortly after Maastricht, Tommaso Padoa-Schioppa traced the evolution of thinking about EMU in the Delors Committee.[5] Initially, he said, monetary union had been viewed in Europe as the inescapable and beneficial consequence of processes already under way – the elimination of capital controls and the transformation of the EMS from a system of adjustably pegged exchange rates to a system of nearly fixed rates. Therefore, the Delors Committee devoted a great deal of attention to the further evolution of exchange rate arrangements. Indeed, its agenda for each stage of EMU included steps to limit exchange rate variability. In Stage One, it said, every EC currency should enter the exchange rate mechanism of the EMS; it did not propose limiting the use of exchange rate realignments but urged that other adjustment mechanisms be made to work more effectively. In Stage Two, it said, the exchange rate band should be narrowed, and realignments should be exceptional. Finally, it said that Stage Three should start with the locking of exchange rates and complete elimination of the band, followed by the introduction of a single currency.

4. The Commission (1990) stresses this difference between the two types of domains, citing Krugman (1984). The share of the dollar in the reserves of EC countries has fallen in recent years, because they have begun to use the deutsche mark when intervening to stabilize EMS exchange rates. They can do this because the deutsche mark is now traded directly for other EC currencies on European foreign exchange markets; it is becoming a vehicle currency. Evidence is provided by the surveys of the London foreign exchange market conducted by the Bank of England (1992). Transactions involving the dollar but not the deutsche mark accounted for 52 percent of total turnover in 1992, compared with 67 percent in 1989, whereas transactions involving the deutsche mark but not the dollar accounted for 13 percent, compared with about 7 percent in 1989. (Direct dollar–deutsche mark transactions accounted for 24 percent of total turnover in 1992 and 22 percent in 1989.)

5. See *IMF Survey*, March 30, 1992, pp. 104–7.

The Committee came quickly to realize, however, that EMU would require a more fundamental change – the introduction of a single monetary policy and the design of new institutions to formulate and implement monetary policy. The shift in the focus of the committee is reflected in the Maastricht Treaty, which is primarily concerned with the constitution of the ECB and ESCB, not the evolution of exchange rate arrangements. Furthermore, institutional change will occur more abruptly under the treaty, which did not adopt the recommendations of the Delors Report that there be a gradual move from the coordination of national monetary policies to the introduction of a single policy, a narrowing of the exchange rate band before the locking of exchange rates, and a gradual change in the rules regarding recourse to exchange rate realignments.

The implementation of the treaty will likewise have large, discontinuous effects on the foreign exchange market, and these could take place earlier than commonly believed. It is widely understood that the introduction of the ECU as the single currency of the EC will take away much business from the foreign exchange market. It will cease to deal in lire, francs, and marks, because they will cease to exist. Fewer people understand, however, that the locking of exchange rates on the first day of Stage Three could have that same effect. It was shown in Chapter 3 that subsequent transactions in the national currencies can and should involve mere bookkeeping entries on the relevant bank balance sheets rather than the use of the foreign exchange market.

The removal of all these transactions from the foreign exchange market will cut down business in that market, but the reduction may be relatively small. Most transactions in that market occur at the interbank level, where traders take and adjust positions from minute to minute and hour to hour. Once the exchange rates connecting the ESCB currencies have been locked irrevocably, with no bands around them, traders will have no incentive to move in or out of those currencies, but they will have no less incentive than before to switch between those currencies, taken as a group, and the other major currencies. Until the ECU replaces the national currencies, traders are likely to use the deutsche mark as their proxy for the whole set of ESCB currencies; hence, trading in that proxy should rise sharply, while trading in all other ESCB currencies should fall sharply.[6]

This concentration of foreign exchange trading, first on the proxy, then

6. The discussion below speaks of effects caused by introducing the ECU, but some could occur at the start of Stage Three, before the introduction of the ECU, with the deutsche mark serving as a proxy for the ECU. Under the arrangements proposed in Chapter 3, moreover, wholesale trading in the ECU could begin on the very first day of Stage Three.

on the ECU, can be expected to have two effects. First, it should cut the costs of trading in the proxy and ECU, compared to the costs of trading in non-ESCB currencies.[7] Second, it should diminish the basic advantage of using a single vehicle currency, challenging the pivotal role of the dollar in the foreign exchange market. The first effect is incremental. The second is not. It will change the functioning of the foreign exchange market and remove one of the main institutional arrangements that has preserved the role of the dollar in the international monetary system.[8]

Other developments will reinforce these tendencies. Countries in Central and Eastern Europe are likely to define the values of their currencies in terms of the ECU. The EC will be their largest trading partner, and they will look to London, Frankfurt, and Paris more than New York or Tokyo for financial services, short-term credit, and long-term capital. They will be natural candidates for membership in an informal ECU zone; they will borrow in ECU, hold most of their reserves in ECU, and peg their currencies to the ECU.[9] The ECU zone may also replace the CFA franc area (which may continue to hold its reserves in Paris but will hold them in ECU), and it may extend to other African countries that have strong trading links to one or more of the EC countries. The size of its domain outside Europe, however, will depend partly on the evolution of pricing practices in the major commodity markets. If some of them shift to the ECU, many commodity-exporting countries may begin to invoice their exports in ECU and will join the ECU zone. One cannot even rule out a shift to the pricing of oil in ECU, rather than dollars, which would extend the ECU zone into the Middle East.

7. See Black (1991), who finds a significant inverse relationship between the bid-asked spread and the volume of trading. But the bid-asked spread and volume may both be endogenous; the main cause of the decrease in cost and increase in volume may be the next factor cited in the text – the reduction in the need for a vehicle currency due to the fall in the *number* of currencies traded.
8. Alogoskoufis and Portes (1992) raise this possibility but ascribe it to the volume of trading in the ECU that will follow the elimination of the national currencies. They miss the two points in the text – that trading in the national currencies may cease before the ECU is introduced, because the maintenance of locked exchange rates need not involve use of the foreign exchange market, and that the decrease in the number of currencies traded should have its own separate and fundamental impact on the informational and search-cost advantages of using a vehicle currency (see Krugman, 1980).
9. See Goodhart (1992b). Mundell (1993), however, is skeptical, because the ECB may "impose too tough a monetary standard," and countries in Eastern Europe may prefer to adopt "the easier standard that would be set by modest U.S. rates of inflation." On efforts to promote the creation of an ECU zone in Central and Eastern Europe, see Collignon (1992) and Davenport (1992). (But Davenport fails to explain why it would be better for the Central European countries to peg to the present basket ECU than to their own trade-weighted baskets of currencies.)

Table 5-1 *Shares of various currencies in total foreign exchange reserves of developing countries (percent)*

Currency	1981	1983	1985	1987	1989	1991	1993
U.S. dollar	64.1	64.6	64.5	59.8	61.3	62.7	62.3
Deutsche mark	12.5	10.3	10.0	11.1	11.3	10.8	11.4
Pound sterling	3.4	4.4	4.3	5.2	5.6	6.0	4.3
French franc	2.1	1.6	1.9	1.8	1.8	2.1	1.6
Dutch guilder	1.4	1.0	0.9	1.1	0.8	0.8	0.8
Japanese yen	4.9	4.7	6.9	8.5	6.9	7.7	9.5
Swiss franc	3.7	3.2	2.6	2.7	2.3	2.2	2.6
Unspecified	7.9	10.3	9.0	9.7	10.0	7.7	7.5

Source: International Monetary Fund, *Annual Report,* 1991, 1994, Table 1.2; may not add to total because of rounding.

The external demand for the ECU

If EMU has some or all of these effects, the ECU will be widely held as a reserve currency. But total reserve-currency holdings of ECU may not be very big at first, compared with reserve holdings of the present EC currencies, and may grow only slowly thereafter. In fact, the share of the ECU in global reserves may be *lower* initially than the share of the present EC currencies. To see how that can happen, one must look separately at three groups of countries – the developing countries and the small industrial countries outside the EC, the EC countries themselves, and the other large industrial countries.

The developing countries and small industrial countries began diversifying their currency reserves in the early 1970s, soon after the breakdown of the Bretton Woods System (see Kenen, 1983). Yet the shares of various currencies in the total foreign exchange reserves of the developing countries have been fairly stable for many years (see Table 5–1). Most of the fall in the share of the dollar occurred before 1981. Unless the advent of the ECU leads to shifts in the pricing of major commodities such as oil, it is unlikely to induce another round of diversification by the developing countries.[10]

10. Note that the countries most closely linked to the EC account for a very small fraction of the developing countries' currency reserves. The distribution of currency reserves at the end of 1993 (percentages of global total) was as follows: Africa, 3.9; Asia, 55.5; Europe, 4.9; Middle East, 12.7; Western Hemisphere, 23.1. Furthermore, five East

The EC countries hold large amounts of ECU in their currency reserves, but those are official ECU, which will turn into dollars and gold on the first day of Stage Three.[11] Their holdings of EC currencies are likewise quite large. In September 1991, for example, their holdings of deutsche marks accounted for 18.2 percent of their total foreign exchange reserves, and their holdings of three other EC currencies accounted for 6.7 percent. Hence, their holdings of all EC currencies must have accounted for more than a quarter of their total foreign currency reserves.[12] But their holdings of EC currencies will cease to function as reserves at the beginning of Stage Three; they will not be needed to support the locking of exchange rates, and they will not be usable for intervention in the markets for the dollar or yen.[13] Furthermore, the advent of the ECU will change those reserve assets into domestic currency claims; deutsche mark reserves of the Banque de France will become ECU claims on the Bundesbank (or on the commercial banks at which they happen to be held). That is why the introduction of the ECU will reduce the fraction of global reserves denominated in ECU, compared with the fraction held in EC currencies just before the ECU is introduced.

Because the EC countries will not have to use reserves to defend their exchange rates after they are locked, their total reserves may be unnecessarily large. A back-of-the-envelope calculation by the Commission (1990) put the surplus between $200 billion and $230 billion, depending on the method used, an amount roughly equal to 4 percent of the Com-

Asian countries (Taiwan, Korea, Malaysia, Singapore, and Thailand) accounted for 80 percent of Asian currency reserves and for 44 percent of the global total. The oil-exporting countries, by contrast, accounted for only 11 percent of the global total.
11. See Article 23 of the EMI Statute.
12. Calculations based on unpublished IMF data; the three other currencies are pounds sterling, French francs, and Dutch guilders. When the numbers are recast as shares of total foreign exchange reserves excluding official ECU, holdings of the same four EC currencies work out at 32.5 percent rather than 24.9 percent. Gros and Thygesen (1992) quote larger figures for 1990. At one point (p. 402), they say that the total reserves of EC countries amounted to ECU 200 billion, of which only ECU 90 billion represented non-EC currencies; these numbers imply that EC currencies accounted for 55 percent of total reserves. Elsewhere (p. 403), however, they say that holdings of non-EC currencies amounted to ECU 120 billion. The EMS crises of 1992 and 1993 probably affected the figures substantially, but current data are not publicly available.
13. The ECB *could* instruct the Banque de France to use some of its deutsche marks to buy dollars, instead of instructing the Bundesbank to "create" additional deutsche marks. In Chapter 2, however, I suggested that the ECB is apt to engage in intervention for its own account, using reserve assets transferred to it under Article 30 of the ESCB Statute, rather than instruct the national central banks to use their residual reserves for that purpose.

munity's GDP.[14] This sum, the Commission said, could be put to better use. But it warned of the need to be careful when disposing of surplus reserves, because of undesirable exchange rate effects.

There is, in fact, no easy way for the EC countries to transform "excess" reserves into more productive assets. Conceivably, they could engage in public capital formation (or stimulate private capital formation); aggregate demand would then rise, producing a current account deficit, and it could be financed by running down reserves. But the necessary increase of aggregate demand could jeopardize other basic aims, such as price stability. It would be even harder for the EC countries to change the composition of their currency reserves without affecting the exchange rates between those currencies, such as the yen–dollar rate.[15] The EC countries may be stuck with redundant dollars, just as they were stuck with gold after it was demonetized officially by the Second Amendment to the Articles of Agreement of the IMF. The United States sold gold in the 1970s; EC countries did

14. The Commission's estimate, however, compares total reserves, including gold, with the reserves that the EC would need, so that the "excess" implicitly includes gold as well as foreign exchange. Furthermore, its calculations make no allowance for the transformation discussed in the preceding paragraph. The figures cited earlier in the text suggest that some $75 billion of EC currencies should be subtracted from the "excess" because they will cease to function as reserves. When both gold and EC currencies are subtracted from the Commission's estimate, the implied "overhang" of external currency reserves turns out to lie between $40 billion and $70 billion. Gros and Thygesen (1992) attack the problem differently but come up with a figure equivalent to some $100 billion. As was noted earlier, however, they use reserve data that show EC countries to hold larger amounts of EC currencies than do the data on which I have relied. Had they used data comparable to my own, their method would have led them to a lower figure. Finally, Leahy (1994) finds that the "overhang" turns into a "shortage" when some well-known models are used to compute the demand for reserves and for individual reserve assets.

15. It would be possible, of course, for the EC countries to sell dollars and buy yen when the United States and Japan wanted to resist a depreciation of the yen in terms of the dollar. (It would also be possible for Japan to sell dollars and buy ECU, adjusting the composition of Japanese reserves, when the EC and the United States wanted to resist a depreciation of the ECU in terms of the dollar.) It would be far more sensible, however, to facilitate off-market diversification by adopting a proposal made many years ago to create a "substitution account" at the IMF, in which governments might deposit unwanted dollars in exchange for SDR-denominated claims on the IMF (see, e.g., Kenen, 1981). Gros and Thygesen (1992) argue that foreign exchange markets are sufficiently large and efficient to cope with the diversification of EC currency reserves, as the size of the net shift out of the dollar would be only a small fraction of the daily turnover in those markets. Williamson (1992a) takes the same view. But turnover is the wrong scalar; one must ask who would want to *hold* the dollars sold by the ECB and the national central banks and would thus be willing to assume the long positions they were trying to liquidate.

not – and they may go on holding dollars just as they went on holding gold.[16]

The options of the other large industrial countries – Japan and the United States – resemble those of the EC countries. They are not free to "optimize" the composition of their reserves. They will, of course, obtain ECU in exchange for EC currencies held as reserves at the start of Stage Three, and they will add to their ECU holdings whenever they buy ECU in the foreign exchange market to keep the ECU from depreciating in terms of the dollar or yen. But they are not apt to buy many ECU in the early years of EMU, because the ECU is more likely to be strong than weak.

All of these considerations lead back to the forecast made at the start of this survey. The ECU will be widely held as a reserve asset, but holdings will grow gradually via accumulation, not rapidly via asset switching.[17]

What can be said about private holdings of ECU and ECU-denominated claims? Two points must be made at the outset. First, individuals, firms, and financial institutions will not be constrained by concerns about the exchange rate effects of their behavior. Second, one must distinguish between the effects of EMU on the demand for the ECU as money and its effects on the demand for ECU-denominated claims. The locking of exchange rates and introduction of the ECU may reduce the demand for the ECU as money. By helping to unify capital markets within the EC, however, EMU may produce a long-lasting increase in the demand for ECU-denominated claims. That is why the ECU is likely to appreciate after Stage Three begins.

The fundamental change in the functioning of the foreign exchange market will increase the demand for ECU, as they will be used in many third-currency transactions for which dollars are used now. This increase in demand, however, may be more than offset by a reduction in demand attending the substitution of the ECU for the national currencies of the ESCB countries.

Participants in the foreign exchange market will need ECU to replace some of their holdings of the national currencies; they will need them to trade ECU for other major currencies. But there will no longer be any

16. Cooper (1992b) comes to the same conclusion.
17. This forecast conflicts with one made by Alogoskoufis and Portes (1991, p. 236), who predict significant substitution into the ECU. And that prediction is weaker than the one they made elsewhere, i.e., "potentially significant substitution of ecu for dollars *by central banks in the EC*" (Alogoskoufis and Portes, 1992, p. 278, italics added). This cannot possibly happen, because the ECB and national central banks will not hold ECU as reserve assets.

trading among the ESCB currencies and no need for ECU to replace the ESCB currencies previously held for that purpose or, more importantly, for taking positions in the ESCB currencies to profit from expected re-alignments. Furthermore, the residents of the ESCB countries will no longer need to hold cash balances in other ESCB currencies. They will not need them for day-to-day transactions or to hedge against exchange rate risk.[18] In brief, there will be a once-and-for-all reduction in the demand for money, and it may occur as soon as exchange rates are locked.

There is no way to estimate the size of this reduction, because of the lack of data on the foreign currency holdings of EC residents. The Bank for International Settlements publishes data on the cross-border deposit obligations of European banks, currency by currency, but does not break them down by currency and holder. Two bits of evidence, how-ever, suggest that these deposits are fairly large.

First, something is known about the foreign currency deposits held by EC residents at their own domestic banks. In December 1993, banks in Europe and Canada had $293 billion of foreign currency obligations to their own residents, of which $214 billion was owed by banks in the EC countries. The breakdown by currency (in billions of dollars) was as follows:

U.S. dollars	146
EC currencies and ECU	106
Japanese yen	10
Swiss francs	12
Other and unallocated	19

Presumably, banks in EC countries accounted for a disproportionate share of the total holdings of EC currencies. Second, information is available on the total cross-border deposit liabilities of EC banks in their own national currencies. In December 1993, these liabilities amounted to $155 billion, of which a significant fraction was probably owed to the residents of other EC countries.[19] Some of these holdings will be redun-dant after exchange rates have been locked.

18. Eichengreen (1992d) carries this last point further. He notes that when the dollar has been weak in terms of the deutsche mark, the latter has been strong in relation to other EMS currencies, and vice versa. Therefore, a French investor whose wealth is denominated mainly in francs has had an incentive to hold both dollars and deutsche marks. Under EMU, by contrast, the investor's wealth will be denominated mainly in ECU, and the investor may then have an incentive to hold additional dollars.

19. Bank for International Settlements, *International Banking and Financial Market Devel-opments*, Basle, May 1994: Tables 3B and 4D for foreign currency liabilities to nonbank residents, and Table 4B for domestic currency liabilities to nonbank nonresidents.

The size of the increase in demand for ECU-denominated assets will depend on the contribution of EMU to the unification and quality of EC asset markets, and this will take place gradually, before and after Stage Three begins. But the effect will be long lasting – a larger flow demand for equities, bonds, and other instruments rather than a once-and-for-all stock adjustment – with enduring effects on the value of the ECU.[20] The ECB can readily offset a once-and-for-all reduction in the demand for ECU balances by reducing the supply. It will be harder to offset the exchange rate effects of an ongoing capital inflow.

EMU and policy coordination

The external effects of EMU will depend in part on the ability of the EC to join with other countries in policy coordination and exchange rate management. Discussions of this issue have focused mainly on coordination among the United States, Japan, and the key countries of the Community.[21]

The case for policy coordination has been debated vigorously ever since the Plaza and Louvre accords. This is not the place to review that debate, apart from noting that there is wide agreement on three points: (1) coordination among the G-7 countries has been sporadic; (2) it has focused too narrowly on exchange rate management and relied too heavily on intervention in the foreign exchange market; and (3) there has been some coordination of monetary policies but little coordination of fiscal policies, despite repeated promises on that score.[22]

The episodic character of coordination and the emphasis on exchange rate management are easily explained and may be inevitable. Governments take to policy coordination only when they believe that something has gone wrong in the linkages among their economies, and changes in

20. The Commission (1990) suggests that EMU will cause a once-and-for-all shift to ECU-denominated assets, which could be as large as ECU 300 billion. Gros and Thygesen (1992) criticize the Commission for not distinguishing between the preferences of EC residents and those of other investors. The latter, they say, hold more dollar assets at present; hence, the shift into the ECU will be correspondingly larger. Their reasoning, however, is weak. They assume that *all* investors will want to hold portfolios equally weighted with dollars and ECU, yet the very point they make – that outsiders hold more dollars – conflicts with that supposition.

21. Another dimension of the problem – the need for coordination between the ESCB countries and the remaining EC countries – is discussed in Chapter 6.

22. Funabashi (1989) provides a detailed discussion of the Plaza and Louvre accords; Dobson (1991) provides a more general account of coordination among the G-7 countries; Kenen (1989) reviews the academic literature, and some of the text below draws on that review.

exchange rates or current-account balances are the most visible signs of trouble. They rarely engage in coordination to improve domestic conditions per se, although that is how economists tend to view the process and how they evaluate the benefits and costs.

It is equally easy to understand why monetary policies have figured more prominently than fiscal policies in the recent history of coordination, despite the many promises to alter fiscal policies. Monetary policies are easier to alter, and the responsibility for monetary policy is less dispersed within most major countries. In those with independent central banks, however, international coordination requires internal coordination, which has not always been achieved. Internal coordination must take place ex ante between each country's government and its central bank before the government can participate in international negotiations, and it is also needed ex post, in the form of a commitment by the central bank to implement a policy bargain after the participating governments have made one. Thus, Dobson (1991) argues that the difference between success and failure in the work of the G-7 has depended crucially on the degree of agreement between Bonn and Frankfurt.[23]

The Commission brushes this problem aside when it discusses the implications of EMU for global coordination:

> For international policy coordination at [the] global level to become more efficient, it is of paramount importance that the definition of responsibilities ensures an efficient handling of [exchange rate] policy. The two major requirements for the Community in that respect are to be able to speak with one voice in exchange rate policy discussion at [the] G7 level, and to ensure consistency between its exchange rate and monetary policy objectives. In what follows, it is assumed that both conditions are fulfilled. (Commission, 1990, p. 190)

Having disposed summarily of this difficult problem, the Commission goes on to argue that EMU will actually promote international coordination by replacing the present asymmetric regime with a more symmetric multipolar regime. At present, it says, Europe comprises a collection of medium-sized policy centers, and the spillover effects of their policy decisions are much smaller than those of U.S. policy decisions. The American economy, it reminds us, is much bigger and less open than the typical European economy. Under this asymmetric arrangement, the Commission argues, the United States has less to gain from policy coordination. It can even exploit the asymmetry by choosing its policies unilaterally without suffering much from similar behavior by Europe.

The Commission goes on to recite and dismiss familiar arguments

23. For detailed accounts of the German experience, see Kennedy (1991) and Henning (1994).

against a multipolar system – that it is unstable and leaderless. It concedes the need for leadership in any system but says that a multipolar system will provide better leadership than a hegemonic system. Alluding to the German role in the EMS, it asserts that:

> . . . the leadership issue arises in any monetary regime, because the overall stance of monetary policy has to be set by a policy centre. However, this kind of *de facto* asymmetry within a formally symmetric system, which does not determine a priori which country should be the anchor of the system, is very different from the structural asymmetry of for example the Bretton Woods system whose rules gave the leadership to a particular country independently of the quality of its policy. Moreover, it can be considered desirable that the operation of the system rewards performance by linking effective leadership to reputation. (Commission, 1990, p. 195)

It is hard to refrain from quarreling with this reading of international monetary history. It is more important to point out, however, that the Commission's main argument can be turned around. If the United States has little interest in policy coordination because its economy is large and relatively closed, why should the EC be expected to behave differently when it comes to resemble a single economy, similar in size and openness to the U.S. economy? Furthermore, Goodhart (1992c) points out that efforts to coordinate national policies have originated chiefly with the United States, and this contradicts the Commission's premise.

Alogoskoufis and Portes (1991) do not assume away the problem of internal coordination, but they pose it as a problem of representation. Who will speak for the EC in the G-7 when national governments are responsible for fiscal policies, the Council of Ministers has something to say about exchange rate policy, and the ECB is responsible for monetary policy and for intervention on foreign exchange markets? They also note that the presidency cannot represent the Council in the G-7, because the presidency rotates semiannually, and the work of the G-7 calls for continuity.

The problem of representation arises directly from the Maastricht Treaty, which does not deal clearly with the problem of internal coordination. The issue stems from Article 109 of the Treaty, which reads in part:

> 1   . . . the Council may, acting unanimously on a recommendation from the ECB or from the Commission, and after consulting the ECB in an endeavour to reach a consensus consistent with the objective of price stability, after consulting the European Parliament, in accordance with the procedure in paragraph 3 . . . , conclude formal agreements on an exchange rate system for the ECU in relation to non-Community currencies. The Council may, acting by a qualified majority . . . and after consulting the ECB in an endeavour to reach a consensus consistent

with the objective of price stability, adopt, adjust or abandon the central rates of the ECU within the exchange rate system.

2   In the absence of an exchange rate system in relation to one or more non-Community currencies as referred to in paragraph 1, the Council may, acting by a qualified majority either on a recommendation from the Commission and after consulting the ECB, or on a recommendation from the ECB, formulate general orientations for exchange rate policy in relation to these currencies. These general orientations shall be without prejudice to the primary objective of the ESCB to maintain price stability.

3   . . . where agreements concerning monetary or foreign exchange regime matters need to be negotiated by the Community . . . , the Council . . . shall decide the arrangements for the negotiation and for the conclusion of such agreements. These arrangements shall ensure that the Community expresses a single position. The Commission shall be fully associated in the negotiations.

    Agreements concluded in accordance with this paragraph shall be binding on the institutions of the Community, on the ECB and on Member States.

4   Subject to paragraph 1, the Council shall, on a proposal from the Commission and after consulting the ECB, acting by a qualified majority decide on the position of the Community at international level as regards issues of particular importance to economic and monetary union and, acting unanimously, decide its representation. . . .

The intergovernmental conference had to work hard on this article, which went through many drafts. Some governments wanted to be absolutely sure that the Council could not force the ECB to intervene on the foreign exchange market in a manner inconsistent with the pursuit of price stability. Other governments wanted to be sure that governments would retain firm control over the Community's exchange rate policy.[24] Even now, the wording of the article is very cumbersome, partly because there is no agreed name for the present exchange rate regime. The term "regime" does not appear in Article IV of the Articles of Agreement of the IMF, which speaks of the "monetary system" and the exchange rate "arrangements" of member countries (and then speaks of a "system of exchange arrangements").

The meaning of the first paragraph is fairly clear. It pertains to the procedure that must be followed before the EC can agree to a binding

---

24. Note in this connection that governments, not central banks, are members of the IMF and that their obligations under its Articles of Agreement cannot be transferred formally to the ECB (see Lastra, 1992; and Burdekin, Wihlborg, and Willett, 1992).

arrangement like that of the Bretton Woods System, which would fix the external value of the ECU. The second paragraph is clear on certain points but not on others. The EC will not make an informal agreement affecting the external value of the ECU unless the agreement is fully compatible with price stability (see, e.g., Italianer, 1993). But it does not say who shall judge that – or how.

The article as a whole, moreover, does not state clearly how the EC will participate in international discussions, such as those in the G-7, on exchange rate management. Paragraph 3, on the conduct of negotiations about exchange rate policy, cannot apply. First, it is cited in paragraph 1 but not in paragraph 2. Second, the final sentence of paragraph 3, on the binding nature of exchange rate agreements, clashes with the careful language of paragraph 2, which speaks of "general orientations" and can even be read to say that the ECB may decide for itself whether the "general orientations" are consistent with price stability.[25] (Indeed, paragraph 2 appears to contemplate "general orientations" adopted unilaterally by the EC rather than guidelines agreed collectively by the G-7, like those in the Plaza and Louvre accords. The two are not mutually exclusive; orientations adopted by the EC could embody guidelines agreed by the G-7. But the path from the one to the other is not clearly marked.) That leaves paragraph 4, concerning EC positions and representation on issues "of particular relevance" to EMU. But it does not say anything about exchange rates or a role for the Commission.

There are two other reasons to be concerned about the influence of EMU on the outlook for policy coordination and exchange rate management among the major industrial countries.[26]

First, the EC may not have much interest in exchange rate management at the global level. It will resemble a single large economy, comparatively closed to the outside world and not very sensitive to fluctuations in ECU exchange rates. Even today, the EC countries show less concern about fluctuations in the dollar values of their currencies than they did five or

25. Feldstein (1993, p. 9) ignores the crucial distinction between paragraphs 1 and 2 when he asserts that Article 109 gives the Council de facto control over monetary policy because a "decision of the Ministers to reduce the value of the ECU relative to the dollar or yen (similar in spirit to the decisions made at the Plaza in 1985 or the Louvre in 1987) would force the European Central Bank to pursue an easier and more inflationary monetary policy."

26. Similar concerns are expressed by Eichengreen (1992d), Goodhart (1992c), Gros and Thygesen (1992), and Pisani-Ferry et al. (1993). Gros and Thygesen go on to note that the fiscal provisions of the Maastricht Treaty may make fiscal policy coordination even more difficult than it is today, and they also call attention to the risk of conflict between the EC and those of its members that belong to the G-7, because the latter may be prevented from participating fully in the work of the G-7.

ten years ago. The locking of exchange rates will compound this effect by immunizing the EC countries from the tensions produced in the EMS by fluctuations in the dollar–deutsche mark rate.

Second, the ECB will want to earn credibility by proving its ability to maintain price stability. Hence, it may resist EC involvement in any attempt at exchange rate management by the G-7 countries, especially if it were seen to require heavy intervention on the foreign exchange market. The Bundesbank has shown the same aversion to large-scale intervention but has felt free to intervene substantially from time to time, because its credibility is firmly established.[27] That will not be true of the young ECB.

In the first years of EMU, then, the G-7 countries may find it harder to agree on policies and strategies for exchange rate management, and EMU may thus lead to exchange rate fluctuations wider than those seen since the Louvre Accord. That would be truly ironic. EMU is meant to replace the EMS, which emerged from the desire to create a zone of monetary stability in Europe. Yet the achievement of that goal may have the effect of producing greater exchange rate instability at the global level.

27. When the threat to price stability became acute during the EMS crisis of 1992, however, the Bundesbank objected to further intervention, even of the sort required in the EMS (see Chapter 7).

CHAPTER 6

The transition to EMU

There has been more debate – academic and official – about Stage Two of EMU than about Stage Three. The recommendations of the Delors Report (1989) regarding the mandate and organization of the ESCB were widely endorsed, but its proposals regarding the transition to EMU were strongly criticized. Some critics questioned the need to require convergence before moving to Stage Three. Others questioned the wisdom of giving the ECB any role in the conduct of monetary policy during the transition to EMU.

The first two sections of this chapter examine those two issues and the debate about them. The remaining sections deal with three other issues: the use of the ECU before it becomes a currency in its own right, the need for "one last realignment" before exchange rates are irrevocably locked, and monetary cooperation between the ESCB countries and the remaining EC countries – those that cannot enter Stage Three initially, as well as those that may opt out.

This chapter does not ask how the EMS crises of 1992 and 1993 have affected the outlook for EMU or bear on the interpretation of the Maastricht Treaty. Those matters, and the crises themselves, are considered in Chapter 7.

The controversy over convergence

The processes and preconditions for starting Stage Three were described in Chapter 2. In 1996, certain convergence criteria will be used to identify the countries that are ready to enter Stage Three, decide whether it is "appropriate" to start that stage, and, if so, to set a date. If no such date is set in 1996, Stage Three will start automatically in 1999. The same convergence criteria will still be used, however, to identify the countries that are ready to participate. But Chapter 2 did not discuss the convergence criteria or examine the rationale for insisting on them.

The case for convergence

A number of economists wanted Stage Three to start without waiting for convergence. Dornbusch (1990), for example, warned that convergence

124

has already "peaked" within the core of the EC, and he called on the core countries, led by France and Germany, to move immediately to monetary union. A two-speed Europe, he maintained, would be better than a no-speed Europe, and that might be the outcome if Stage Three were delayed.[1] Others also wanted Stage Three to start quickly, but they denied the need to leave any country out. Stage Two is bound to be hazardous, they said, and is unnecessary; convergence will take place automatically as soon as Stage Three begins.[2]

The crises of 1992 and 1993 demonstrated clearly that Stage Two will be hazardous, but there were reasons for concern even before those crises erupted. I cited four such reasons in my earlier monograph (Kenen, 1992b).[3]

First, the EC countries may still try to pursue what Padoa-Schioppa (1988) has described as the "inconsistent quartet" of policy objectives – free trade, free capital movements, fixed exchange rates, and independent monetary policies. They are supposed to coordinate their monetary policies in the EMI, but that will be difficult, for reasons given later.

Second, several EC countries will have much trouble meeting the convergence criteria. They will face political and economic problems as they seek to reduce their inflation rates and cut their budget deficits before Stage Three begins, even if it is delayed until 1999.

Third, markets may come to expect that some countries will try to exploit their independence before they must surrender it – that the high-debt countries, for example, will engineer inflations and devaluations in a final effort to cut down their debt burdens – and the markets' response to those expectations will induce exchange rate crises.[4]

---

1. Swoboda (1991) took a similar position.
2. See, e.g., Giovannini (1990a), who proposed a quick "currency reform" by all the EC countries and a quick move to monetary union. The Commission also favored a short transition, because the EMS might prove to be fragile; see Italianer (1993).
3. Other authors offered some of the same reasons; see, e.g. Masson and Taylor (1992) and Currie (1992b). Gros and Thygesen (1992, p. 164) were more optimistic. After reviewing the theory of speculative crises, including the paper by Obstfeld (1986) on self-fulfilling forecasts of devaluation, they concluded that it is "extremely unlikely that the EMS would be subject to random and self-fulfilling speculative attacks of this sort in the future." They also warned, however, that a crisis could arise early in Stage Two, because some countries might want to devalue before the beginning of the two-year "examination period" in which a country's exchange rate policy will affect its ability to enter Stage Three.
4. This argument has two variants. One says that markets will expect the EC countries to undertake "one last realignment" before Stage Three begins, in order to offset cost and price disparities before the locking of exchange rates. This possibility cannot be precluded and will be discussed below. The other says that markets will expect the high-debt countries to devalue unilaterally, although that could bar them from entering

Finally, the next several years may be very turbulent for reasons unrelated to EMU and all that. The EC countries cannot expect the world to leave them alone while they work their way through the effects of previous shocks and mistakes. The world is not an economist's model, into which one can inject a single shock or policy change, then watch the economy move to a new steady state. Shocks do not queue up like aircraft in a holding pattern, each waiting for the one ahead to clear the runway. They come in quick succession from many directions. Will the price of oil remain unchanged in the 1990s? Was German unification the last shock from the East or perhaps the first of many?

Nevertheless, Stage Two may be necessary, because convergence itself may be necessary, and convergence will take time. Fiscal convergence may be needed to stave off political and market pressures of the sort discussed in Chapter 4, and a close convergence of inflation rates may likewise be needed to stave off political pressures.

A single monetary policy aimed at achieving price stability will tend to equalize price levels and inflation rates in all of the ESCB countries.[5] That will not happen instantaneously, however, nor will it happen costlessly in the high-inflation countries, where output and employment may be affected heavily. The speed and cost of the adjustment will depend crucially on the speed and size of the change in private sector behavior induced by the move to EMU.

If the Bundesbank could transfer credibility to the ECB by transferring responsibility to it, private sector behavior might change dramatically in every ESCB country. The convergence of national inflation rates could then be regarded as an outcome of Stage Three, not as a precondition for it. If indeed the ECB could acquire credibility instantaneously, it would be easier for the ECB to achieve price stability in Stage Three than for the individual EC countries to achieve it in Stage Two. Unfortunately, it is far harder to transfer reputations than to transfer obligations. The ECB will have to earn its own credibility, and that may be more difficult without convergence in Stage Two.[6] If

Stage Three (see, e.g., Cukierman, 1991; and Froot and Rogoff, 1992). Nevertheless, both variants imply that the risk of an exchange rate crisis will increase as the start of Stage Three approaches.

5. But Eichengreen (1993a) cites recent studies showing that inflation rates within a monetary union can vary across regions by as much as 1½ percent a year, though not persistently in one direction.

6. Even with high credibility, the costs of fighting inflation can be very high. Dornbusch (1990) computes "sacrifice ratios" for the EC countries. (The sacrifice ratio divides the change in the unemployment rate by the change in the inflation rate and thus measures the rise in unemployment that goes with reducing inflation by one percentage point.) The sacrifice ratios were higher for Germany and the Netherlands than for other EC

inflation rates are allowed to differ until Stage Three begins, skepticism may persist, and the ECB will have to prove that it is truly independent and able to bear the blame for imposing the costs of fighting inflation – costs that will, in turn, be high if there is much skepticism.

The same basic point can be made without mentioning credibility. It is a matter of responsibility. If the EC countries are truly committed to creating an ECB with the primary aim of maintaining price stability, they should start to reduce inflation before Stage Three begins. They should show themselves willing to impose the economic costs and bear the political risks of fighting inflation. That is how to prove that they will give the ECB the independence it will need to maintain price stability. A decision to move quickly to Stage Three, without reducing inflation first, and thus depend on the ECB to achieve price stability, not merely maintain it, would be an abdication of responsibility. The ECB would have to bear the blame for the costs of reducing inflation – and would have to work harder. Hence, any such abdication would raise serious doubts about the commitments made at Maastricht.

Corden (1993) puts the point clearly. Those who believe in the paramount importance of price stability, especially those in Germany, require proof that policy preferences have converged in Europe and that it is thus safe to enter EMU. The convergence criteria are meant to elicit such proof.[7]

Defining convergence

Article 109j of the Maastricht Treaty contains four convergence criteria, and they are explained in a protocol to the treaty:[8]

> countries whose central banks are commonly believed to have less credibility. This result may cast more doubt on the usefulness of the sacrifice ratio than on the conventional wisdom about credibility, but Eichengreen (1993a) cites work by Bini-Smaghi and Del Giovane that is consistent with it; an effort by the ECB to reduce inflation rapidly would cause the largest output losses in the low-inflation countries. Fratianni and von Hagen (1992) maintain that the locking of exchange rates, by itself, will affect private sector behavior, reducing the cost of disinflation immediately. I am less optimistic, because the locking of exchange rates will not by itself confer credibility on the ECB or quell all doubts about the permanence of EMU.

7. It must nevertheless be noted that the convergence of inflation rates and other indicators of economic performance cannot supply firm proof that policy preferences have also converged. Before drawing any such conclusion, one would need to know how costly it was to achieve the convergence in performance.

8. The italicized passages paraphrase the language of Article 109j; those beneath them are direct quotations from the protocol.

1   *Achieving a high degree of price stability*, which the protocol interprets as

. . . an average rate of inflation, observed over a period of one year before the examination, that does not exceed by more than 1½ percentage points that of, at most, the three best performing Member States in terms of price stability. Inflation shall be measured by means of the consumer price index (CPI) on a comparable basis . . . .

2   *Achieving a sustainable financial position*, which the protocol interprets as meaning that

. . . at the time of the examination the Member State is not the subject of a Council decision . . . that an excessive deficit exists.

3   *Maintaining the country's exchange rate within the normal EMS band*, which the protocol interprets as meaning that

. . . the Member State has respected the normal fluctuation margins . . . without severe tensions for at least the last two years before the examination. In particular, the Member State shall not have devalued its currency's bilateral central rate against any other Member State's currency on its own initiative for the same period.

4   *Achieving a long-term interest rate indicative of durable convergence and of the country's participation in the EMS*, which the protocol interprets as meaning that

. . . over a period of one year before the examination a Member State has an average nominal long-term interest rate that does not exceed by more than 2 percentage points that of, at most, the three best performing Member States in terms of price stability.

The treaty goes on to say, however, that when the Commission and the EMI measure convergence, they should also examine current account balances and the evolution of unit labor costs and other price indexes.[9]

9. But there is an ambiguity in Article 109j. It instructs the Commission and EMI to report to the Council of Ministers on "the progress made in the fulfilment by the Member States of their obligations regarding the achievement of economic and monetary union." It goes on to say that those reports should "also examine the achievement of a high degree of sustainable convergence by reference to the fulfilment by each Member State of the [convergence] criteria." But when it sets out the process by which the Council will decide on the eligibility of each EC country, it makes no further reference to the four criteria but confines itself to the reports of the Commission and EMI. "On the basis of these reports," it says, the Council shall assess, "for each Member State, whether it fulfils the necessary conditions for the adoption of a single currency" (i.e., is ready for Stage Three). But it does not list those "necessary conditions" or say that the Commission and EMI, when preparing their reports, should treat the convergence criteria as "necessary conditions" (i.e., that each country should be expected to fulfill each and every one of them). In 1996, Belgium will probably fulfill

The first two criteria summarized above are related very clearly to the basic rationale for achieving convergence – the need to hand on to the ECB a sustainable situation and not make it bear the blame for imposing the costs of achieving one.[10] But the case for the exchange rate criterion is weaker, and the interest rate criterion may be redundant or misleading.

What can be learned by asking a country to keep its exchange rate stable when the entire convergence exercise is aimed at deciding whether the country is ready to enter a monetary union in which it will have no exchange rate of its own? If it has paid a high price to defend its currency, it may deserve praise for its tenacity. If it has suffered silently, moreover, without blaming its partners for its problems, it may be expected to honor the independence of the ECB and thus continue to be silent if the ECB's monetary policy causes it more pain. But past performance on this score may not be a good predictor. Attitudes change. So do governments.[11]

There is perhaps another rationale for the exchange rate criterion. The ability of the EC countries, as a group, to avoid exchange rate realignments during the two-year run-up to Stage Three may say something about their ability to adjust to asymmetric shocks after exchange rates have been locked and further realignments ruled out. A judgment on that matter will have to be made in 1996, when the EC must decide if it is "appropriate" to start Stage Three. But the test should be applied to the EC as a whole, not used to ask whether each country individually is ready to enter Stage Three.[12]

The exchange rate criterion may have been meant to serve a third

the exchange rate, inflation rate, and interest rate criteria, and it may have cut its budget deficit to 3 percent of GDP; nevertheless, it may still be deemed to have an excessive deficit under Article 104c, because of its high debt ratio. Has the Council to decide that Belgium does not fulfill the "necessary conditions" for entering Stage Three? For reasons discussed in subsequent chapters, it would be prudent to suppose that the Council will indeed treat the convergence criteria as "necessary conditions" and insist that each country meet all of them fully. But that is a decision that the Council itself must take; it is not clearly mandated by Article 109j.

10. They may not suffice for this purpose, however, as sustainability may also require narrow differences in price and cost *levels*, not merely an equalization of the rates at which they change. This point will come up again in connection with the case for realigning exchange rates before Stage Three begins.

11. Begg et al. (1991) take a different view of the exchange rate criterion. It is the *only* criterion to which they would pay attention, because they appear to believe that the success of the EC countries in avoiding realignments during the run-up to Stage Three is an adequate test of their ability to bear the costs of reducing inflation in Stage Three itself.

12. It will be used in that broad way in 1996, when the EC must decide whether to begin or postpone Stage Three. But it cannot serve that purpose later, when Stage Three will start automatically.

purpose – to reduce the risk of realignments during Stage Two so as to confer credibility on the locking of exchange rates at the outset of Stage Three and thus protect the nascent monetary union from exchange rate crises before it has moved to using the ECU as its single currency.[13] Realignments in Stage Two might cast a shadow on Stage Three. If that was a reason for including it, however, the authors of the treaty did not ask themselves how currency conversions should take place after exchange rates have been locked but before the shift to the ECU. Conversions can and should take place through the ECB and the national central banks, as shown in Chapter 3, without recourse to the foreign exchange market. Accordingly, the ECB will not have to defend the locked exchange rates by intervention, and there is little reason to worry about exchange rate crises in Stage Three. Concerns of that sort, then, cannot really justify using an exchange rate test as a measure of convergence.

What can be learned from examining long-term interest rates? Unlike other numbers used in the convergence criteria, they are forward-looking. They contain information about expectations – but many sorts of expectations. When a country's long-term interest rate exceeds other countries' rates, it may be because markets expect a larger increase in the country's short-term rate or in its inflation rate, or expect it to devalue its currency or default on its debt.[14]

All of these are "bad things" from the standpoint of convergence. But most of them are covered by the other criteria. It may be reassuring for governments to know that the markets' views do not differ from their own – those that they have based on the other criteria.[15] And when there

13. De Grauwe (1992a) and Langfeldt (1992) stress this need; Fratianni and von Hagen (1992) make a similar point when they interpret the introduction of the ECU as a way to impede exit from EMU.

14. Eichengreen (1993a) notes that default risk can be the only important cause of an interest rate difference when exchange rates are credibly fixed and that the interest rate criterion is therefore redundant unless a future default would threaten the viability of a monetary union. In Chapter 4, however, I argued that a default could indeed threaten the integrity of the ECB's monetary policy. Furthermore, the exchange rate criterion does not by itself require a credible fixing of exchange rates during Stage Two, so that differences in long-term interest rates may not be due exclusively to differences in default risk.

15. This was, indeed, the rationale for including the criterion (see Bini-Smaghi, Padoa-Schioppa, and Papadia, 1994). On that same rationale, however, the criterion is badly designed. If the markets' views about future inflation differ from those of the governments (which are supposed to be based on the actual inflation rates cited in the inflation rate criterion), then the interest rate criterion should not use the interest rates of the three countries having the lowest inflation rates; it should use those of the countries having the lowest interest rates. Jenny Wilkinson drew my attention to this point, but it is also made by Artis (1994).

is a difference between the two views, governments may want to reassess their own. But the markets' views may be badly biased. They will be affected by the markets' forecasts concerning the decisions that the governments are making. If the markets come to believe that a particular country will be unable to enter Stage Three, they may forecast high inflation, devaluation, or default on the country's debt, and the country's long-term interest rate may rise. Conversely, if markets conclude that a country is ready to enter Stage Three, the country's interest rate may fall. Governments should not rely very heavily on information that can be contaminated by the markets' forecasts of the governments' own intentions.

Measuring convergence

When the Maastricht Treaty was adopted at the end of 1991, it was already obvious that some countries would not be ready to enter Stage Three, not in 1997 nor in 1999, so that there would be a two-track path to EMU. In fact, the treaty contains provisions, discussed at the end of this chapter, to govern relations between the ECB and the national central banks of the slow-track countries. No government, however, was ready to concede that it would have to take that track. The governments' optimism was based partly on the progress they hoped to make in meeting the convergence criteria and partly on the belief that their partners would interpret the criteria liberally, to preserve solidarity in the Community. Italians, for example, insisted that their country, a founding member of the EC, could not possibly be excluded from Stage Three. But the outlook has changed, because some EC countries, particularly Germany, are committed to applying the criteria strictly and because the economic situation has worsened.

How far were the individual countries from meeting the convergence criteria in 1992, just after the Maastricht Treaty was signed, and where are they now? Their situations can be assessed by applying the criteria one by one, starting with the exchange rate criterion.

At the start of 1992, the drachma and escudo were the only EC currencies outside the exchange rate mechanism of the EMS. But the pound and peseta had not yet entered the narrow band, and they would have had to do that quickly in order to keep their exchange rates within the "normal" band during the two-year period prior to the time at which the Commission and EMI must start to prepare their reports to the Council.[16] The other EC countries were firmly committed to the EMS,

16. Because the Council must render its decision on moving to Stage Three before the end of 1996, that two-year period was due to start before the end of 1994. (The escudo

and there had been no significant realignments in 1990 or 1991. Further-more, the debate at the end of 1991, after the sharp increase in German interest rates, showed that most of the EC countries were strongly op-posed to any realignment, even one produced by revaluing the deutsche mark. (But it was not clear even then that they would be able to defend their exchange rates "without severe tensions.")

A few months later, however, in September 1992, the lira and pound dropped out of the exchange rate mechanism, and three other EC curren-cies, the escudo, peseta, and punt, were devalued thereafter. In August 1993, the very notion of a "normal" band was called into question, when the band was widened "temporarily" from 2¼ percent to 15 percent.

It is easier to say how far countries must travel to meet the inflation rate and interest rate criteria. In 1991, the three best-performing coun-tries in terms of inflation were Denmark, Luxembourg, and France (which was tied with Belgium and Ireland); their inflation rates averaged 2.9 percent, and their long-term interest rates averaged 8.9 percent. Therefore, the inflation rate cutoff would have been 4.4 percent, and the interest rate cutoff would have been 10.9 percent.[17] Hence, Greece, Italy, Portugal, and Spain would have failed to meet both the inflation rate and interest rate criteria, and the United Kingdom would have failed to meet the inflation rate criterion.[18] Recent data on inflation rates and interest rates are shown in Table 6–1. There, the three best-performing countries are Denmark, Ireland, and the United Kingdom, the inflation rate cutoff would be 3.0 percent, and the interest rate cutoff would be 9.6 percent. Hence, Greece, Italy, and Portugal would fail to meet both criteria, and Germany, Luxembourg, and Spain would fail to meet the inflation rate criterion.

Although Table 6–1 lists the budget deficits and debts of the EC countries and compares them with the corresponding reference values, the fiscal criterion does not use them mechanically. It applies the test set out in Article 104c of the treaty and discussed in Chapter 4. If the

entered the exchange rate mechanism in April 1992, on the same terms as the pound and peseta.)

17. The treaty does not explain how to use the numbers for the three best-performing countries; it is commonly assumed that the numbers should be averaged, as they are here, and the permissible margin (1½ percent for the inflation rate and 2 percent for the interest rate) should then be added to the average. (A different interpretation is possible, however, because the protocol refers to the inflation rates of "at most" the three best-performing countries. If their inflation rates are very different, attention may focus on those of the one or two countries having the lowest rates.)

18. There is no comparable long-term interest rate for Greece, but its short-term rate was very high, suggesting that its long-term rate would have been much higher than the cutoff level. The same supposition is made below for the most recent period.

Table 6-1 *Convergence indicators for the EC countries, 1994*

Country	Inflation Rate[a]	Interest Rate[b]	Fiscal Deficit[c]	Public Debt[d]
Belgium	2.6	7.0	**5.5**	**140.1**
Denmark[e]	1.4	8.2	**4.3**	**78.0**
France	2.0	6.5	**5.6**	50.4
Germany	**3.9**	6.1	2.9	51.0
Greece	**13.4**	na	**14.1**	**121.3**
Ireland[e]	1.4	7.2	2.4	**89.0**
Italy	**4.4**	**10.3**	**9.6**	**123.7**
Luxembourg	**3.3**	6.7	−1.3	9.2
Netherlands	2.7	6.5	**3.8**	**78.8**
Portugal	**6.0**	**11.6**	**6.2**	**70.4**
Spain	**4.8**	9.2	**7.0**	**63.5**
United Kingdom[e]	1.7	7.4	**6.3**	50.4

Note: Numbers in bold type exceed the numerical limits or reference values set out in the Maastricht Treaty.

[a]Measured by the average percentage change in the consumer price index in the twelve months ending with March 1994 (February 1994 for Ireland); German figure is for West Germany alone. The criterion for compliance is obtained by taking the average for the three countries having the lowest inflation rates and adding the 1½ percent margin allowed by the treaty; it works out as 3.0 percent.

[b]Measured by the average interest rate on long-term government bonds in the twelve months ending with March 1994; no such figure available for Greece. The criterion for compliance is obtained by taking the average for the three countries having the lowest inflation rates and adding the 2 percent margin allowed by the treaty; it works out at 9.6 percent.

[c]Forecast by EC Commission of net borrowing by general government in 1994 expressed as a percentage of GDP. The reference value is 3.0 percent.

[d]Forecast by EC Commission of gross debt owed by general government at the end of 1994 expressed as a percentage of GDP; see notes to Table 4-2. The reference value is 60.0 percent.

[e]Country with one of three lowest inflation rates.

Source: EC Commission; data are not yet harmonized fully to conform to the provisions of the Maastricht Treaty.

Council has found that a country is running an "excessive" budget deficit, pursuant to Article 104c, and the finding has not been rescinded, the country does not fulfill the fiscal criterion. In September 1994, the Council found that ten countries had excessive deficits (Luxembourg and Ireland were the exceptions), and the outlook for some of those countries was not very bright. The numbers in Table 6–1 suggest that Greece and Italy may find it impossible to persuade the Council that they are no longer running excessive deficits, even in 1998, before the final deadline for starting Stage Three. Other countries may have trouble too. Belgium and Denmark may be able to reduce their deficits to 3 percent of GDP, but not fast enough to engineer appreciable reductions in their debt ratios and thus show that those ratios are "sufficiently diminishing and approaching the reference value at a satisfactory pace" (i.e., meet the test applied to Ireland in 1994). Portugal and Spain may have trouble bringing their deficits down, and their debt ratios will continue to rise in the interim.[19] Economic recovery will help the EC countries to reduce their deficits, but it may not suffice.

It is thus unlikely that a majority of EC countries will be ready for Stage Three in 1997, when a majority is required to set a starting date, and it may be hard to muster a majority in 1999 – although a majority is not needed then.[20]

The road map in the treaty

As soon as it was decided that the ECB would not be established in Stage Two – that the EMI would take its place – the intergovernmental conference began to debate the character and mandate of the EMI. Italy and France were concerned to maintain political momentum, so they wanted the EMI to resemble the ECB as closely as possible. Britain and Germany sought to maintain national control over monetary policy until it was transferred to the ECB, so they wanted to limit the mandate of the EMI.[21] The outcome was a compromise, but it was tilted toward the Anglo-German view.

19. Germany's debt ratio will also rise in 1995, when the German government must take over the debt of the Treuhand, but the Commission's forecasts, shown in Table 4–2, indicate that the German debt ratio will not quite reach 60 percent of GDP.
20. The situations of Austria and Finland are somewhat better than those of the present EC members – but that is not true for Sweden. The Commission does not provide comparable data on those countries, but similar data appear in the Organisation for Economic Co-operation and Development's *Economic Outlook*. Pursuing the approach adopted in Table 6–1 (but using 1993 data for inflation rates and interest rates, rather than the more recent data used in Table 6–1), one finds that Austria and Sweden would have failed the inflation rate criterion, but all three countries would have met the interest rate criterion. Austria, Finland, and Sweden were expected to run budget deficits larger than 3 percent of GDP in 1994, although Austria's was not expected to be much larger. Furthermore, Sweden was the only country having a debt ratio above 60 percent in 1993. When Bayoumi and Eichengreen (1993) examined the shocks affecting these and other countries of the European Free Trade Association (EFTA), they found that those of Austria, Sweden, and Switzerland are highly correlated with those of the core EC countries, but those of the other EFTA countries have been more idiosyncratic.
21. See Crockett (1991a) and Bini-Smaghi, Padoa-Schioppa, and Papadia (1994).

The intergovernmental conference had to decide other issues as well. What might be done to intensify policy coordination among the EC central banks? Should steps be taken in Stage Two to make the ECU as basket more attractive as an asset, to pave the way for the ECU as currency in Stage Three? Should the EMS band be narrowed in Stage Two, to pave the way for the locking of exchange rates in Stage Three?

What must happen in Stage Two

Stage Two began on January 1, 1994, the EMI was established, and several new rules took effect. There is to be no "monetary financing" or "bailouts" of public entities (Articles 104 and 104b of the treaty) and, as already mentioned, the EC countries must endeavor to avoid excessive deficits (Article 104c), although sanctions cannot be imposed until Stage Three. Finally, governments needing to grant independence to their own central banks have to initiate the process during Stage Two (Article 109e), and some, including France, have already done so.

The structure and functioning of the EMI

The role of the EMI is described by Article 109f of the treaty and by its own Statute, appended to the treaty. It is governed by a Council comprising a president, vice-president, and the governors of all the EC central banks. The president is appointed to a three-year term by the "common accord" of the heads of state or government, on a recommendation from the EMI Council.[22] The Council itself chooses the vice-president from among the central bank governors. At the Brussels Summit in December 1993, Alexandre Lamfalussy was chosen as the first president; Maurice Doyle, governor of the Bank of Ireland, was chosen as vice-president. The Committee of Central Bank Governors was dissolved when Stage Two began, because the EMI has assumed its duties.

Article 4 of the EMI Statute instructs the EMI to strengthen cooperation among the central banks and the coordination of their monetary policies, aimed at ensuring price stability; to hold consultations on issues falling within the central banks' competence and affecting the stability of financial institutions and markets; to monitor the functioning of the

22. Unlike the president of ECB, the president of the EMI can be reappointed. As in the case of the ECB, the president of the EC Council and a representative of the Commission may participate in the deliberations of the EMI Council but may not vote, and the president of the EMI may attend meetings of the EC Council when it discusses matters related to the work of the EMI. The EMI president may also appear before committees of the European Parliament.

EMS and assume the tasks of the European Monetary Cooperation Fund (EMCF), which administers the EMS credit facilities; and to facilitate the use of the ECU and oversee the development and smooth functioning of the ECU clearing system. National monetary authorities are expected to consult the EMI before taking decisions about monetary policy.

But the EMI has another major task. By the end of 1996, it must specify the "regulatory, organizational and logistical framework necessary for the ESCB to perform its tasks" (EMI Statute, Article 4) and must submit it for decision to the ECB when the latter is established. Specifically, the EMI shall:

- prepare the instruments and the procedures necessary for carrying out a single monetary policy in the third stage;

- promote the harmonization, where necessary, of the rules and practices governing the collection, compilation and distribution of statistics in the areas within its field of competence;

- prepare the rules for operations to be undertaken by the national central banks in the framework of the ESCB;

- promote the efficiency of cross-border payments;

- supervise the technical preparation of ECU bank notes.

Under Article 15 of its statute, the EMI may adopt guidelines for the national central banks on "the implementation of the conditions necessary for the ESCB to perform its functions" (but these will not be binding, as they will have to be approved by the ECB).[23]

Finally, Article 6 of the EMI Statute allows the EMI to receive monetary reserves from the national central banks and issue ECU against them in order to implement the EMS agreements. It may also hold and manage reserves at the request of national central banks, but only as their agent and at their risk. The French finance minister said at Maastricht that France will place some of its reserves with the EMI, but that has not yet happened.[24]

23. Unanimity is required for the EMI Council to adopt the "framework" for the ESCB. It is also required for decisions on certain financial matters and for decisions to publish opinions and recommendations concerning monetary policy. A two-thirds majority is required to adopt an opinion or recommendation concerning monetary policy and the "guidelines" addressed to the national central banks. Otherwise, the EMI Council uses simple majority voting.

24. More recently, the president of the Bundesbank has said that Germany will not place reserves with the EMI and that he knows of no country that is planning to do so (*Financial Times*, January 31, 1994).

Article 8 of the EMI Statute declares that the central bank governors shall act "according to their own responsibilities" when participating in the work of the EMI Council, and the Council itself "may not seek or take any instructions from Community institutions or bodies or Governments of Member States." These provisions echo Article 7 of the ESCB Statute.

Chapter 3 examined some of the problems that the EMI will have to resolve when designing the "framework" for the ESCB and "guidelines" for the national central banks. But more must be said about the role of the EMI in coordinating monetary policies, the ECU in Stage Two, and the long-term future of the EMS.

Monetary policies in Stage Two

The EMI will not make decisions about monetary policies; they will remain in national hands. Nevertheless, it may "formulate opinions or recommendations on the overall orientation of monetary policy and exchange rate policy" and on national monetary policies, and it may address them to the Council of Ministers or to individual governments and central banks.[25] The EMI Statute, however, says nothing about the criteria that should used to appraise the "overall orientation" of monetary policy or the policies of individual countries, apart from stating that policy coordination should be aimed at price stability.

The convergence criteria will be helpful, of course, in appraising and coordinating monetary policies. Countries with high inflation rates will have to reduce them. Furthermore, participation in the EMS will impose constraints on the setting of national interest rates, although the constraints were weakened by the widening of the band in 1993. These requirements, however, can serve mainly to limit the freedom of individual countries to deviate from the general tenor of monetary policies in the EC as a whole. They do not provide a basis for setting or appraising that general tenor.

This was not a problem in the late 1980s. The Bundesbank pursued a

---

25. Article 5 of the EMI Statute. An opinion or recommendation addressed to an individual government or central bank can be adopted over the opposition of that country's governor, because unanimity is not required. Gros and Thygesen (1992) note that the powers of the EMI in the monetary field are not greater than those of its predecessor, the Committee of Central Bank Governors (although the chairman of the Committee of Governors could decide on his own to publicize its deliberations). The Bundesbank also draws attention to the similarity between the institutions (Deutsche Bundesbank, 1992); unlike Gros and Thygesen, however, the Bundesbank is pleased with it.

monetary policy aimed at price stability, and the other EMS countries pursued monetary policies aimed at maintaining stable exchange rates in terms of the deutsche mark. But these arrangements were based implicitly on German fiscal policies and wage-setting practices that permitted the Bundesbank to control inflation without resorting to high interest rates. They helped other EMS countries to adapt to German monetary policy and to justify that strategy. After German unification, fiscal and wage pressures mounted in Germany, inflation accelerated, and the Bundesbank had to raise interest rates sharply. These events helped to set the stage for the EMS crises of 1992 and 1993. But even before the first crisis, the costs imposed on other EMS countries by the German policy mix gave rise to widespread discontent, reinforcing the case for EMU itself and inspiring new proposals for the closer coordination of monetary policies.

Some of those proposals called on the Bundesbank to broaden its own policy domain – to aim at price stability in the EC as a whole, not in Germany alone.[26] But the Bundesbank rejected that idea, citing its constitutional obligation to pursue price stability within Germany and noting that a widening of its domain would have forced it to accept more inflation in Germany in the early 1990s. Furthermore, this approach did not offer a satisfactory basis for coordinating monetary policies; it was aimed exclusively at one country's policies. Another approach was more appealing from this particular standpoint and has been widely endorsed as a basis for policy coordination in the EMI, especially since the EMS crises (see, e.g., Gros and Thygesen, 1992; Bofinger, 1993; Collignon et al., 1993; and Ludlow, 1993). This approach is based on the framework proposed by McKinnon (1982, 1984) in his plan for monetary coordination at the global level. The EC central banks would choose an appropriate path for an intermediate policy target – an interest rate average or monetary aggregate for the EC as a whole. Each national central bank would then choose a path for its local counterpart of the target variable. They would not necessarily choose identical paths, as some might have higher inflation rates than others, but the *sum* of their decisions would have to be consistent with the path chosen for the EC variable. Further-

26. Kenen (1992a), Mundell (1993), and Artis (1994). See also the simulations cited in Chapter 1, note 15, in which EMU was modeled as an arrangement under which the Bundesbank stabilized EC prices while other EC countries stabilized their exchange rates in terms of the deutsche mark. Hughes Hallett and Ma (1994) look closely at the welfare effects of such an arrangement by running simulations that include the years following unification; there would have been small welfare losses for Germany (where the inflation rate would have been higher) but large welfare gains for the other EC countries (where output losses would have been smaller).

more, a country might have to depart temporarily from the medium-term path for its target variable, because of developments in the foreign exchange market, but such departures would take place symmetrically and would therefore cancel out at the EC level.

McKinnon's own framework envisaged the use of a global monetary aggregate, and all of the national deviations were produced symmetrically and automatically by nonsterilized intervention on the foreign exchange market. It was, in effect, a gold standard without gold. The rationale was McKinnon's finding that national inflation rates are affected more strongly by the global money supply than by national money supplies, but other studies failed to confirm that finding (see Spinelli, 1983; and Goldstein and Haynes, 1984). The currencies of the EMS countries, however, may be closer substitutes than those of the major industrial countries with which McKinnon was concerned, and there are reasons for believing that the total money supply of the EMS countries has more influence on the inflation rates of individual countries than do their own national money supplies.[27]

Because EC central banks rely mainly on interest rates, not monetary aggregates, to influence aggregate demand, they may prefer to focus on an average EC interest rate than on an EC monetary aggregate. It is unrealistic, moreover, to ask the Bundesbank to refrain completely from sterilizing the money supply effects of intervention on the foreign exchange market. Those effects greatly affected the Bundesbank's policies during the 1992 EMS crisis and affected the subsequent evolution of the EMS itself.[28] But some such framework will have to be devised if the EMI is to have much influence on monetary policies during the remainder of Stage Two.

27. See Bayoumi and Kenen (1993) and Cassard, Lane, and Masson (1994); the latter show that the German inflation rate is responsive to an M3 aggregate for the core countries of the EC, which suggests that the Bundesbank should welcome the use of such an aggregate as the basis for policy coordination. (They also point out that the use of a core-country aggregate for coordination, rather than an EC-wide aggregate, may be awkward politically when no EC country has yet been declared ineligible to enter Stage Three.) The results cited above are consistent with those of Kremers and Lane (1990), Monticelli and Strauss-Kahn (1992), and Artis, Bladen-Hovell, and Zhang (1993), all of whom find that there is a stable demand function for the total money supply of the EMS countries. For a survey of recent work on the demand for money in the EC countries and in the EC as a whole, see Fase (1993); for critical assessments, see Sardelis (1993) and the exchange between Barr (1992) and Kremers and Lane (1992).

28. Rieke (1994) sets out the Bundesbank's views; the role of money supply effects in the 1992 crisis and in the evolution of the EMS are discussed in Chapter 7, which also examines some other proposals for monetary coordination.

The ECU in Stage Two

Anticipating the shift to the ECU in Stage Three, several proposals were made to enhance the attractiveness of the existing ECU and thus to encourage its use.[29] There were proposals to "harden" the ECU and strengthen the system for settling interbank claims produced by transfers of ECU-denominated balances. But Schulmann (1993) rightly suggests that these issues have attracted more attention than they deserve. Why encourage the use of the existing ECU when Stage Three will bring about a fundamental change in the very nature of the ECU, from being a basket of national currencies to being a currency in its own right?

Attempts to make the ECU more attractive would have been quite sensible had the EC decided to pursue an evolutionary approach to monetary union of the sort proposed by the United Kingdom. The pace and success of the process would have depended crucially on the ability of the ECU to compete with the various national currencies. Under the approach adopted at Maastricht, however, the attractiveness of the ECU used in Stage Two will not greatly affect the outcome in Stage Three, when the ECU as currency replaces the ECU as basket. Present arrangements for clearing and settling transactions in ECU will not be important in Stage Three, which must be concerned primarily with redenominating and linking arrangements previously used to clear and settle transactions in national currencies, not with replacing them by the arrangements used for the ECU as basket.

Care must be taken in Stage Two to guard against a breakdown of the system for clearing and settling ECU transactions. Such a breakdown could impair public confidence in the ECU and make it harder to move to the ECU in Stage Three. No one can object, moreover, to eliminating legal and other impediments to wider use of the ECU. But ambitious efforts would waste time and energy.

Two proposals were advanced to harden the ECU in Stage Two. The first one sought to prevent any future exchange rate realignment from reducing the value of the ECU basket in terms of the strongest EMS currency. This could have been done by adjusting the currency composition of the basket after any realignment (i.e., increasing the number of units of the currencies being devalued to offset their depreciation in terms of the strong currencies, or even raising uniformly the number of units of every currency). Previously, the composition of the basket was adjusted at five-year intervals in a manner that maintained its value in

---

29. On the existing ECU and its uses, see Allen (1992); on the pricing of the ECU in financial markets, see Folkerts-Landau and Garber (1992b).

terms of each national currency but raised the shares of the currencies that had been devalued since the previous adjustment. This technique exposed the ECU to gradual "softening" because it raised the amount by which any subsequent devaluation of those same currencies would reduce the value of the ECU in terms of the strong currencies. The second proposal was to fix the composition of the basket. That would not have prevented a realignment from reducing the value of the ECU in terms of the strong currencies. In fact, it would have precluded any adjustment in the basket designed to achieve that result. But it would have ended the previous practice, by which periodic changes in the composition of the basket exposed the ECU to gradual softening with repeated devaluations of the weaker currencies.

The first proposal would have done more to harden the ECU but would have produced uncertainty about the timing of future changes in the basket, which would have been keyed to the timing of future realignments. Furthermore, the second proposal was seen to simplify the terms of contracts denominated in ECU and was strongly endorsed by participants in the ECU markets. Accordingly, Article 109g of the Maastricht Treaty fixes the currency composition of the ECU basket, and it took effect when the treaty was ratified.

Exchange rates in Stage Two

Recall the recommendations of the Delors Report (1989) about exchange rates in Stage Two. The EMS band would be narrowed, and realignments would be made only in exceptional circumstances.

The narrowing of the band was seen as a step toward the locking of exchange rates at the start of Stage Three. It might have been useful as a way of proving progress and capturing in advance some of the benefits expected in Stage Three from suppressing the band completely. But the actual benefits would have been small – far less than proportional to the compression of the band – because a mere narrowing of the band would not have banished the need for currency conversions or the fixed costs of making them.

Furthermore, a narrower band might have interfered with the targeting of monetary policies on price stability. Exchange rate stability and price stability usually go together over the medium run. The currencies of countries with high inflation rates are apt to come under pressure in the foreign exchange markets, forcing those countries to keep their interest rates higher than those of low-inflation countries. But the two objectives may come into conflict in the short run. The maintenance of exchange rate stability within a very narrow band can require higher interest rates than those that a country might want to maintain with a view to reducing inflation over the longer term. Conversely, a country seeking to reduce its inflation rate quickly may have to keep its interest rates higher than those of its EMS partners.[30] By defining exchange rate stability ambitiously, a narrowing of the band might have raised the likelihood of those conflicts, and the recommendation was not adopted. The issue will arise again, however, in a different form. Should the present wide band be narrowed before Stage Three begins? I answer that question in Chapter 7.

What does the Maastricht Treaty say about exchange rate realignments? It does not limit them to "exceptional circumstances," but a country that devalues unilaterally in the two years prior to mid-1996 will run afoul of the convergence criteria. Yet the treaty left three windows open. The first was wide open at the start of Stage Two; a country was free to devalue unilaterally before mid-1994, the earliest date for starting the "examination period" in which its exchange rate policy will come under scrutiny. The second is half-open throughout Stage Two; a country is always free to *revalue* its currency during Stage Two. The third is open narrowly at the end of Stage Two; nothing can prevent the EC countries from undertaking a general realignment before the permanent locking of exchange rates, if the realignment is agreed unanimously and is designed in a way that does not affect the external value of the ECU.[31]

The case for "one last realignment" arises from concern that the locking of exchange rates may leave some countries in disequilibria, which they could rectify thereafter only by enduring a period of low growth and high unemployment. Article 109j of the treaty appears to acknowledge this risk when it instructs the Commission and EMI to take account of unit labor costs and other price indexes when assessing the degree of

---

30. That was, of course, the German case after unification, but there have been others, such as the Spanish case in the late 1980s.
31. This last option is often ignored; Begg and Wyplosz (1993) and Eichengreen (1993a) both appear to believe that realignments are ruled out permanently after the beginning of the two-year examination period. But Article 109l of the treaty contains this language: "At the starting date of the third stage, the Council shall, acting with the unanimity of the Member States without a derogation . . . , adopt the conversion rates at which their currencies shall be irrevocably fixed and at which irrevocably fixed rates the ECU shall be substituted for these currencies, and the ECU shall become a currency in its own right. This measure shall by itself not modify the external value of the ECU." The meaning of the final sentence is unclear, because the "external value" of the ECU depends on the (floating) exchange rates between the EC currencies, as a group, and all other currencies. The sentence is sometimes read to mean that there must be no realignment like that suggested in the text – perhaps because it is hard to attach any other operational meaning to it. Gros and Thygesen (1992) agree that it does not rule out one last realignment, but they deplore that fact.

convergence, although it does not tell them how to interpret those numbers. The size of the problem will depend on the time it will take for the EC countries to converge on a common inflation rate; the longer it takes, the larger will be the cumulative gaps between national price levels on the date when exchange rates are locked.[32] The costs of dealing with the problem will depend in turn on the degree to which the EC countries fall short of being an optimum currency area in the sense described in Chapter 4.

Four arguments are made against another realignment. First, experience in the EC suggests that changes in nominal exchange rates cannot change real rates for long; the EC economies are too tightly linked by trade, and real wage rates are too rigid.[33] Second, the EC will be an optimum currency area by the beginning of Stage Three, because the single market will have come into being; hence, the cost of adjusting to an initial disequilibrium will not be as large as one might anticipate. This was the view of the Commission (1990). Third, a realignment just before Stage Three would call into question the credibility of the commitment to lock exchange rates irrevocably and could impair the credibility of the ECB. Fourth, expectations of a final realignment would produce specula-

32. The size of the problem will also depend on the degree of exchange rate flexibility during the last years of Stage Two and on the way in which exchange rates are locked. If the wide band is not narrowed, if exchange rates are allowed to move freely through it, and if exchange rates are locked at the market rates prevailing on the first day of Stage Three, rather than the corresponding central rates, the size of the problem may be reduced. (It could be amplified instead if market forces have driven exchange rates far from their long-term equilibrium levels – which is not impossible with quasi-floating rates.) Thygesen (1993a) believes that the exchange rate changes of 1992 and 1993 have already reduced the size of the problem by correcting the worst misalignments.

33. Giovannini (1991) advances an odd version of this argument. Because the ECB will be expected to pursue a noninflationary monetary policy, the move to Stage Three will banish expectations of inflation, so that prices and wages will become more flexible. With flexible prices, however, a change in nominal exchange rates will not change real exchange rates. This argument has some validity. If goods and labor markets are in equilibrium initially and prices are flexible, a change in nominal exchange rates will generate disequilibria that will lead to offsetting changes in prices and wages; there will then be no lasting change in real exchange rates. But the case for a realignment is usually based on the supposition that goods and labor markets are in disequilibrium initially – that real exchange rates are misaligned. In that case, the reduction in real-wage rigidity produced by the credibility of the ECB's monetary policy should allow a change in nominal rates to produce a lasting change in real rates. (This point reappears below, where a distinction is drawn between "active" and "reactive" changes in exchange rates.) A different version of the argument is offered by Britton and Mayes (1992). Because real wages are rigid, inflation rates will rise in countries that devalue their currencies. Hence, those countries will be hard hit right after the start of Stage Three, when the ECB imposes a monetary policy aimed at price stability.

tive pressures in Stage Two, making it harder for some countries to satisfy the exchange rate convergence criterion.

No one can know whether real exchange rates will be badly mis- aligned just before Stage Three, but something can be said about the various arguments against a final realignment. When appraising the first argument, that realignments are ineffective in the EC context, it is important to distinguish between an "active" exchange rate policy, aimed at improving a country's competitive position, and a "reactive" policy, aimed at correcting an earlier deterioration. The difference is very important in the European context, because some of the same economists who warn against using the exchange rate actively have nevertheless favored using it reactively. This may reflect incipient schizophrenia – but probably not. An active devaluation can create disequilibria in goods and labor markets, which are likely to produce inflationary pressures and thus vitiate the real effects of the devalua- tion. A reactive devaluation is less risky when it is aimed at correcting a misalignment that has already produced a disequilibrium of the oppo- site sort – excess supply in the traded-goods sector and the labor market – and this is the case contemplated by those who would not rule out a final realignment.

Another distinction is needed to assess the second argument, concern- ing the effects of the single market. The removal of barriers to factor movements is, of course, necessary to raise factor mobility and bring the EC closer to being an optimum currency area. As pointed out in Chap- ter 4, however, the mere removal of barriers will not be sufficient, because other inertial forces will continue to impede factor mobility. The narrowing of income differences and other disparities among U.S. regions – a process driven partly by factor movements – has taken many decades even in the absence of formal barriers to interregional factor mobility (see Barro and Sala-i-Martin, 1991).

The third argument has already been answered. Realignments in Stage Two are not apt to undermine the fixed exchange rates in Stage Three. Once Stage Three begins, currency conversions will take place at par on the books of the ESCB, not in the foreign exchange market. The general public may be slow to understand this, but those who have the power to influence exchange rates by moving their money around will quickly realize that the game is over.

The fourth argument, however, is hard to answer. If a final realign- ment is widely expected, it will be increasingly difficult to combat specu- lation in the run-up to Stage Three, and governments may then be unable to meet the convergence criteria regarding exchange rates and interest rates. If they try to meet the exchange rate criterion, they may violate the interest rate criterion. One is therefore tempted to suggest that the final realignment take place soon, before expectations build up, but that will not work. No one can truly guarantee the finality of an early realignment.[34] Hence, the exchange rate criterion must be interpreted in a way that will avoid the need to narrow the EMS band before the locking of exchange rates, as a wide band is the best feasible defense against speculative pressures.

Dealing with the slow-track countries

As a two-track path to EMU seems inevitable, it is worth asking whether the slow-track countries will have any way to influence the policies of the ECB. Some governments, notably those that had reason to fear that they will be on the slow track, wanted all of the national central bank governors to participate in the deliberations of the ECB's Governing Council, even if some of them could not vote on policy matters. Other governments wanted to exclude the nonparticipants from any formal role. A compromise was reached by the intergovernmental conference, and it is reflected in Article 109l of the Maastricht Treaty, which provides for the creation of a General Council as a third decision-making body of the ECB, and in Articles 44 to 47 of the ESCB Statute, which define its role.

The president and vice-president of the ECB and all of the central bank governors will be voting members of the General Council, and the president will chair it. (Other members of the Executive Board may take part in its meetings but may not vote.) The General Council will "contribute" to the work of the ECB in various areas (e.g., by collecting statistics and making personnel policy) but will have no role in making monetary policy. It will be "informed by the president of the ECB of decisions of the Governing Council" and will, no doubt, discuss them. But the statute does not give it any right to be informed about matters *pending* before the Governing Council.

The nonparticipants will not have to transfer any foreign exchange reserves to the ECB and will not be subject to its jurisdiction. They will "retain their powers in the field of monetary policy according to national

---

34. Begg et al. (1991) tried to solve the problem by proposing that the final realignment take place before the Maastricht Summit and that the treaty include an outright ban on any subsequent exchange rate change. There are two problems with this solution: (1) the prohibition would not have taken effect until the treaty was ratified; and (2) the case for a final realignment depends in part on the size and duration of future inflation rate differences, which cannot be known in advance.

law" (Article 43 of the ESCB Statute).[35] They *will* be subject to the bans on monetary financing, on bailouts of public entities, and on excessive budget deficits (but they will not be subject to sanctions if they fail to correct excessive deficits).

What about policy coordination? What about the management of exchange rates between the ECU and the nonparticipants' currencies? The treaty and ESCB Statute do not answer these questions. The General Council will "take over those tasks of the EMI which . . . have still to be performed in the third stage" (Articles 44 and 47 of the ESCB Statute), and the tasks of the EMI include fostering policy coordination and monitoring the EMS. But the treaty and statute do not say that the General Council will inherit the *powers* of the EMI – the right to make policy recommendations to individual countries and to be consulted in advance about the future course of monetary policies.[36]

Furthermore, the General Council is poorly designed to coordinate monetary and exchange rate policies. Suppose that Canada, Mexico, and the United States were to set up a committee for that purpose. Surely, the governors of the Bank of Canada and Banco de Mexico would expect to meet with the chairman of the Board of Governors of the Federal Reserve System, not sit among the presidents of the Federal Reserve Banks, with the chairman of the Board of Governors presiding at the opposite end of the table. If Canada and Mexico asked to join the Federal Reserve System, their governors would become the presidents

---

35. But countries with derogations are required to make their national laws compatible with the treaty and ESCB Statute and to appoint their central bank governors for terms no shorter than five years. The United Kingdom will not be subject to these requirements if it does not choose to enter Stage Three.

36. Article 44 of the ESCB Statute, which transfers residual tasks from the EMI to the ECB, was presumably designed to transfer the EMI's responsibilities for managing the credit facilities of the EMS. Furthermore, Articles 4 and 5 of the EMI Statute, which give the EMI the rights listed above, refer to the "national" monetary authorities; they cannot readily be construed as giving the General Council the right to make recommendations to the ECB itself. Nevertheless, an EC official very familiar with the history and language of these provisions wrote to me as follows: "I do not share your pessimistic view that the General Council will not inherit the powers of the EMI. In Treaty language, 'tasks' means 'powers' (see Article 4a of the ESCB Statute). The only reason for the current formulation of Article 44 of the ESCB Statute is that some tasks of the EMI simply cannot be executed any longer (e.g., development of the ECU). The intention of this article is clearly that all of the tasks of the EMI except those which are logically impossible are performed, *mutatis mutandis*, by the General Council. This would include *ex ante* monetary policy coordination and the monitoring of the functioning of the successor to the EMS." I am not fully convinced, although I hope that he is right.

of the thirteenth and fourteenth Federal Reserve Banks, but that is a different story.

The practical importance of these organizational matters will depend on the number and size of the slow-track countries. If they are few and small, there may be little need for consultations about monetary and exchange rate policies. They will have to adapt their policies to those of the ECB and peg their currencies to the ECU if they wish to qualify for eventual participation. If they are numerous and some of them are large, policy coordination may matter greatly, not only to them but also to the ESCB countries. Questions remain, moreover, about the manner in which exchange rates should be managed.

The Maastricht Treaty is virtually silent on these matters. Article 109m calls on the EC countries to treat their exchange rates as matters of common interest in Stage Two and to "take account of the experience acquired" in the EMS – an injunction that might be read differently now than it did when the treaty was drafted. In Stage Three, these obligations will apply "by analogy" to countries with derogations. Furthermore, Article 109k says that countries with derogations cannot enter Stage Three until they meet conditions "on the basis of" the criteria in Article 109j, and those criteria include "observance of the normal fluctuation margins" of the EMS. Countries with derogations are thus expected to assume an exchange rate obligation of some sort, if not to preserve the formal framework of the EMS. But the treaty does not impose any reciprocal obligation on the ECB with regard to the management of the exchange rates between the ECU and the nonparticipants' currencies. There are, of course, two basic ways of managing those rates.

The nonparticipants might peg their currencies unilaterally to the ECU and take responsibility for keeping their exchange rates within predetermined bands. They would then use their own reserves for intervention and set their interest rates at the levels required to maintain exchange rate stability. They would probably intervene in ECU and hold some of their reserves with the ECB. If they assumed those responsibilities, however, they might also insist on the right to change their exchange rates whenever they saw fit, without the consent of the ECB or the EC as a whole.[37]

Alternatively, decisions and duties could be shared between the ECB and the nonparticipants' central banks, under a residual version of the

---

37. Some countries, such as the United Kingdom, might even opt for indefinite floating rather than unilateral pegging. The long-term consequences for the EC, especially for the single market, are discussed in Chapter 8.

EMS in which the ECU would be one of the currencies involved, together with the nonparticipants' currencies. Central rates would be chosen collectively, the ECB would have to intervene whenever the ECU reached the limit of its band, and it might be expected to alter its interest rates to maintain exchange rate stability.[38] Finally, there would be short-term credit facilities like those of the EMS.

Several economists have expressed support for a residual EMS (see, e.g., Britton and Mayes, 1992; and Mundell, 1993). But Gros and Thygesen (1992) have objected, because a residual EMS might interfere with the pursuit of price stability by the ECB. It was for this very reason that the intergovernmental conference gave so much attention to the roles of ECB and the Council of Ministers in choosing exchange rate arrangements vis-à-vis third currencies – a matter discussed in Chapter 5. Unilateral pegging, however, would have much the same effect if the nonparticipants intervened in ECU and held their reserves with the ECB; whenever a nonparticipant's central bank sold ECU in order to defend its currency, it would increase bank liquidity in the ESCB countries. The monetary effect would not differ from that of a sale by the ECB itself under a cooperative exchange rate arrangement.[39]

Unilateral pegging might also burden the nonparticipants heavily. Consider a country that had failed to satisfy the exchange rate criterion for entering Stage Three. Should it be expected to do better on its own, without the benefit of the credibility conferred by collective arrangements, the obligation of the ECB to intervene, and large credit lines?

The EMS crises have made it hard to answer this question firmly. On the one hand, the crises have made it more likely that there will be several slow-track countries, including some large countries. Hence, intervention by those countries could have appreciable effects on the monetary situation in the ESCB countries. It may also be imprudent to

38. It would still be possible for the nonparticipants to define their central rates in terms of the ECU, just as they would with unilateral pegging, but the bands for the bilateral exchange rates between the nonparticipants' currencies would have to be defined differently from the bands for the rates between the ECU and each such currency. To use the metaphor of the 1960s, the bands for the rates involving the ECU would form a "tunnel," while the bands for the other bilateral rates would form a "snake" and undulate within the tunnel.

39. The size of the effect will depend, of course, on the sizes of the countries involved. If all of the nonparticipants are small countries, the effect will be too small to disrupt the monetary policy of the ECB. If some of the countries are large, the effect will be large, whether it results from unilateral intervention or a cooperative exchange rate arrangement. (Note that the balance sheet of the ECB will be much bigger than that of the Bundesbank, even if EMU includes only a few countries initially. Hence, intervention should be less threatening to the ECB than it has been to the Bundesbank.)

leave decisions about realignments entirely to the slow-track countries, because the realignments could have large effects on the ESCB countries. On the other hand, the EMS crises have greatly weakened the reciprocal commitments made to the present EMS. Therefore, a residual EMS might not give much comfort to the slow-track countries. Austria has pegged the schilling to the deutsche mark without help from the Bundesbank, but several EC countries could not defend their EMS parities despite help from the Bundesbank.

CHAPTER 7

Reconsidering the transition

The transition to EMU proposed in the Maastricht Treaty and discussed in Chapter 6 was based on the belief that there could be a "seamless" path to monetary union. Inflation rates and long-term interest rates could be made to converge gradually; budget deficits and debt ratios could be made to conform to the requirements of the treaty; and exchange rates could be kept within the "normal" EMS band without "severe tensions." Realignments were not ruled out, but they should take place only in "exceptional" circumstances (Delors Report, 1989). There had been several realignments within the EMS, but the last one had occurred in January 1987, five years before the signing of the Maastricht Treaty.

There were reasons to question the plausibility of this scenario, even when it was widely accepted; some of them were cited in Chapter 6. But the reasons began to multiply shortly after the treaty was signed. On June 2, 1992, Danish voters rejected the treaty in a national referendum, and critics of the treaty were growing more vocal in Britain. In August, tensions began to develop in the EMS, focused chiefly on the lira, and they intensified early in September, when public opinion polls began to suggest that French voters might also reject the treaty in a referendum on September 20. That did not happen, although the vote was very close. Before the outcome was known, however, the lira and pound had been withdrawn from the exchange rate mechanism of the EMS, the peseta had been devalued, and other EMS currencies had come under attack. The peseta was devalued again in November, along with the escudo, and the punt was devalued in January 1993. The French franc and Danish krone were defended successfully, but their fate was in doubt for some time.

Tensions subsided in the first months of 1993, but they reemerged in April. The peseta and escudo were devalued again in May, and the French franc came under attack in July. On August 1, the EMS band was widened hugely, from 2¼ percent to 15 percent. The foreign exchange markets had torn up the seamless scenario.

The crises of 1992 and 1993 have been described at length elsewhere, and there is no need to tell the whole story here.[1] Figure 7–1 offers a chronology. The causes and effects of the crises deserve attention, however, because of their implications for the path to EMU and for the ultimate benefits and costs of EMU. This chapter, then, deals with four questions:

- What were the underlying causes of the crises?
- Why did the crises begin in 1992, not earlier or later?
- What can be done to prevent future crises?
- Must the Maastricht Treaty be revised to cope with the consequences of the crises?

Another issue is raised in Chapter 8 – whether the crises have strengthened or weakened the basic case for EMU.

The causes of the crises

Two reasons are commonly given for the "hardening" of the EMS in the late 1980s. First, there was growing support for using a fixed exchange rate as a nominal anchor and, in the particular context of the EMS, "borrowing credibility" from the Bundesbank by pegging to the deutsche mark. Second, there was concern that the relaxation of capital controls and their forthcoming abolition, required by the Single European Act, would expose the EMS to massive speculative pressures unless foreign exchange markets could be convinced that there would be no more realignments. It is often argued, moreover, that the rapid progress made on the design of EMU had sustained the hardening of the EMS.[2] By 1992,

1. See especially BIS (1993), Eichengreen (1993c), Eichengreen and Wyplosz (1993), Goldstein et al. (1993), Group of Ten (1993), IMF (1993), and Cameron (1994). I draw on these accounts and some of my earlier papers (Kenen, 1993b, 1994b, and 1995). My interpretation of the EMS crises has also been influenced by the recent writings of officials closely involved in the crises, including Hoffmeyer (1993), Padoa-Schioppa (1994), and Rieke (1994).
2. Gros and Thygesen (1992), Eichengreen and Frieden (1993), Garrett (1993), Jacquet (1993), and Portes (1993). There is strong evidence that the hardening of the EMS led to an appreciable change in the markets' views about the likelihood of realignments, although no one can prove that this change reflected the progress toward EMU (see Frankel, Phillips, and Chinn, 1993; and Svensson, 1993). The willingness of investors to take long positions in the lira and other EMS currencies also testifies to confidence in the fixity of EMS exchange rates; see Goldstein, et al. (1993), who describe the use of "proxy hedging," by which investors who switched from dollar to lira assets to earn higher interest rates sold deutsche marks forward for dollars to hedge against a future depreciation of the EMS currencies against the dollar but did not sell lire forward for deutsche marks to hedge against a future depreciation of the lira against the mark.

Figure 7-1 *A chronology of the EMS crises, June 1992 to September 1993*

1992

June 2   Danish referendum rejects Maastricht Treaty; tensions develop in EMS, leading to sharp increases in short-term interest rates

June 3   France schedules referendum on Maastricht Treaty for September 20

July 2   Federal Reserve reduces discount rate to 3 percent

July 16   Bundesbank raises discount rate to 8¾ percent but leaves Lombard rate at 9¾ percent; gap between German and U.S. short-term interest rates widens to 6¾ percent

August 20   Pound falls close to EMS floor; dollar falls to historic low against deutsche mark

August 27   Record levels of intervention fail to raise pound appreciably

August 28   Lira falls below EMS floor

September 3   Britain borrows $14.5 billion in deutsche marks to augment reserves; pound rises above DM 2.8

September 4   Bank of Italy raises official interest rates sharply, but lira remains below EMS floor

September 5–6   At Bath meeting of EC officials, Germany rejects British call for lower German interest rates, but communiqué affirms support for existing EMS parities; Bundesbank pledges not to raise interest rates in present circumstances

September 8   Finnish markka floated; Swedish central bank raises marginal lending rate to 75 percent

September 10–11   Lira remains below EMS floor despite heavy intervention by Bank of Italy and Bundesbank

September 12–13   Meetings between German and Italian authorities lead to announcement that lira will be devalued by 7 percent and Bundesbank will lower interest rates

September 14   Bundesbank lowers discount rate to 8¼ percent and Lombard rate to 9½ percent; lira moves to top of new EMS band; pound strengthens

September 15   Lira falls below new EMS parity; pound and peseta depreciate

September 16   Bank of England raises minimum lending rate to 12 percent and announces that it will rise to 15 percent on next day, but pound falls below EMS floor despite intervention by Bank of England, Bundesbank, and Bank of France; Britain suspends participation in EMS and rescinds second rise in minimum lending rate; intervention fails to raise lira; Swedish central bank raises marginal lending rate to 500 percent

---

Figure 7-1 (continued)

September 17 Italy suspends participation in EMS; peseta devalued by 5 percent; punt and Danish krone fall to EMS floors; Bank of England lowers minimum lending rate to 10 percent

September 19 Britain announces that pound will not return to EMS until it is reformed

September 20 French referendum endorses Maastricht Treaty by narrow margin; franc appreciates

September 21 Bank of France and Bundesbank intervene as franc falls close to EMS floor

September 22 French franc, peseta, and escudo remain weak; punt falls below EMS floor despite intervention

September 23 Bank of France and Bundesbank suport franc by intramarginal intervention, and Bank of France raises official interest rate to 13 percent; Spain imposes capital controls

September 24 Ireland imposes capital controls, but punt remains below EMS floor despite continuing intervention

October 3–31 Official interest rates lowered gradually in most countries affected by crisis (and some rates lowered again in November), but most remain above precrisis levels

November 19 Swedish krone floated

November 22 Peseta and escudo devalued by 6 percent, and Spain rescinds capital controls

November 23 Norwegian, Irish, and Spanish central banks raise official interest rates

December 3–28 Continued market pressures against French franc, Danish krone, and punt; official interest rates lowered in Belgium, Italy, the Netherlands, and Scandinavian countries

December 10 Norwegian krone floated; Bundesbank announces that it will raise M3 target for 1993

December 13 Edinburgh Summit adopts growth initiative and grants Denmark binding exemptions from Maastricht Treaty

December 16 Portugal rescinds all capital controls

1993

January 5 Bank of France and Bundesbank intervene to support franc, and Bank of France raises official interest rates

---

Figure 7-1 (continued)

January 6   Irish central bank raises official interest rate to 50 percent (and raises it again to 100 percent on January 8)

January 12–26   Several central banks lower official interest rates, with Bank of England lowering minimum lending rate to 6 percent

January 28   After having cut its official interest rate in mid-January, Irish central bank raises it again to 100 percent

January 30   Punt devalued by 20 percent

February 1   Danish central bank raises official interest rate, pushing overnight rate above 100 percent

February 4   Bundesbank lowers discount rate to 8¼ percent and Lombard rate to 9 percent (and lowers discount rate again to 7½ percent on March 18)

April 13   Spain schedules election for June 7, and peseta weakens; Bank of France lowers official interest rate (and does so again on April 19 and on May 6, 13, and 25)

April 22   Bundesbank lowers discount rate to 7¼ percent and Lombard rate to 8½ percent

April 23   Six EC central banks intervene to support peseta

May 13   Peseta and escudo devalued by 8 and 6½ percent, respectively

May 18   Second Danish referendum endorses Maastricht Treaty

June 14   Bank of France lowers official interest rate (and does so again on June 21 and July 2)

June 24   French economics minister convenes Franco-German meeting to plan concerted interest rate cuts, but German finance minister cancels meeting; deutsche mark falls against most major currencies, including French franc

July 1   Bundesbank lowers discount rate to 6¾ percent and Lombard rate to 8¼ percent

July 9   Bank of France intervenes to support franc

July 12   French franc falls close to EMS floor; German finance minister pledges support; Bundesbank says that it has intervened to support franc

July 16   Six central banks intervene to support Danish krone

July 22   French franc, Danish krone, peseta, and escudo come under more pressure because of uncertainty about outcome of next Bundesbank council meeting; Bank of France raises official interest rate; Bundesbank intervenes to support franc

---

Figure 7-1 (continued)

July 28 Bundesbank lowers repurchase rate, and markets expect cuts in official rates at next day's council meeting

July 29 Bundesbank lowers Lombard rate to 7¾ percent but does not change discount rate, disappointing markets; central banks intervene to support Belgian franc, Danish krone, French franc, peseta, and escudo, but they remain close to EMS floors

July 30 Belgian franc, French franc, and Danish krone falls below EMS floors

July 31–August 1 EC finance ministers and central bank governors examine measures to cope with crisis; decide to widen EMS band from 2¼ percent to 15 percent effective August 2

August 9–23 Bank of France lowers overnight lending rate five times, by total of 2¼ percentage points, but leaves 5–10 day rate unchanged

September 9 Bundesbank lowers discount and Lombard rates to 6¼ and 7¼ percent, respectively; Bank of France lowers 5–10 day rate from 10 to 7¾ percent but leaves intervention rate at 6¾ percent

---

Source: Adapted and condensed from International Monetary Fund, *World Economic Outlook: October 1993*, pp. 42–47.

"governments and markets were beginning to behave as if all the EMS participants were in a quasi-monetary union with fixed rates" (Thygesen, 1993a, p. 24).

Two problems posed threats to the sustainability of the situation – the shift in the German policy mix after unification and the apparent deterioration in the cost competitiveness of certain EC countries, notably Italy and Spain.

Having failed to raise taxes by enough to meet the costs of unification, Germany was running bigger budget deficits and starting to encounter inflationary pressures. Therefore, some economists began to recommend that the deutsche mark be revalued against the other EMS currencies; the expenditure-raising effects of unification should be diverted partly to the outside world by the expenditure-switching effects of a realignment.[3]

There was also a narrowing of the spread between the market price of the basket ECU and of the corresponding currency basket; Folkerts-Landau and Garber (1992b) link it to the hardening of the EMS, but Fratianni and von Hagen (1992) ascribe it to the clause in the Maastricht Treaty freezing the composition of the basket and to the common view that the treaty precluded a final realignment that might alter the value of the ECU abruptly just before Stage Three.

3. See Portes (1993) and the references there.

France, however, objected strenuously to any devaluation of the franc, even one resulting from a revaluation of the mark. Why should the franc be devalued, it was asked, when France has less inflation than Germany? Some of the other EMS countries also opposed a revaluation of the mark, and the threat – or promise – of a realignment did not materialize.

Many accounts of the crisis, especially those of official bodies, argued that certain EMS currencies were clearly overvalued on the eve of the crisis:

> One important factor that contributed to market pressures against some currencies was the apparent deterioration of international cost competitiveness. In the years preceding the crisis, limited adjustments of parities and a lack of full convergence of inflation rates resulted in significant real appreciations of the lira, the escudo, and the peseta, as well as of the Swedish krone, which was unilaterally pegged to the ECU. Although inflation declined rapidly and the pound sterling did not appreciate substantially in real terms after the United Kingdom joined the ERM in October 1990, its central parity came to be perceived by some in the market as ambitious. The widening of current account deficits, . . . given relative cyclical positions, also suggested to financial markets that exchange rate parities might eventually need to be corrected. (IMF, 1993, p. 30)

Summarizing, the document went on to say that the currencies attacked initially were those of countries "where the longer-run sustainability of the central rate was in doubt because convergence with the low-inflation EMS countries was still unsatisfactory, or because the initial choice of the rate had been too ambitious" (IMF, 1993, p. 32).

But another official account conceded that, for as long as EMU seemed to be on track, officials and markets may have believed that "these misalignments might in time be corrected by further adjustments in domestic costs and prices rather than by a deliberate exchange rate realignment" (BIS, 1993, p. 192). Failing that, a realignment might be needed later, but not in 1992. For this and other reasons, Eichengreen and Wyplosz (1993) conclude that movements in prices and labor costs did not play a large part in the 1992 crisis.[4]

4. Eichengreen and Wyplosz note that the pattern of forward exchange rates in the months before the crisis does not suggest that markets predicted devaluations by the countries having weak competitive positions. In fact, forward rates did not signal a shift in expectations until polls began to predict a no vote in the French referendum, and the shift was not pronounced (see Rose and Svensson, 1993). But Edison and Kole (1994) find that expectations of devaluation emerged earlier in the summer for the lira, pound, and peseta. Furthermore, interest rates on lira-denominated bonds rose right after the Danish referendum. It should also be noted that the deutsche mark was already appreciating in real terms because of the increase in the German inflation rate, and BIS economists have shown that the Italian, Spanish, and British competitive positions

In June 1992, however, the Danish referendum sowed seeds of doubt about the future of the Maastricht Treaty and, more immediately, the willingness of certain EMS countries, especially Italy, to solve their macroeconomic problems without changing their exchange rates – not only to adopt the fiscal reforms demanded by the treaty but also to live with the high short-term interest rates that German monetary policy was imposing on the rest of the EMS countries.

Several accounts of the subsequent crisis have used a model developed by Obstfeld (1986) to show how expectations of a devaluation, arising sui generis, can actually produce the devaluation; by leading to capital outflows that eat up a country's reserves, they can force the country to devalue its currency.[5] There are, in effect, two equilibria in Obstfeld's model, with and without devaluation, and each one would be sustainable if it were left alone. Obstfeld (1994) himself has warned that his model should not be applied mechanically to the 1992 crisis. Italy and Britain suffered huge reserve losses when trying to defend their currencies, but that is not why they quit.[6] Two other factors were at work.

First, the countries' ability to intervene on the foreign exchange market was not constrained by the finite size of their own reserves; under the credit arrangements of the EMS, they could borrow from the Bundesbank if they had to intervene to prevent their currencies from leaving the EMS band. But they were constrained effectively by the concern of the Bundesbank itself about its ability to keep the German money supply from rising as a result of its lending to its partners and of its own intervention. More will be said on that point shortly.

Second, the countries themselves could not afford to pay the economic and political price of raising their short-term interest rates by enough to prevent speculation against their currencies – not when they were suffering deep and long recessions, with high and rising unemployment.[7]

After adapting Obstfeld's model to allow for the second factor, Eichengreen applies it to the case of France in 1993. The Balladur government, he says,

were somewhat stronger than commonly believed; see Turner and Van't dack (1993), especially Graphs 10 and 17, on comparative export profitability and relative profitability in the traded-goods sector.

5. The first model of this sort was provided by Flood and Garber (1984).
6. Estimates of total intervention from June through December 1992 cluster around $175 billion, with half of it occurring in September (BIS, 1993, p. 188).
7. The potential cost was especially high for Britain, where the recession had been very long and deep, and where an increase in short-term interest rates is translated quickly into higher mortgage rates. There is no such direct link in other EMS countries. (In France, banks were persuaded to hold down their lending rates when money market interest rates were raised to defend the franc.)

. . . was prepared to hold out – that is, to live with German interest rates despite their consequences for unemployment – indefinitely if necessary, in order to defend the narrow bands of the ERM and continue down the Maastricht path to EMU. In the absence of speculative pressure, doing so would have been a political equilibrium, in that the benefits of the franc fort policy, which maximized the chances that a relatively early monetary union would be achieved, more than compensated French politicians for the costs. In the absence of speculative pressure, this was also an economic equilibrium, in that there were no problems of price competitiveness producing balance-of-payments deficits. . . . But what the Balladur Government was not capable of doing was living with interest rates significantly above German rates. . . . Once speculative pressure was brought to bear, a political equilibrium in which current costs (in terms of unemployment) were dominated by deferred benefits (in terms of early . . . monetary union) was transformed into a political disequilibrium in which the costs . . . dominated. (Eichengreen, 1993c, pp. 33–4)

Writing before the 1992 crisis, Gros and Thygesen (1992, p. 124) made the same point in general terms:

. . . if the market believes that the authorities are not willing to contemplate high domestic interest rates purely in defense of their exchange rates in the EMS, capital flows might become unstable. In such a situation any small shock – whether it be a shock to the fundamentals or just a shift in portfolio preferences – could trigger a crisis.

They went on to predict, however, that a strong commitment "is not even likely to be tested and can therefore ensure the stability of the EMS."

Although they were too optimistic, their reference to a "small shock" calls attention to a flaw in the Obstfeld model, even when modified by Eichengreen and others. Without introducing a shock or the advent of new information that changes the markets' views about the sustainability of the initial situation, the model cannot readily explain the timing of a crisis – why markets attacked the franc in July of 1993, not in May or June. Therefore, it is necessary to ask what markets may have learned – why they may have thought there was just one equilibrium in June, with no devaluation, but changed their minds in July.

In this particular case, three bits of information became available. Late in June, the German finance minister refused to attend a meeting called by his French counterpart to discuss concerted interest rate cuts. A few weeks later, new forecasts for the French economy warned that it would grow more slowly than had been expected. Finally, on July 29, the

Bundesbank council adjourned for its summer vacation having made a small cut in the Lombard rate but no change in the discount rate. Hence, markets concluded that German interest rates would not fall sharply or quickly, which meant that France could not afford to reduce its own interest rates, and it might be unwilling to raise them, given the gloomy outlook for growth.[8]

Going back to 1992, the same framework can be used to show how the Danish referendum and the forecasts of a no vote in the French referendum helped to trigger the September crisis. They said that the Maastricht Treaty might not take effect, which said, in turn, that Italy would have less incentive to meet the terms of the treaty – that fiscal retrenchment was less likely and a devaluation of the lira was more likely than when the outlook for EMU was brighter. All this seems obvious now, but it was not so obvious before the Danish referendum.[9]

Other events and mistakes contributed to the 1992 crisis. The weakness of the dollar underscored and aggravated the weak competitive positions of countries such as Britain, which compete directly with the United States in international markets.[10] The problems of the Scandinavian countries, beginning with Finland, which had suffered a sharp fall in its exports to Russia, alerted markets to the fragility of the EMS itself. Most important, the 7 percent devaluation of the lira on September 14, 1992, was badly bungled. It may have been large enough to restore Italy's competitive position, but it was too small to seem decisive. It evoked an inadequate response by the Bundesbank – a 25 basis-point cut in the discount and Lombard rates. And it should have been the occasion for a general realignment – a modest revaluation of the deutsche mark combined with selective devaluations of the lira, peseta, escudo, and pound. The BIS has said that this was the "only conceivable way out," although very hard to arrange. The failure to agree on a realignment allowed "official positions to be misunderstood

8. Melitz (1994) examines French policies during the crises, including the failed attempt to win an anchor role for the franc by cutting French interest rates in the weeks before the 1993 crisis.
9. Some writers reject the "obvious" interpretation. Thus, Spaventa (1993) says that the prospect of EMU – not the dimming of the prospect – was a chief cause of the crisis, because the conditions imposed by the Maastricht Treaty were seen as being too onerous for certain countries; see also Papadia and Saccomanni (1994).
10. European accounts of the crisis emphasize this point. Buiter, Corsetti, and Pesenti (1993) note, in fact, that many Europeans saw the turmoil that began in August 1992 mainly as a dollar crisis, caused by the weakness of the U.S. economy, efforts by the Federal Reserve to bring down U.S. interest rates, and the apparent indifference of both presidential candidates to the fate of the dollar. Edison and Kole (1994) offer some supporting evidence.

or misrepresented" and let markets conclude, rightly or wrongly, that there were disagreements among governments and institutions (BIS, 1993, pp. 198–9).[11]

In the event, the crisis spread contagiously from currency to currency as markets came to understand that the EMS had been weakened and its members could not afford to defend it.

Eichengreen and Wyplosz (1993) report the results of a survey of foreign exchange traders, which sums up the story. Some 68 percent of the traders blamed the crisis mainly on high German interest rates; a smaller number blamed inflation in the weak-currency countries, the erosion of support for the Maastricht Treaty, or the inevitability of a realignment. When asked why central banks had ceased to defend their currencies, 65 percent cited the economic cost of high interest rates. When asked when the traders had begun to believe that exchange rate changes were imminent, 22 percent said "before the Danish referendum," but 47 percent said "after the Danish referendum," and another 15 percent said "upon hearing about public opinion polls in France." When asked whether the weakness of some currencies in the summer of 1992 had caused them to expect other currencies to weaken, 90 percent said yes, and 77 percent of those explained that markets had "tasted blood."

Drawing lessons from the crises

There are remarkable similarities between the EMS crises of 1992–3 and the crises of 1971–3, which led to the collapse of the Bretton Woods System.

In both cases, the country at the center of the system suffered a large political shock, underestimated the fiscal implications, and declined to pay the political price of correcting its mistake. In the late 1960s, Lyn-

---

11. The Germans were apparently interested in a more general realignment but pursued the matter rather casually – too casually perhaps to impress the French with the urgency of the issue. Norman (1992), Muehring (1992), and Cameron (1994) provide accounts of the events surrounding the Italian devaluation, differing in emphasis but not much in substance. It may be objected that France would have vetoed a general realignment, even if Germany had pressed for one, because the French believed that the franc was immune to contagious speculation. What would have happened, however, if the German chancellor had warned the French president that the Bundesbank could not be expected to support the franc – if he had called attention to the so-called Emminger letter discussed later in this chapter? (One might also ask what would have happened if the German chancellor, not the Italian prime minister, had telephoned John Major about the devaluation of the lira – and added the same sort of warning about future Bundesbank support for the pound.)

don Johnson had tried to finance the Vietnam War without sacrificing the Great Society or raising taxes. He was also misled by Defense Department forecasts that minimized the cost of the Vietnam buildup. In the early 1990s, Helmut Kohl tried to finance German unification without greatly raising taxes. And he was misled by optimistic forecasts about the speed at which East Germany could be transformed. The two mistakes had different exchange rate effects, because the central banks responded very differently. As the cost of the Vietnam War mounted, there was at first a tightening of monetary policy in the United States, which ran balance of payments surpluses in 1968–9; but monetary policy was reversed thereafter, driving the balance of payments back into deficit. In Germany, by contrast, the Bundesbank tightened monetary policy right after unification and did not cut its interest rates until the eve of the EMS crisis.

In both cases, the game played between markets and governments had ossified the exchange rate regime, although the architects of both regimes had tried to combine short-term stability with long-term flexibility. Furthermore, the center country in each system was unable to arrange an orderly exchange rate realignment and resorted instead to methods that undermined the system. Their tactics were different, but the outcomes were quite similar. In 1971, Richard Nixon and John Connally acted provocatively by shutting the gold window and imposing an import tax. In 1992, Helmut Schlesinger and other Bundesbank officials expressed their doubts about certain EMS currencies, mobilizing market forces to put pressure on them.[12]

There is also a distressing similarity between the conclusions drawn by official bodies after the crises were over. In the wake of the Bretton Woods crises, governments established the Committee of Twenty to design a system of "stable but adjustable" exchange rates. In the wake of the 1992 EMS crisis, the Monetary Committee and the Committee of Central Bank Governors issued reports that said that more "timely" realignments would help to ward off future crises (Monetary Committee, 1993; Committee of Governors, 1993b).

These two EC reports were undoubtedly influenced by the view expressed in every official account of the 1992 crisis, that the crisis was due

---

12. Eichengreen and Wyplosz (1993) and Garrett (1993). Eichengreen and Wyplosz also suggest that the Bundesbank actually threatened to limit its intervention, but I have found no evidence that it refused to intervene or grant reserve credit to its partners. No such accusation was made publicly, not even in the trading of recriminations after the pound left the EMS. (Bundesbank officials were very reluctant to make any such threat, because it would be tantamount to threatening the withdrawal of the deutsche mark from the EMS.)

to the weak competitive positions of the countries whose currencies came under attack at the start of the crisis. But when one asks authors of the reports whether their own countries' currencies should have been devalued in 1990 or 1991, all of them say no. Furthermore, the reports failed to explain how governments can contemplate "timely" realignments without reinforcing the EMS against speculative attacks. The central bank governors raised the issue obliquely when they stressed the need to make markets "aware of the risk of, and possible losses from, speculation." But they did not go on to ask whether, with narrow exchange rate bands and more frequent realignments, the risks of speculation can be raised sufficiently.

More important, the two reports acknowledged that the 1992 crisis had exposed a big gap in the defenses of the EMS. The intervention rules and credit arrangements of the EMS had been designed to guarantee that countries with weak and strong currencies would bear joint and symmetric responsibility for the defense of the system. Whenever a country's currency reached the edge of its band vis-à-vis one of its partners' currencies, the partner was supposed to intervene unstintingly to keep the exchange rate from leaving the band (or lend the weak-currency country as much of the partner's currency as the weak-currency country needed to intervene on its own).[13] In effect, the system was meant to protect a weak-currency country from exhausting its reserves and being forced to devalue. The system would then be immune to attacks of the sort modeled by Obstfeld (1986) and others. But there was a crucial qualification to those rules and arrangements – the so-called Emminger letter.

The Bundesbank has always been concerned about the risk of conflict between its basic mandate to maintain price stability and the need to intervene on the foreign exchange market to honor commitments made by the German government. It had faced one such conflict in the final days of the Bretton Woods System, when it withdrew from the foreign exchange market, allowing the deutsche mark to float. When faced with the risk of future conflict under the rules of the EMS, Otmar Emminger, president of the Bundesbank, sought assurances from the German government regarding the Bundesbank's obligations:[14]

13. Under the 1987 Basle–Nyborg Agreement, a weak-currency country was even entitled to expect that it could borrow from its partners for intramarginal intervention, not just mandatory intervention at the limit of the band, if it did not abuse the privilege. (But it was expected to permit its currency to move more freely through the band and rely more heavily on interest rate changes to defend its currency.)
14. Emminger (1986), pp. 361–2; quoted and translated by Eichengreen and Wyplosz (1993, p. 109), who go on to quote a public statement by the minister of economics

The autonomy in monetary policies of the Bundesbank would particularly be put in jeopardy if strong imbalances with the future EMS resulted in extreme intervention obligations which would then threaten the value of the currency. This would make it impossible for the Bundesbank to carry out its legal obligations. Referring to the repeated assurances from the Chancellor and the Finance Minister, the Bundesbank is starting from the premise that, if need be, the German government will safeguard the Bundesbank from such a situation, either by a correction of the exchange rate in the EMS or, if necessary, by discharging the Bundesbank from its intervention obligations.

In other words, the Bundesbank could not be required to support its partners' currencies, even though failing to do so would violate the rules of the EMS.

This exception went largely unnoticed for many years, and the obligation to undertake open-ended intervention was seen to be the unique feature of the EMS.[15] Even those who say, with hindsight, that the EMS rules were unrealistic did not say so before September 1992, when the Bundesbank invoked the Emminger letter and asked the German government to negotiate a devaluation of the lira.

The reports of the Monetary Committee and the Committee of Central Bank Governors did not mention the Emminger letter, but they came very close. The governors warned that "there cannot be an automatic and mechanistic response to market tensions, involving symmetrical action on the part of the authorities of countries with weak and strong currencies." Voluntary action was possible but must not interfere with "control over domestic monetary conditions in the country issuing the intervention currency," and it must be "consistent with the primary objective of achieving price stability in the Community."

Thygesen (1993a, p. 50) has criticized both reports for failing to affirm support for the postcrisis EMS parities, and he cites the passage just quoted, because it "was not apt to convince market participants of any great firmness in the defence of the parity grid." But he misses the point. There could no longer be such firmness after the Bundesbank had in-

that the Bundesbank "has the responsibility to intervene, and the option not to intervene if it is its opinion that it is not able to do so." Begg and Wyplosz (1993) wonder how the German government could make two inconsistent commitments – one to its EMS partners and the other to the Bundesbank. Talks with participants in the EMS negotiations of 1978–9 have led me to conclude that Germany's partners were not informed officially about the agreement with the Bundesbank. (They must have been aware of the minister's statement but may not have seen it at the time as a firm promise by the German government to relieve the Bundesbank of its obligations.)

15. In 1981, however, the German government (not the Bundesbank) threatened to halt intervention to support the Belgian franc when the Belgian government opposed a large devaluation of the franc (see Henning, 1994).

voked the Emminger letter. Yet the quotation is noteworthy for another reason. It explicitly renounces the notion of symmetry, on which the EMS was based. Having done that, it should have looked at other ways to fortify the EMS.

Two responses to the crisis

The path to EMU in the Maastricht Treaty is mined with deadlines like the date of the French referendum that helped to trigger the 1992 crisis. The one most often cited is the final deadline – the date on which exchange rates will be locked, after which there can be no more realignments. But other deadlines in the treaty may also trigger crises in the foreign exchange markets. Having found that ten countries have excessive budget deficits, the Council of Ministers will soon have to decide whether some of those countries have corrected their deficits. Before the end of 1996, the Council will also have to decide which countries have met the convergence criteria, whether a majority has met them and, if so, whether to start Stage Three.[16] Meanwhile, there may be more realignments, and though they may occur in a "timely" way, markets are not likely to be taken by surprise.

These concerns have generated two groups of proposals – those that would accelerate the move to EMU or emulate the workings of the monetary union before it has begun, and those that would fortify the EMS against the shocks that could occur along the Maastricht path to EMU.[17]

Proposals to accelerate or emulate EMU

These proposals can be treated briefly, because most of them were examined earlier in the book, and they have already been rejected by Germany.

Right after the 1992 crisis, there was a flurry of talk about a "dash" to EMU.[18] France and Germany would fix the exchange rate between their currencies and eliminate the band completely. Their central banks would then adopt a common monetary policy aimed at price stability. The Benelux countries would join in, accompanied perhaps by Denmark.

16. Even before that, the German Bundestag will debate the question and adopt a resolution advising the German government on the position it should take in the Council of Ministers. I say more on this matter below.
17. Artis (1994) provides an excellent survey of these proposals.
18. See, e.g., Pisani-Ferry (1992) and the plan in Pisani-Ferry et al. (1993). Eichengreen and Frieden (1993) also view a dash to EMU as the first-best scenario on economic grounds and believe that Germany might accept it in exchange for tighter political union. For a sympathetic German view, see Nölling (1993).

The idea of a mini-EMU was popular in France, because the fixing of the franc–mark rate was seen as a way to fend off future attacks on the franc. But little was said about three basic questions: (1) Would the central banks create a mini-ECB to formulate and execute monetary policy, or would they merely adopt guidelines for interest rates or monetary aggregates? (2) Would the fixing of exchange rates be defended in the foreign exchange market, or would central banks move quickly to the ECU as their unit of account – to over-the-counter convertibility and the other arrangements listed in Chapter 3? (3) Who would determine the eligibility of other EC countries and what criteria would be used?

The credibility and solidarity of a mini-EMU would depend on the answers to the first and second questions. If the central banks did nothing more than reach agreement on guidelines for interest rates or monetary aggregates, and each one used its own techniques to implement the guidelines, the system as a whole could experience severe strains. The central banks could then be forced to engage in large-scale intervention to keep their exchange rates fixed. The system would resemble what Corden (1972) called a pseudo-union, and it might break down.[19]

The future of the Community itself could be affected by the answer to the final question. Chapter 6 pointed out that the Maastricht Treaty contemplates a two-track path to EMU, as some of the EC countries are not likely to meet the convergence criteria, even in 1999. Nevertheless, the treaty says that every EC country will enter EMU as soon as it meets those criteria. In fact, the Council of Ministers must review the situation of each nonparticipant every other year (TEU, Article 109k). But if a self-selected group of countries form a mini-EMU outside the framework of the treaty, they may insist on the right to decide whether other EC countries should be allowed to join it later, and they may be quite strict. If the low-inflation countries form a monetary union, they will have an incentive to exclude other countries that are not as strongly committed to price stability. This might happen even though an all-inclusive union would be better for each country than no union whatsoever.[20]

19. Eichengreen and Wyplosz (1993) make the same point, and it echoes a point made by De Grauwe (1993a) about Stage Three of EMU (because he assumes that the locking of exchange rates would be defended by intervention before the shift to the ECU). It must also be noted that the Bundesbank could not commit itself to implement such guidelines without a modification of its basic mandate. (The legislation by which Germany ratified the Maastricht Treaty amended the German constitution to permit a transfer of monetary sovereignty, but only to the ECB in accordance with the treaty.)
20. Alesina and Grilli (1993). Their conclusion, however, derives from strong assumptions about the governance of the union and the behavior of the economies involved; see Eichengreen and Wyplosz (1993) and Levine and Pearlman (1994). But Rogoff (1991) reaches a similar conclusion without invoking those assumptions.

Much has been written recently about the benefits and costs of a two-speed Europe.[21] But the arguments for that approach do not carry over to the notion of "variable geometry" in the EC. If an individual EC country can opt in or out of particular commitments or can be excluded from them, it will become much harder to obtain unanimous participation in *any* EC enterprise and for the Community to speak with a single voice when dealing with the outside world. Furthermore, Martin (1993) points out that the scope for cross-issue bargaining will be greatly reduced. Hence, a mini-EMU could harm the Community as a whole.[22]

Talk about a dash to EMU died down at the end of 1992, when the German Bundestag adopted a resolution that said, in effect, that Germany must not sacrifice the deutsche mark unless and until the requirements of the Maastricht Treaty have been completely satisfied. The convergence criteria must be "narrowly and strictly interpreted," and their fulfillment "may not be merely verified by reference to statistics but rendered credible by the convergence process." The resolution also declared that the German government will require the "consenting vote" of the Bundestag to cast its own vote in the Council of Ministers on the eligibility of countries to enter Stage Three, and it asked the government to promise that it will "respect" the Bundestag's opinion.[23] The resolution of the Bundestag figures importantly in the opinion of the German Constitutional court upholding the constitutionality of the Maastricht Treaty.

Although the Bundestag has taken a tough line, and the Bundesbank has said repeatedly that German monetary policy will aim at achieving price stability in Germany, not at meeting the needs of other EC countries, many economists continue to propose arrangements designed to

21. Barber (1994) provides an excellent guide to the recent debate, which was triggered by a document issued on behalf of the governing parties in the German Bundestag. The document urged the formation of an EC core consisting of countries that would adhere fully to all EC arrangements and obligations, and it seemed to imply that a country which does not adhere to some of those arrangements might be excluded from others. Several EC governments objected vehemently, and the proposal was not endorsed by the German government.

22. Pisani-Ferry et al. (1993) recognize this problem. Therefore, they present their own plan for a mini-EMU as a way for the core countries to emulate EMU, not as a substitute for the plan in the treaty. For that very reason, their answers to my questions (1) and (2) are not reassuring.

23. These quotations come from the version of the resolution contained in the official translation of the ruling by the Federal Constitutional Court affirming the constitutionality of the Maastricht Treaty. (I have already noted, however, that Article 109j of the treaty says that questions pertaining to the start of Stage Three will be decided by qualified majority voting. Hence, the German government cannot block decisions on those questions, even if the Bundestag tells it to do so.)

emulate EMU before it actually begins. Some of those proposals were reviewed in Chapter 6, including the suggestion that the EC central banks, working through the EMI, should base the coordination of their monetary policies on a monetary aggregate for the EC as a whole (or for the group of countries most likely to move to EMU). But some economists would go further. Thygesen (1994, p. 61) still believes that the policy-making environment "can be modified in ways that shift the incentive for voluntary coordination strongly toward collective action and management." Hence, he makes two proposals: (1) the EMI should monitor (but not dictate) the extent to which the central banks should sterilize their interventions on the foreign exchange market; and (2) individual central banks should enter into bilateral contracts with the EMI to manage their domestic money market operations.

The first proposal is, of course, a faint echo of the plan borrowed from McKinnon and discussed in Chapter 6, whereby the EC central banks would agree on a common monetary target, implement it individually, and engage symmetrically in nonsterilized intervention so that their transactions in the foreign exchange market would not affect the money supply of the EC as a whole. Even in that strong form, however, an effort to emulate EMU will not fortify the EMS unless the central banks can make a credible commitment to it. The close coordination of monetary policies might prevent a rerun of 1992–3, when the Bundesbank's monetary policy was too strict for its partners. But it might not preclude a crisis triggered by a deadline in the Maastricht Treaty that leads the market to expect a devaluation or a general realignment.

Proposals to fortify the EMS

There are three ways to fortify the EMS against future crises: reviving or replacing the original commitment to unlimited intervention, restricting capital movements, and raising the riskiness of speculation by declining to narrow the present wide band until the locking of exchange rates.

Reviving the commitment to intervention

What might be done to revive confidence in the ability of the EMS countries to conduct unlimited intervention in the face of speculative pressures or to make intervention more effective?

There is by now clear evidence that joint or concerted intervention is more effective than unilateral intervention by a weak-currency country.[24] In 1992, for example, the Bundesbank's commitment to support the French franc was surely important in defending the franc against the first wave of speculation, and joint intervention by six central banks helped to defend the Danish krone in July 1993. (Similar support for the peseta in April, however, did not avoid the devaluation in May.) Hence, Thygesen (1993b) has suggested that the EMI be made responsible for the organization or conduct of intervention in the EMS (see also Gros and Thygesen, 1992).

There are two problems – legal and practical. Article 6 of the EMI Statute allows the EMI to "hold and manage foreign exchange reserves as an agent for and at the request of national central banks." It may not do so, however, until it adopts rules to make sure "that transactions with these reserves shall not interfere with the monetary policy and exchange rate policy" of any EC country. Hence, there are reasons to wonder whether the EMI can use the reserves entrusted to it to engage in intervention. First, the word "manage" may mean "invest" rather than something broader.[25] Second, a country that places reserves with the EMI might let the EMI decide how they should be used to support its currency but might not let the EMI use them to support another country's currency. Finally, the passage quoted above says clearly that the EMI may not buy or sell a member's currency, even for the purpose of managing reserves, let alone for intervention, if that would undermine the monetary policy of the country issuing the reserve currency. The EMI cannot use deutsche marks to buy lire if that would raise the German money supply in a manner opposed by the Bundesbank.

This brings up the practical problem. The Bundesbank will not engage in unlimited intervention – and its stance has been endorsed by the report of the central bank governors – not because it objects to the exchange rate effects but because it objects to the money-supply effects. It is worried about its ability to sterilize the intervention. It would therefore insist on having close control over any intervention by the EMI.[26]

24. See Dominguez (1990) for evidence deriving from G-7 experience.
25. Article 30 of the ESCB Statute draws a distinction between management and use when it says that the ECB shall "manage and hold" reserves transferred to it and "use them for the purposes set out in this Statute."
26. This objection applies a fortiori to the suggestion by Bofinger (1993), endorsed by Collignon et al. (1993), that a country committed firmly to EMU should be allowed to draw on the credit facilities of the EMS without being made to repay its drawings. There would then be no limit whatsoever on the country's appetite for deutsche mark credit and, therefore, a greater threat to the Bundesbank's control over the German money supply.

Restricting capital flows

In the early years of the EMS, capital controls helped to defend it against speculative attacks. The EMS did not collapse when the controls were dismantled, because its members had made a commitment to the "new" fixed-rate EMS, which was then reinforced by the commitment to EMU. When those commitments were called into question in 1992, the EMS succumbed to speculative pressures. It has therefore been argued that capital flows should be restricted, if not actually controlled, to protect the EMS during the rest of the transition to EMU.[27]

The capital controls used by France and Italy prevented banks and other financial institutions from making loans to foreigners, even to their affiliates in the Eurocurrency market. They also prevented individuals from holding foreign currency assets, such as bank accounts in other EC countries. But there were no restrictions on foreigners, who could move their own funds freely in and out of France or Italy. These controls were not very strict compared with those obtaining right after the Second World War. In fact, capital outflows from France and Italy were not smaller, on average, than the outflows from countries that did not use controls. Furthermore, interest rates in countries with capital controls did not always differ greatly from the corresponding rates in the Eurocurrency market, even though those countries' banks were not able to arbitrage freely between domestic and offshore markets.[28] Nevertheless, large differences emerged whenever realignments were expected.

Those large differences are often adduced as proof that capital controls "really bite" when realignments are expected (Begg and Wyplosz, 1993, p. 31).[29] There is no way to know, however, by how much they reduced the volume of capital flows or held down reserve losses during turbulent periods. France experienced very large losses before the devaluations of 1982 and 1983 (though smaller than its losses in 1992 and 1993). Furthermore, the effectiveness of the controls was due partly to conditions that no longer prevail.

27. The best statement of this view will be found in Eichengreen, Tobin, and Wyplosz (1995), but see also Eichengreen and Wyplosz (1993) and Eichengreen, Rose, and Wyplosz (1994).
28. On average outflows, see Gros and Thygesen (1992); on interest rates, see Giavazzi and Giovannini (1989) and Fratianni and von Hagen (1992). The interest rate differences were larger and more volatile, however, than those for countries without controls.
29. This assertion seems paradoxical, because an impending realignment should make evasion more attractive. Gros (1987) tries to resolve the paradox by arguing that the channels normally used to evade controls cannot handle a sudden surge of capital outflows, so that more expensive channels have to be found; see also Gros and Thygesen (1992).

In the early 1980s, the deutsche mark was the only world-class currency in the EMS. Few foreigners held large amounts of other EMS currencies. To speculate against them, then, foreigners had either to borrow them and sell them spot or to sell them forward. Capital controls, however, prevented French and Italian banks from making loans to foreigners, directly or via the Eurocurrency market, so that the supply of credit was very inelastic. Hence, Eurocurrency interest rates rose very sharply when realignments were expected. When those rates were high, moreover, it was expensive for foreign exchange dealers to cover their forward positions, which made it expensive for their customers to sell francs or lire forward.[30]

Under these circumstances, it was not necessary to raise domestic interest rates in France and Italy in order to defend the franc and lira. Controls kept residents from selling their own countries' currencies, and foreigners were not greatly affected by French or Italian interest rates, because they did not have large franc or lira holdings. At the start of the 1990s, however, foreigners began to take large long positions in several EMS currencies to earn higher interest rates than those available on deutsche mark or dollar assets, and the liquidation of those positions played a major role in the 1992 crisis. The resulting capital outflow could not have been halted by high Eurocurrency interest rates. Domestic interest rates had to be raised hugely.

There was talk of imposing controls after the 1992 crisis, but it did not attract much official support or last very long. Capital controls would violate the Single European Act and the Maastricht Treaty.[31] Attention has come to focus instead on taxing foreign exchange transactions or requiring those engaged in certain capital transactions to make domestic currency deposits with the central bank, on which they would earn no interest.[32]

---

30. Dealers who buy francs forward from those who want to speculate against the franc typically cover their positions by borrowing francs and selling them spot. When the supply of franc credit is inelastic, so that dealers must pay high interest rates to cover their own positions, dealers must quote large discounts on their offers to buy francs forward. See Goldstein et al. (1993) or Garber and Taylor (1995) for a detailed account of the transactions involved.

31. Under Article 73e of the treaty, countries still having capital controls must rescind them before 1996; under Article 73f, controls may be imposed on capital flows to or from outside countries if they "cause, or threaten to cause, serious difficulties for the operation of economic and monetary union," but only if they are "strictly necessary" and only temporarily.

32. Eichengreen and Wyplosz (1993) suggested that these requirements should be imposed on holdings (or purchases) of foreign currencies; Eichengreen, Tobin, and Wyplosz (1995) suggest that they should be imposed on domestic currency loans to nonresidents, which would be more sensible.

A tax on foreign exchange transactions would be easy to evade unless it was adopted globally, and because it would be levied on *all* transactions, not merely those connected with short-term capital movements, it could not be levied at a rate high enough to discourage speculation without also harming trade and long-term capital movements.

Foreign exchange transactions typically leave traces on the books of banks in the countries issuing the currencies involved. A sale of francs for deutsche marks, for example, usually requires a transfer of francs on the books of French banks and a transfer of marks on the books of German banks. Much netting may take place before the transfers occur, however, and banks cannot readily identify the transfers that reflect foreign exchange transactions. Therefore, a tax on those transactions cannot be collected without the cooperation of all countries in which trading can take place, not just those whose currencies are being traded.

A low tax would not be a heavy burden on trade or long-term capital flows. Eichengreen and Wyplosz (1993) note that a 1 percent tax (2 percent on a round-trip transaction) represents a cost of nearly 8,000 percent per annum on a one-day shift but only 0.2 percent on a ten-year investment. Suppose, however, that markets begin to forecast a 6 percent devaluation of the franc, with probability 0.5, one week from now. The expected gain on a bet against the franc will be 3 percent, which will exceed the 2 percent tax cost of selling the franc now and buying it back later. In other words, Eichengreen and Wyplosz have shown that a low tax cannot greatly affect the return on a long-term investment, but they have not demonstrated that it can offset the expected gain from betting on a near-term devaluation.[33] Finally, a tax high enough to deter traders and investors from betting on large exchange rate changes would also deter them from betting on small exchange rate changes. Therefore, it could interfere with the ordinary two-way trading that limits exchange rate volatility.

A deposit requirement would be easier to enforce and more effective. If a bank lending francs to foreigners had to deposit the same number of francs with the Banque de France, on which it would earn no interest, such lending would be less profitable. Furthermore, the implicit tax would rise automatically and thus "bite harder" whenever domestic interest rates rose, and that would not happen with a tax on

---

33. Eichengreen, Tobin, and Wyplosz (1995) concede this point, but they turn it around. A transactions tax, they say, would not protect misaligned parities, because the gains expected from "inevitable near-term realignments would far exceed the tax costs." Thus do defects become virtues.

foreign exchange transactions. But this also means that a deposit requirement would not obviate the need to raise domestic interest rates whenever offshore rates were rising. Nor would it discourage residents or foreigners from using the forward market to speculate against the franc. French foreign exchange dealers could still borrow francs to hedge their own long positions and could then satisfy their customers' desire to take short positions.[34] Finally, deposit requirements could not discourage foreigners from liquidating long positions, as they did in 1992.

Living with the wide band

When the Monetary Committee met on July 31, 1993, to cope with the attack on the French franc, it canvassed many options but could not reach agreement. The Bundesbank would not engage in unlimited intervention, so the French said that the deutsche mark should be allowed to float. It was Germany, after all, that could not meet its obligations under the EMS rules. To be sure, the franc would depreciate against the mark, but France would not have devalued its currency. (Furthermore, the departure of Germany would leave France as the anchor country of the EMS.) But that plan was unacceptable. One by one, the smaller countries, such as the Netherlands, said that they would continue to peg their currencies to the mark if it left the EMS. The Germans proposed that the EMS band be widened temporarily to 6 percent – the wide band used by Italy before 1990 and by Spain, Britain, and Portugal when they joined the EMS.[35] And other countries went even further, proposing the suspension of all intervention – in other words, a float. But that suggestion was rejected by those who believed that the EMS should be kept in being, albeit in looser form. (Some may have been worried about the risk of tying their currencies to a soaring deutsche mark.)

The whole matter was referred to the ministerial meeting that convened on August 1. After much debate and bilateral consultations, the ministers agreed to widen the EMS band temporarily, but to move all the way to 15 percent, rather than 6 percent. The decision was greeted

---

34. Therefore, a deposit requirement on loans to foreigners would have an odd effect. Offshore transactions would move onshore instead. Foreign banks would use their French affiliates for all of their trading in francs; the affiliates would qualify as French residents, and loans to them would be exempt from a deposit requirement.

35. The idea was not new; the Bundesbank had made the same suggestion during an earlier discussion of "fault lines" in the EMS (see Brittan, 1993).

enthusiastically by European financial markets, because it was taken to mean that France and other EC countries would then follow the British example and reduce their interest rates below those of Germany.[36] But that did not happen. French interest rates fell after the crisis, but the Banque de France did not cut them aggressively, and the franc did not depreciate greatly. Instead, it moved gradually back into the old narrow band (see Figure 7–2). Even as it did so, however, central bankers began to predict that the band would not be narrowed soon, because the wide band could prove to be an effective safeguard against speculation (see, e.g., Rieke, 1994).

The case for a wide band is usually made by showing why a narrow band makes it safe to bet on a realignment. Consider the case of the old EMS band, having a total width of 4½ percent (i.e., 2¼ percent on each side of the central rate). When a currency sits at the weak edge of the band, anyone who bets that it will be devalued by 10 percent cannot lose more than 4½ percent if the currency is not devalued but cannot gain less than 5½ percent if it is devalued, even if it moves to the strong edge of the band after it has been devalued.[37] But when the band is wider than 10 percent, the results change dramatically. If the currency is not devalued, the largest possible loss will rise from 4½ to 10 percent, and if the currency is devalued, there will no longer be a guaranteed gain; if, indeed, the currency moves to the strong edge of the band after it has been devalued, even those who bet correctly will suffer losses. Williamson and Henning (1994) thus formulate two "golden rules" for exchange rate management: (1) never get locked into defending a misaligned rate; and (2) never change a parity by more than the width of the band.

The two reports discussed earlier in this chapter were concerned with the first rule when they recommended more "timely" realignments. The decision to widen the band, although taken *faute de mieux*, gave belated recognition to the second rule.[38] The two rules together provide the best defense for the EMS during the rest of Stage Two.

36. This expectation was widely held, even in official quarters. In October 1993, the International Monetary Fund expected governments to "take advantage of the greater flexibility offered by the wider bands," making it both "likely" and "appropriate" that interest rates would fall significantly (IMF, 1993, p. 28).
37. That is quite likely to happen, because those who have bet that the currency will be devalued will want to cover their short positions by purchasing the currency, causing it to move to the strong edge of the band. There were several episodes of this sort during the early years of the EMS (see, e.g., Kenen, 1988b).
38. Williamson (1992b) invoked the two rules in a plan for reform of the EMS proposed shortly after the 1992 crisis. By contrast, Pisani-Ferry et al. (1993) recommended more frequent realignments and the narrowing of the band from 2¼ to 1 percent.

Figure 7-2 *Daily exchange rates for the French franc, Italian lira, and pound sterling against the deutsche mark, January 1992 through June 1994*

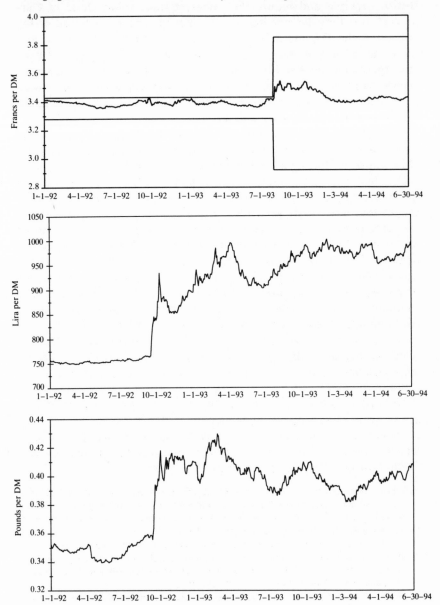

Source: Datastream. Vertical scales differ in relative width; EMS band not shown for lira or pound.

The wide band and the Maastricht Treaty

Many economists endorse this conclusion, but some of them believe that it is incompatible with the requirements of the Maastricht Treaty.[39] That is not strictly true.

Recall the language used in Article 109j of the treaty. When it decides whether a country is ready to enter Stage Three, the Council of Ministers must ask whether the country has "observed the normal fluctuation margins" of the EMS. But "normal" is not defined in the treaty or in the relevant protocol. It would therefore be possible for the EC countries to decide that the wide band is now "normal." Alternatively, they could embody that decision in the legislation that is supposed to replace the protocol.[40]

Objections might come from those who would say that, when they endorsed the treaty, they understood normal to mean narrow. The objection would be justified inasmuch as the term was used in the treaty to distinguish the "normal" 2¼ percent band from the "exceptional" 6 percent band used by new entrants to the EMS. Had that distinction not been necessary, the treaty and protocol might have referred to "the band" without any qualifying adjective (and the EC countries might have been free to say that "the band" was the new wide one, not the old narrow one). A lethal objection, however, might come from the Bundestag, which has called for a "strict and narrow" reading of the convergence criteria. The Bundestag might also argue that any decision to modify the exchange rate criterion, even if taken unanimously by the Council of Ministers, would violate the rights of the national parliaments – and, in some cases, the voters – that ratified the treaty. (The Bundestag might be mollified, however, if the Bundesbank declared itself firmly against any narrowing of the band during the remainder of Stage Two.)

A different approach was proposed by Henning Christopherson, vice-president of the Commission (*Financial Times*, December 15, 1993). Governments could seek to keep their currencies within the old narrow band, without saying so in advance or deciding formally to narrow the band, and they could then apply the convergence criterion accordingly. This is an attractive option, and it has been widely endorsed. Unfortunately, it has one flaw. When markets realize that this is how the conver-

---

39. See, e.g., De Grauwe (1994), Fratianni, von Hagen, and Waller (1992), Ludlow (1993), and Melitz (1994).
40. According to the protocol, the Council of Ministers, acting unanimously on a proposal from the Commission and after consulting various bodies, must adopt "appropriate provisions to lay down the details of the convergence criteria." That legislation will then replace the protocol.

gence criterion will be interpreted, they may start to test the governments' de facto commitment to the narrow band, and the wide band will no longer protect the EMS from speculative attacks. Therefore, the governments may have to decide formally that "normal" means "wide," even if that calls for an amendment to the treaty. Amendments may be needed for other reasons, too. They come up in Chapter 8.

The EC governments must also decide how they will move from the wide band to the irrevocable locking of exchange rates – whether to lock them at the market rates prevailing on the eve of Stage Three or at the corresponding central rates, which may be quite different if the band stays wide. It may be best to declare in advance that they will use the central rates, then count on the credibility of that declaration to drive the two sets of rates together as the deadline approaches. If they do not narrow the band, they can adjust the central rates before the deadline without necessarily affecting market rates abruptly.[41]

41. For variants, see Kenen (1994b) and Cobham (1995). For plans to move from freely floating rates directly to the ECU, see Fratianni, von Hagen, and Waller (1992), Fratianni (1993), and De Grauwe (1994).

CHAPTER 8

Getting on with EMU

Events and issues examined in Chapter 7 raise two questions. Is the case for EMU stronger or weaker than it was when the Maastricht Treaty was adopted? What might be done to make sure that an appreciable number of EC countries will be able to enter Stage Three in 1999, when it is due to start automatically? This chapter answers those questions.

The case for EMU

When asking whether EMU would be a good thing, one must first answer the economist's favorite question: "Compared to what?" Until recently, EMU was often compared with the "hard" EMS that prevailed from early 1987 until September 1992. Today, it should be compared with the wide-band EMS born in August 1993. The two benchmarks are quite different and thus pose different questions.[1]

Comparing EMU with the hard EMS

When EMU was compared with the hard EMS, there was little point in asking whether Europe resembles an optimum currency area – whether the EC countries are likely to suffer large asymmetric shocks, and whether price flexibility and labor mobility are sufficiently high to limit the costs of adjusting to those shocks.

Exchange rate changes were not ruled out under the hard EMS, although governments had renounced them to preempt speculative attacks, and they were successful until 1992. Their success, however, was largely due to the growing expectation of a "seamless" transition to EMU and the concomitant belief that external imbalances would henceforth be corrected by changing domestic policies rather than changing exchange rates. When that expectation was called into question, so was the viability of the hard EMS. When comparing EMU with the hard EMS, then, the latter was viewed – or should have been viewed – as a

---

1. This point was stressed by Thygesen (1993a) even before the EMS band was widened and has been echoed frequently in the recent literature. See, e.g., Viñals (1994).

fixed-rate system, whose members, apart from Germany, had given up the use of monetary policy to pursue domestic economic objectives. Nevertheless, their commitment to fixed exchange rates should not have been deemed to be perfectly credible. For as long as each country had its own currency, it could still change its exchange rate or drop out of the system entirely.

Although the EMS crises of 1992–3 shattered the expectation of a seamless transition to EMU, they also served to highlight the advantages of EMU when it was contrasted with the hard EMS.

First, the crises demonstrated forcefully that a fixed-rate system cannot be immune to speculative pressures and that, ironically, the pressures will be amplified when, as in the early 1990s, the system acquires enough credibility to generate huge financial flows in response to uncovered interest rate differences. The subsequent reversal of those flows, consequent upon a blow to confidence, can then cause a massive attack on the system – which is, of course, the tale of 1992.

Second, the crises demonstrated that the most virtuous leader can make big mistakes, and these can impose enormous costs on its partners when the leader is not sufficiently solicitous of its partners' interests or committed firmly to the fixed-rate system. Reverting to language used before, no such system can survive indefinitely when the leader's policy domain is narrower than the domain of the system itself. Its survival can likewise be threatened when the leader's policy preferences differ from those of its partners. In a monetary union, by contrast, there can be no difference between domains, and the union's policy preferences are, in a sense, an average of its members' preferences.[2]

These two lessons, by themselves, imply that EMU would not be worse than a fixed-rate system like the hard EMS and might be much better, as it would be more durable. But there are two qualifications and additional considerations.[3]

2. This will happen when the union's policy-making body consists of national representatives who reflect their own countries' preferences and take account of conditions at home, as in the models used by Martin (1992) and von Hagen and Suppel (1994). But it can also happen when the members of that body are supposed to be independent but are chosen by a legislature consisting of national representatives, as in the model used by Alesina and Grilli (1992), or by an institution like the European Council, which takes decisions by "common accord" but in which there is bound to be bargaining.
3. The following list is not exhaustive; the Commission (1990) and De Grauwe (1992a) consider other benefits and costs. There is, in addition, the EC version of the "bicycle" theory, which says that the process of trade liberalization must never stop; otherwise, we topple into protectionism. The EC version warns that Europe must never stop moving toward an "ever closer union" (TEU, Article A); otherwise, it will topple into nationalism. See also the discussion in Chapter 5 of the international dimensions of EMU.

The first qualification has figured in every cost–benefit analysis of EMU: Germany will lose its monetary leadership and, therefore, its freedom to pursue price stability within Germany. This result will be costly to Germany whenever inflationary pressures are stronger in Germany than in other EC countries, even if the European Central Bank proves to have policy preferences no different from those of the Bundesbank, and it would be even more costly to Germany if the ECB proved to be more tolerant of inflation. The same qualification holds for countries such as France that have acquired a taste for strict price stability; they, too, will suffer losses if the monetary policy of the ECB is, on average, less austere than the policy "exported" by the Bundesbank under the hard EMS.[4]

The second qualification applies to every EC country. The ECB cannot expect to inherit the credibility of the Bundesbank, even if it is seen to have the very same policy preferences. In its early days, moreover, the ECB may be unable to execute its monetary policy strictly or consistently. The move to EMU is likely to produce unexpected changes in the demand for money, and the instruments of monetary policy will not be perfectly harmonized across the EC countries. Hence, EMU may fail to deliver price stability or – what is more likely – may do so more expensively in terms of output and employment.

Two additional considerations have been cited frequently. First, EMU will eliminate all of the transaction costs imposed by the coexistence of separate national currencies. The Commission (1990) suggested tentatively that those costs may be as large as 0.5 percent of GDP. Second, EMU can banish completely the risk of future exchange rate changes – a risk that cannot be dismissed in a putatively fixed-rate system.[5] The elimination of exchange rate risk should, in turn, have two effects:

- It should help to integrate capital markets and should reduce long-term interest rates in countries that have had chronically weak currencies.

4. The asymmetric sacrifice of sovereignty is stressed by Nölling (1993); on the size of the resulting loss to Germany, see Currie (1992a, 1992b) and the comment by Hughes Hallett (1992). The loss to like-minded countries is not cited as often; critics of EMU tend instead to warn that the "peripheral" countries will suffer if price stability is imposed on them before they are ready for it. (This point is also stressed by Nölling and by the manifesto of German economists opposing EMU, published in the *Frankfurter Allgemeine Zeitung* on June 10, 1992.)

5. This assumes, of course, that EMU is forever, which is a strong assumption; see Cohen (1993) on the demise of monetary unions. His survey suggests, however, that such unions usually break down for political reasons (although the collapse of the ruble zone reflected an explicit cost–benefit assessment by the Russian government). It should nevertheless be noted that the German Constitutional Court held that Germany could withdraw from EMU if the ECB failed to deliver price stability.

- It should foster trade within the Community and, more important, should stimulate investment in tradable-goods industries.

But very little is known about the sizes of these effects.

When the Commission (1990) sought to demonstrate that EMU might be better than the hard EMS, it depended heavily on the first effect. In fact, Masson and Symansky (1992) have shown that much of the net benefit ascribed to EMU by the Commission's simulations reflected the way in which the Commission had modeled the impact of EMU on the exchange rate risk premium and, therefore, on interest rates and capital formation. More conservative methods greatly reduce the net benefit from EMU, whether one compares it with the hard EMS or with a less rigid exchange rate regime.

The effects of exchange rate risk on trade, production, and investment are still subject to debate. Studies conducted in the early 1980s found few effects, if any, and even those that found them did not claim that they were large.[6] Most of those studies, however, looked at the wrong source of risk. They asked whether short-term exchange rate volatility depresses trade or capital formation, and there are ways to hedge against that sort of volatility. It is far harder – but more important – to look at the effects of longer-term changes in exchange rates, because it is harder to hedge against them. If a firm could be perfectly certain about its future foreign currency receipts, it could readily convert them into its own currency by selling the foreign currency forward (or borrowing in that currency). But no firm can know what its receipts will be when the profitability of trade itself depends on future exchange rates. Recent studies focusing on this sort of risk have found that it has trade-depressing effects.[7] Yet they cannot be said to weigh heavily for EMU when it is compared with the hard EMS, in which there was not a great deal of uncertainty about medium-term exchange rate trends.

Finally, a single currency could make pricing more transparent within the EC and could thereby intensify competition. In that sense, the Commission (1990) was quite right to say that a single market needs a single currency. But the size of the resulting efficiency gain cannot be readily quantified.

There is thus a quixotic twist to this whole comparison. The progress toward EMU during the early 1990s tended to weaken the case for EMU by making the hard EMS seem viable. It was rather hard to argue that

6. Surveys will be found in IMF (1984) and Gotur (1985); see also the papers by Cushman (1983), Kenen and Rodrik (1986), and Thursby and Thursby (1987).
7. These studies are surveyed by Kumar and Whitt (1992); also the paper by Chowdhury (1993).

each and every EC country would benefit from EMU in strictly economic terms. The case for EMU gets stronger, however, when it is compared with the present EMS.

Comparing EMU with the wide-band EMS

When the EMS band was widened abruptly in 1993, it looked at first as though the EMS was giving way to a floating-rate regime, at least temporarily. The new band seemed too wide to matter. To the dismay of some, however, and the relief of others, exchange rate changes were quite small under the new regime. Short-term fluctuations were larger than before, but not like those attaching to the lira or the pound (see Figure 7–2).[8] When comparing EMU with the wide-band EMS, however, it would be prudent to assume that the present EMS can and will accommodate larger changes in exchange rates over the long term, including realignments of the central rates themselves. Therefore, it is time to take up issues that were set aside when EMU was compared with the hard EMS and to reexamine certain other issues.

The wide-band EMS has given the EC countries freedom to pursue monetary policies appreciably different from the Bundesbank's policy. But they have not chosen to use it. They appear to believe that the strenuous pursuit of exchange rate stability is still the surest way to achieve price stability. One may wonder about that. But if they are right, the wider band should make EMU more attractive. With the passage of time, some EC governments will come under growing pressure to strike out on their own – to abandon their orthodox stance and exploit their independence. The pressure will be especially strong in countries with stubbornly high unemployment rates. Hence, countries that are truly committed to price stability will find it cheaper to buy credibility from the ECB by entering EMU than to go on renting it from the Bundesbank.

The wide-band EMS has also given every country the freedom to deal with asymmetric shocks by letting their exchange rates change or by realigning them. The standard objection to that policy response, that

8. During the first twelve months of the wide-band EMS, the day-to-day variability of the DM–lira rate was almost three times as large as that of the DM–franc rate, and the variability of the DM–sterling rate was more than twice as large. (The mean of the squared daily change was 0.172 percent for the DM–lira rate, 0.159 percent for the DM–sterling rate, and only 0.065 percent for the DM–franc rate.) Yet some Europeans are not impressed by the difference in behavior. "We look upon European currencies," says Rutbert Reisch, treasurer of Volkswagen, "as a freely floating exchange rate system. We treat the pound, the lira, the peseta and the French franc just like the U.S. dollar, the Canadian dollar or the yen." (*Financial Times*, December 13, 1993, p. 13)

real wage rates are too sticky, is an equally valid objection to the chief alternative – depending on changes in relative prices to offset asymmetric shocks.[9] From this standpoint, the wider band could make EMU less attractive. If the EC falls short of being an optimum currency area, because prices are not flexible enough and labor is not mobile enough, the costs of EMU may seem higher than when it was compared with the hard EMS. But one new bit of evidence is relevant here.

Previous efforts to ascertain whether the EC resembles an optimum currency area have typically compared the shocks affecting EC countries with the shocks affecting U.S. states or regions. But Ghosh and Wolf (1994) have taken the next step. By adopting two strong assumptions, that the shocks are unaffected by the exchange rate regime and that the output-reducing effect of an asymmetric shock can be offset perfectly by changing the exchange rate, they have been able to measure the cost of forming a monetary union, in which exchange rates cannot change. In the U.S. case, the average annual output loss amounts to 2.6 percent of total U.S. GDP when the existing U.S. monetary union is compared with a hypothetical situation in which every U.S. state is able to change its exchange rate. In the EC case, the output loss is virtually the same – about 2.5 percent of total EC GDP – when an EMU involving the twelve EC countries is compared with a situation in which every EC country has its own exchange rate. Furthermore, these are high-end estimates of the costs involved, because exchange rate changes cannot be expected to offset fully the output-reducing effects of all shocks.[10]

Another consideration pertains importantly to Germany. When the EMS was founded in 1978, some people asked why Germany was interested in joining. The answer most commonly given at the time stressed the risk that the deutsche mark might otherwise appreciate steadily against other EC currencies, undermining Germany's competitive posi-

9. Note, further, that the real effective exchange rates for the pound and lira changed by more – not less – than their nominal effective rates during the two years after they left the EMS.

10. The output costs of other monetary unions are larger than those obtained for the U.S. and EC cases. For the twelve former Soviet republics (i.e., all but the Baltic states), they amount to about 4.5 percent of GDP; for the twelve CFA franc countries, they amount to about 11 percent. (Ghosh and Wolf go on to show that a smaller EMU would be less costly than one that included all twelve EC countries, but their algorithm produces an odd outcome: Germany should not join EMU. That is because Ghosh and Wolf measure the cost of EMU by adding up the costs incurred by each EC country, whether or not it joints a particular version of EMU. Hence, the ability of Germany, the largest EC country, to change its own exchange rate, thus keeping German shocks from reducing total EC output, hugely reduces the cost to all twelve EC countries of forming an EMU without Germany.)

tion (see, e.g., Melitz, 1994). The risk was not greatly reduced, however, until the EMS had been hardened, nearly a decade later, and it rose again in 1992. From a German standpoint, then, the hard EMS looked better than EMU, but the wide-band EMS may be less satisfactory – a point that escapes German critics of EMU. Nölling (1993) wonders why Europe should want a single currency when it has the EMS; but the present EMS is not the one it had before – the one that tied down the deutsche mark but did not hugely interfere with the Bundesbank's autonomy. Germany has now to make a harder choice – whether to rely on the ECB for price stability or rely on foreign exchange markets to hold down the deutsche mark.

Although the effects of exchange rate risk cannot be quantified, they may be larger today than under the hard EMS. Hence, the efficiency gains from EMU may be correspondingly larger.[11] Concerns have been expressed, moreover, about the effects of exchange rate flexibility on the gains to be achieved from the single market and, indeed, the threat it poses to the survival of the single market.

Economists in the United States frequently point out that U.S. and Canadian markets for goods, services, and assets are more closely integrated than those of the EC countries, even though the Canadian dollar floats freely against the U.S. dollar. There is no need, they say, for fixed exchange rates, let alone a single currency. Europeans rarely reply as they should, by asking what would happen to the U.S. economy if all fifty states (or, for that matter, the twelve Federal Reserve Districts) had their own currencies and exchange rates floated freely. The question is somewhat unfair; it leads one to think immediately about the huge costs of adjusting to the new regime, not about the smaller costs of living with it permanently. Yet the permanent costs could be quite large, even if the breakup of the U.S. monetary union did not cause a breakup of the

11. Fratianni and von Hagen (1992) have shown that exchange rate risk was not much lower in the early years of the EMS, when realignments were common, than in the previous floating-rate period, but that it fell thereafter. Their results are especially striking because their calculations do not cover the whole hard-EMS period. Ayuso, Jurado, and Restoy (1994) have examined exchange rate risk under the hard EMS, during the crisis period, and after widening of the band. They find that it rose for the pound and lira after they left the EMS and rose for other EMS currencies during the crisis period. But their results also suggest that, for some of those currencies, especially the peseta and escudo, exchange rate risk has been smaller in the wide-band EMS than it was in the hard EMS; there is more short-term volatility, but markets appear to believe that realignments are less likely than before. (Markets may merely be saying, however, that the realignments of 1992–3 reduced the probability that there will be more of them soon. If that is the case, exchange rate risk may rise with the passage of time.)

single U.S. market – the risk that cannot be ignored in the European case:

> Completing the Single Market in commodities and factors of production, economists agree, will deliver significant efficiency gains. Even if the majority of those gains are technically obtainable despite the maintenance of separate national currencies, a single currency may be required to suppress the political resistance that economic integration would otherwise provoke. The argument runs as follows. The more integrated are national markets, the larger are the import surges that accompany exchange-rate induced shifts in relative prices, and the greater is the pain experienced by impacted firms and workers. The complaints over competitive depreciation and exchange dumping that followed the departure of sterling and the lira from the EMS in 1992 illustrate the point. Monetary union that prevents "capricious" exchange rate swings, thereby ruling out the associated costs, may be necessary to prevent impacted sectors from lobbying against economic integration and to insure the political viability of the Single Market process. In addition, the intricate set of transfers and side payments that makes the Single Market acceptable to all the countries concerned is more difficult to administer when exchange rates vary. (Eichengreen, 1994, pp. 127–8)

The wide band, this same author warns, could be "corrosive" of the single market over the long run.[12]

Finally, it is worth noting that economists' views about the gains from the single market, as well as the gains from a single currency, differ from those of many European business leaders. In February 1994, the *Financial Times* reported their answers to questions about the future of Europe. When asked whether their own firms had benefited from the single market, 77 percent said no. When asked whether a single European currency would improve the competitiveness of the EC, 51 percent said yes.[13]

Moving beyond Maastricht

How, then, can the Community get on with EMU? Chapter 7 rejected the case for a "dash" to EMU, because of German objections and because it could gravely damage the political cohesion of the Community. But the

---

12. Eichengreen (1994), p. 131; the same concern has been expressed by Buiter, Corsetti, and Pesenti (1993), Fratianni and von Hagen (1993), Jacquet (1993), and Viñals (1994). Cameron (1994) poses the issue differently; he asks whether the EC countries would have committed themselves to the single market had there been no EMS.

13. *Financial Times*, February 24, 1994, p. 10. But attention must be paid to the wording of the second question; it asked about the competitiveness "of" the EC, not about competitiveness "within" the EC. Furthermore, McNamara (1994) finds that business leaders are not deeply committed to EMU – even those who express support for it.

Maastricht path to EMU will be hard to follow. One cannot have great confidence in the ability of the EC countries to agree on a date for starting Stage Three when, at the end of 1996, they must consider that possibility. And though the treaty says that Stage Three will start automatically at the beginning of 1999 if a different date has not been chosen, a way might be found to stop that from happening if, as the deadline approaches, there is strong opposition in one or two key countries.

Some of the problems that loom large now were obvious and worrisome early on, even before the treaty was adopted. For that very reason, the treaty says that an intergovernmental conference shall be convened to review it in 1996. The new conference, however, is supposed to focus on those parts of the treaty that deal with the powers of the Parliament and the development of a common foreign policy (TEU, Article N.2). Those who had concerns about the provisions pertaining to EMU were reluctant to reopen them; they hoped that the political commitment to EMU would lead to workable interpretations. They hoped, for example, that the EMI would have enough influence on monetary policies to defend the transition to EMU from shocks, despite the decision at Maastricht to reject the "gradual transfer of responsibility" proposed in the Delors Report. They also hoped that some EC countries would deposit reserves with the EMI, which might then play an active role in defending the EMS.

Most important, advocates of EMU believed initially that Article 104c of the treaty, on excessive budget deficits, would be construed liberally, allowing the Council of Ministers to decide that a majority of EC countries was ready to enter Stage Three in 1997 or, at least, to let most of them enter in 1999, when Stage Three is to start automatically. Governments having large budget deficits expected to show that their deficits had "declined substantially" or were "only exceptional and temporary." Governments having high debt ratios expected to show that those ratios were "sufficiently diminishing and approaching the reference value at a satisfactory pace."

Furthermore, it was feared that any attempt to improve the EMU provisions of the treaty might be counterproductive. There might be a retreat from automaticity – a return to the process proposed in the Netherlands Draft and described in Chapter 2, by which the Council of Ministers would have to consider periodically whether to start Stage Three but could always decide to defer it. The situation has changed, however, and the cost of refusing to reconsider the EMU provisions of the treaty may by now exceed the possible cost of reopening those provisions. Three reasons support that conclusion.

First, the resolution adopted by the Bundestag and cited by the German Constitutional Court will require the German government to insist on a "strict and narrow" interpretation of the convergence criteria, including Article 104c, because an excessive budget deficit will be cause for the Council of Ministers to decide that a particular country is not ready to enter Stage Three.

Second, the reference value for debt, 60 percent of GDP, was unrealistic initially and is absurdly so today. At the end of 1993, Ireland and Portugal were the only two countries having debt ratios smaller than when the Maastricht Treaty was signed. Furthermore, four of the six countries having debt ratios higher than 75 percent of GDP in 1993 ran bigger budget deficits in 1994 than in 1992. Hence, they must make even larger cuts in their deficits before they can start to reduce their debt ratios.

Third, an agreement to treat the wide band as "normal" in the exchange rate convergence criterion, even if taken unanimously by the EC governments, may not sit well with the Bundestag unless the change is part of a balanced package – one that cannot be attacked for making the entry to EMU too easy.[14]

Other objections to the Maastricht Treaty raised in earlier chapters should also be addressed in 1996 if the new intergovernmental conference is instructed to reconsider the EMU provisions of the treaty. Two of them deserve particular attention:[15]

- There must be close policy coordination between the ECB and the central banks of the countries that do not enter Stage Three right away.
- The "democratic deficit" in the treaty should be narrowed by giving the European Parliament additional responsibilities.

I consider these issues later, after proposing a "balanced" package of changes in the convergence criteria and the need for a small change in the timing of the automatic move to EMU.

14. An acceptable package cannot be adopted in time to affect a decision to start Stage Three in 1997. The intergovernmental conference cannot be expected to complete its work quickly. (It has indeed been suggested that the conference should not try to finish its work before the next British election, because the present British government cannot possibly agree to significant changes in the treaty.) Furthermore, amendments to the treaty will have to be ratified by every EC country. Changes could be made, however, in time to affect the decisions that have to be taken in 1998, on the eligibility of individual EC countries to enter Stage Three in 1999.

15. Most of the remaining matters raised in earlier chapters do not pose basic issues of principle. Article 109, on exchange rate policy, needs clarification. Something should also be said about the responsibilities of the ECB under the Articles of Agreement of the International Monetary Fund if, eventually, the ECB is to hold and manage IMF reserve positions or SDRs under Article 30 of the ESCB Statute. Finally, the role of the ECB in prudential supervision will have to be reconsidered eventually, but the treaty provides for that possibility.

The convergence criteria and the transition to EMU

The problem posed by the widening of the EMS band is fairly easy to solve. One of two bodies, the Council of Ministers or the EMI, could be given the right to decide the size of the "normal" band. The initial decision might be taken by the Council after consulting the EMI; any subsequent change might then be made by the EMI.[16]

More difficult problems are posed by the need to amend the criteria used in Article 104c to characterize an excessive budget deficit. It is tempting to suggest that the debt criterion be deleted completely and other ways be found to insulate the ECB from the pressures that might be produced by an incipient or actual debt crisis in an EC country. But that solution would be too radical and too hard to balance by tightening other convergence criteria. There is, however, a second-best solution. The debt criterion can be used to *condition* the deficit criterion, not, as now, to stand beside it. A low-debt country might be made to satisfy the present test – a budget deficit not larger than 3 percent of GDP. A high-debt country might be made to satisfy a more stringent test – a deficit not larger than, say, 2 percent of GDP. It would not be necessary to alter the "indents" in Article 104c, which pertain to the existing deficit criterion, but the qualifications concerning the trend in the debt ratio could be dropped.[17] The new text might then read this way:[18]

> The Commission . . . shall examine compliance with budgetary discipline on the basis of the following requirement:

16. Questions arise here and later about the types of majorities that should be required to take various decisions. But these are political matters on which an economist has little to say – least of all an economist whose own nationality insulates him from the consequences of those decisions.
17. A different solution is suggested by Italianer (1993). Article 104c of the treaty instructs the Council of Ministers, acting unanimously on a proposal from the Commission, to adopt "the appropriate provisions" to replace the protocol that contains the reference values for deficits and debt. Italianer interprets this passage to mean that the Council can change the reference values. If so, it would be possible to raise the reference value for debt. That would not be a balanced change, however, unless the Council also reduced the reference value for the budget deficit. Without changing the language of the treaty itself, moreover, it would be impossible to apply the reduced reference value selectively to the high-debt countries. Finally, it would be necessary to make a very large increase in the reference value for debt to put it within reach of the high-debt countries or spare them the need to reduce their deficits sharply in order to shrink their debt ratios. Raising the reference value for debt does not, by itself, solve the problem.
18. The text that follows inserts into Article 104c the reference values that appear in the Protocol on the Excessive Deficit Procedure. There may be juridical reasons for keeping them apart, but they need not concern us here.

    (a)   for a Member State having a ratio of government debt to gross domestic product that does not exceed 60 percent, that the ratio of the planned or actual government deficit to gross domestic product does not exceed 3 percent;

    (b)   for a Member State having a ratio of government debt to gross domestic product that exceeds 60 percent, that the ratio of the planned or actual government deficit to gross domestic product does not exceed 2 percent.

A Member State shall be deemed to fulfill the appropriate requirement, however, whenever
— either the ratio of the deficit to gross domestic product has declined substantially and continuously and reached a level that comes close to the level required at (a) or (b) above,
— or, alternatively, the excess over the level required at (a) or (b) above is only exceptional and temporary and the ratio remains close to that level.

If a Member State does not fulfill the appropriate requirement at (a) or (b) above, the Commission shall prepare a report. . . .

The changes proposed in Article 104c are, in a sense, self-balancing, in that a high-debt country would have to run a smaller budget deficit. But something more can be done to balance the package of changes in the convergence criteria. The present price-stability test is relative, not absolute. A country can meet it by having an inflation rate "that does not exceed by more than 1½ percentage points that of, at most, the three best performing Member States." Critics object that this test is not strict enough.[19] Should EMU begin, they ask, before really taming inflation? What if the three best-performing countries are running two-digit inflation rates?

This objection can be answered by adding an absolute test: A country's inflation rate must not exceed the smaller of two numbers: the one based on the showing of the three best performers and the other fixed at, say, 2½ percent per year. This seemingly small change is not innocuous. Under the present test, the three best performers are likely to enter Stage Three in 1999 if they meet the other convergence criteria.[20] Under the proposed two-part test, however, Stage Three can not even start automatically in 1999 unless two or more countries have inflation rates below 2½ percent.[21]

19. See the manifesto of the German economists cited in note 4, above.
20. They are likely but not certain to enter Stage Three, because one, or even two, might still have inflation rates that exceed the three-country average by more than 1½ percent. (If two of them do, of course, EMU can not start.)
21. For this reason, the proposed change in the inflation rate criterion would require a modification of the passage in Article 109j concerning the 1999 deadline. Other

A more mundane problem appears to have escaped attention. If Stage Three is to start automatically in 1999, the eligible countries should be identified by the beginning of 1998, if not earlier. Otherwise, their governments, central banks, and financial institutions may not begin to make the necessary changes, including those proposed in Chapter 3 to permit the introduction of the ECU at the "wholesale" level. The ECB would then face serious problems in its attempt to implement a single monetary policy.[22] Hence, it would be prudent to modify Article 109j, without abandoning automaticity.

There are two ways to do that: (1) settle the question of eligibility by the beginning of 1998 (not, as now, by the middle of the year) and leave the actual starting date unchanged, or (2) make no change in the date for settling the question of eligibility but postpone the start of Stage Three itself to mid-1999 or to the beginning of the following year.

Policy coordination with the nonparticipants

The package of changes proposed in the previous section could conceivably permit the majority of EC countries to qualify for EMU in 1997 and should permit the majority to qualify by 1999. For that very reason, the changes may not be acceptable to those who believe that the existing convergence criteria are not strict enough. The Bundestag may balk. Nevertheless, some countries will not qualify for EMU even in 1999, not

changes proposed below might likewise require conforming changes elsewhere in the treaty. The actual inflation rates shown in Table 6–1 produced a 3 percent ceiling, and six countries did not meet it (Germany, Greece, Italy, Luxembourg, Portugal, and Spain); but two more countries would have failed to meet the 2½ percent absolute test (Belgium and the Netherlands). Only four countries (Denmark, France, Ireland, and the United Kingdom) would have met the more stringent absolute test. There is, of course, another way to tighten the inflation rate criterion – by reducing the size of the present 1½ percent margin. Had it been cut to 1 percent, the two tests would have coincided perfectly for the numbers in Table 6–1. This alternative, however, does not answer the basic objection to the present relative test – that it does not rule out the possibility that the three best performers will be running high inflation rates when it is time to decide which countries are ready to enter Stage Three. (The interest rate convergence criterion is also based on a relative test, but the addition of an absolute test to the inflation rate criterion does not necessarily call for a corresponding change in the interest rate criterion.)

22. This problem would not arise acutely if the decision to start Stage Three were taken in 1997; the qualifying countries would have to be chosen by December 31, 1996, but Stage Three itself would not have to start at the very beginning of 1997. If no such decision is taken, the subsequent decision-making sequence is compressed; the qualifying countries do not have to be chosen before July 1, 1998, but Stage Three must start six months later (TEU, Article 109j).

under the present criteria nor those proposed above. Furthermore, two countries may opt out (Denmark and the United Kingdom). Soon after the start of the new century, moreover, the EC may admit more members. Therefore, relations between the ESCB countries and the nonparticipants will require close attention for many years to come.

The framework available for that purpose, the General Council of the ECB, was described in Chapter 6, which posed objections to the organization of that body and raised questions about its powers and duties. The General Council will include, as equals, the president of the ECB, the central bank governors of the ESCB countries, and the central bank governors of the nonparticipating countries. This, I said, would be much like asking the governors of the Canadian and Mexican central banks to sit with the presidents of the twelve Federal Reserve Banks when meeting with the chairman of the Federal Reserve Board to coordinate monetary policies among the North American countries. More important, the General Council will not have to be consulted in advance about matters pending before the Governing Council of the ECB and may not be entitled to advise the ECB or the nonparticipants on monetary matters, even though it is supposed to continue the work of the EMI that must still be done after Stage Three starts.

If some large EC countries do not enter Stage Three immediately, the ECB will have reasons of its own for wanting to consult closely with their central banks, and they, in turn, will want to consult closely with the ECB. If, indeed, the nonparticipants will be expected to link their national currencies tightly to the ECU in order to qualify for Stage Three eventually, they will have to communicate effectively with the ECB, and the ECB will have to listen to them. It may insist, in the manner of the Bundesbank, that they do not fall within its policy domain. But the ECB will be a creature of the Community, and it cannot be completely deaf to the views and concerns of any EC country.

Therefore, the treaty should be amended to establish a new body comprising the president of the ECB and the governors of the central banks of the nonparticipating countries. It should not replace the General Council, which will have duties of its own, but should have responsibilities and powers similar to those of the EMI. It should have the right to be consulted in advance concerning important policy decisions by the Governing Council of the ECB and the right to give advice to individual central banks, including the ECB. Furthermore, it should be made responsible for managing exchange rate arrangements linking the ECU with the nonparticipants' national currencies.

What form might those arrangements take? A comprehensive, formal arrangement resembling the present EMS was considered in Chapter 6, where two objections were raised. First such an arrangement might not be necessary or sufficient for the nonparticipants to tie their currencies tightly to the ECU. Second, the ECB might oppose any arrangement that imposes open-ended obligations on it. It would most certainly be reluctant to make open-ended commitments in respect of a world-class currency such as the pound. Nevertheless, the ECB should want to have some influence on the exchange rate policies of the nonparticipants, and they, in turn, are likely to want some sort of support from the ECB. But they may be better off with credit facilities of fixed but known size than with facilities that are meant to be open-ended but could be shut off abruptly by the ECB.

The details can be worked out by the ECB and the nonparticipants' central banks; there is no need to add them to the treaty or draft a new protocol to deal with them. But Article 109m of the treaty should be amended; it raises the issue but drops it in the laps of the nonparticipants.[23] It should instead encourage the ECB to work closely with the central banks of the nonparticipants to achieve the objectives that they used to pursue through the EMS.

Accountability and the democratic deficit

For reasons given in Chapter 2, the ECB will be more independent than the Bundesbank or Federal Reserve System. Its statute is part of the treaty, which cannot be amended without the consent of every EC country (including the nonparticipants).[24] The ECB must submit an annual report to various EC bodies, including the European Parliament, and the president and other members of the Executive Board may appear before appropriate committees of the Parliament at its request or on

23. The first paragraph says that, until Stage Three, each EC country shall treat its exchange rate policy "as a matter of common interest" and to that end shall take account of the experience acquired in the EMS. But the next paragraph says that after Stage Three has started, these obligations shall fall entirely on the nonparticipants. This makes no sense. The exchange rate connecting two currencies cannot be the concern or responsibility of a single country; it must in principle be the joint concern of the two countries issuing those currencies.

24. It was noted, however, that certain articles of the ESCB Statute can be amended by the Council; it will act by qualified majority on a recommendation from the EC and after consulting the Commission or will act unanimously on a proposal from the Commission and after consulting the ECB. Under both procedures, however, it must have the assent of the Parliament. But the articles in question relate mainly to administrative and financial matters and the use by the ECB of certain policy instruments. The Council cannot alter the objectives or tasks of the ESCB or the provisions regarding its independence.

their own initiative. But the Parliament cannot exercise much influence on the policies of the ECB, because it cannot threaten to amend its mandate or modify its powers. Furthermore, it has only an advisory role in selecting the president of the ECB and the other members of the Executive Board.

These arrangements are stoutly defended by those who believe that monetary policy should be totally insulated from political pressures. But they disturb those who believe that "accountability" should mean something more than the mere rendering of a report and that the treaty goes too far in its attempt to define and defend the independence of the ECB.[25] On this view, the EMU provisions of the treaty deepen the existing "democratic deficit" in the Community. Therefore, two changes should be contemplated.

First, the European Parliament should be entitled to initiate amendments to the ESCB Statute. These should be submitted to the Council of Ministers, which should consult the Commission and the ECB. If they do not raise objections, the Council should decide whether to submit the amendments to the EC governments for ratification. If the Commission or the ECB objects to the amendments, in whole or in part, they should be returned to the Parliament for reconsideration and possible modification. If the Parliament reaffirms its support for them, with or without modification, the Council should have to decide whether to submit them for ratification. These procedures would not replace those in the present treaty; they would merely supplement them.[26]

Second, the Parliament should be given a larger role in selecting the Executive Board of the ECB, including the president and vice-president. Under Article 158 of the treaty, the president and other members of the EC Commission whose terms begin in January 1995 will be nominated by

25. Citations on both sides of the argument are given in Chapter 2.
26. Under Article N of the treaty, the Council does not vote on individual proposals to amend the treaty. Amendments can be proposed by a member state or by the Commission. After consulting the European Parliament and, if appropriate, the Commission, the Council must then "deliver an opinion" on the calling of an intergovernmental conference to consider the amendments. Amendments will not be submitted for ratification by the individual countries unless adopted by the "common accord" (i.e., unanimous consent) of the conference. The procedure proposed in the text would bypass the calling of a conference. (In some cases, amendments to the ESCB Statute will require amendments to the treaty itself; these should not be treated differently from other amendments to the statute.) In a previous note, I promised not to make suggestions about voting. In the present case, however, decisions by the Council would have to be unanimous; it would make no sense for the Council to submit amendments for ratification if any EC government opposed them. To do so might provoke a constitutional crisis within the country opposing the amendment.

the EC governments (the president by common accord and the rest by their own governments). The whole slate, however, must then be approved by the Parliament. This procedure cannot be copied exactly when selecting the Executive Board of the ECB. Because its members will be appointed to staggered eight-year terms, there will be no slate to put before the Parliament. Therefore, each nomination would have to be submitted separately, and the Parliament would have to vote on it separately. But this should not constitute an overwhelming objection. It could force the governments to pay attention to geographic diversity when choosing individual candidates, as the Parliament would probably insist on it. (At present, the treaty and statute do not require diversity; they speak only of the need to choose persons "of recognized standing and professional experience in monetary or banking matters.") But the issue is bound to emerge, even under the present treaty, because every appointment to the Executive Board must be approved unanimously, and each government is thus able to make sure that its nationals – and national interests – are not ignored persistently.

Some will surely say that the European Parliament cannot be entrusted with these responsibilities. It is not a "serious" body. Thygesen (1993a) said this more diplomatically in the passage cited at the end of Chapter 2. The assertion itself is debatable, but the response is obvious. The Parliament is not likely to become a "serious" body until it has serious work to do. The cure for the "democratic deficit" is more democracy, not less.

A final note

Will EMU succeed? Will EMU even happen? These are the important questions, but no one can answer them now. Yet it is not too early to ask whether the blueprint for EMU makes sense, and the answer to that is clear. It does. The blueprint is imperfect and incomplete, because compromise sometimes triumphed over clarity. But one more analogy between the United States and Europe may be appropriate. The Federal Reserve System was likewise a compromise, balancing the needs of an emerging continental economy against regional interests and concerns, and it took many years for that institution to solve the problems generated by the need for compromise. Nevertheless, the imperatives of economic integration produced solutions eventually, and the political system responded by changing the structure, mandate, and powers of the Federal Reserve System. That is bound to happen in Europe, and the adolescent ESCB may be quite different from the newborn institution. The speed of adaptation will depend on the further development of the Community as a political entity.

The move to EMU, however, should not be delayed until that political entity has been developed fully or because the economies of the EC countries have not converged completely. Papadia and Saccomanni (1994) warn that reasons of this sort can always be used to justify further delay. The mechanical hare, they say, is used at racetracks to keep the hounds running without being able to eat it, but the prospect of a never-ending race is clearly inconsistent with the letter and spirit of the Maastricht Treaty. Indeed, it is inconsistent with the whole history of the Community, which has been built by taking risks, not by waiting until they have vanished.

References

Aizenman, J. (1994), "On the Need for Fiscal Discipline in a Union," NBER Working Paper 4656, Cambridge: National Bureau of Economic Research.

Alesina, A., and V. Grilli (1992), "The European Central Bank: Reshaping Monetary Politics in Europe," in Canzoneri, Grilli, and Masson, eds., *Establishing a Central Bank: Issues in Europe and Lessons from the US*, Cambridge: Cambridge University Press.

(1993), "On the Feasibility of a One or Multi-speed European Monetary Union," *Economics & Politics* 5.

Allen, P. R. (1992), "The ECU and the Transition to European Monetary Union," *International Economic Journal* 6.

Alogoskoufis, G., and R. Portes (1991), "The International Costs and Benefits from EMU," in "The Economics of EMU," *European Economy*, Special Edition 1.

(1992), "European Monetary Union and International Currencies in a Tripolar World," in Canzoneri, Grilli, and Masson, eds., *Establishing a Central Bank: Issues in Europe and Lessons from the US*, Cambridge: Cambridge University Press.

Angeloni, I., C. Cottarelli, and A. Levy (1991), "Cross-Border Deposits and Monetary Aggregates in the Transition to EMU," paper presented at the Milan Conference on Monetary Policy in Stage Two of EMU (processed).

Artis, M. J. (1991), "Monetary Policy in Stage Two of EMU: What Can We Learn from the 1980s?" paper presented at the Milan Conference on Monetary Policy in Stage Two of EMU (processed).

(1994), "Stage Two: Feasible Transitions to EMU," CEPR Discussion Paper 928, London: Centre for Economic Policy Research.

Artis, M. J., R. C. Bladen-Hovell, and W. Zhang (1993), "A European Money Demand Function," in Masson and Taylor, eds., *Policy Issues in the Operation of Currency Unions*, Cambridge: Cambridge University Press.

Artis, M. J., and D. Nachane (1990), "Wages and Prices in Europe: A Test of the German Leadership Thesis," *Weltwirtschaftliches Archiv* 126.

Ayuso, J., M. P. Jurado, and F. Restoy (1994), "Is Exchange Rate Risk Higher in the ERM after the Widening of Fluctuation Bands?" Working Paper 9419, Madrid: Banco de España.

Baer, G. D., and T. Padoa-Schioppa (1989), "The Werner Report Revisited," paper annexed to the Delors Report (1989).

Bank for International Settlements (BIS) (1993), *63rd Annual Report*, Basle.

Bank of England (1992), "The Foreign Exchange Market in London," *Bank of England Quarterly Bulletin* 32 (November).

Barber, L. (1994), "Fresh Meat from Europe's Stable," *Financial Times*, September 8.

Barr, D. (1992), "The Demand for Money in Europe: Comment on Kremers and Lane," *IMF Staff Papers* 39.

Barro, R., and X. Sala-i-Martin (1991), "Convergence across States and Regions," *Brookings Papers on Economic Activity* 1.

195

Batten, D. S., M. P. Blackwell, I. S. Kim, S. E. Nocera, and Y. Ozeki (1990), *The Conduct of Monetary Policy in the Major Industrial Countries*, Occasional Paper 70, Washington: International Monetary Fund.

Bayoumi, T. (1993), "The Effects of the ERM on Participating Economies," *IMF Staff Papers* 39.

Bayoumi, T., and B. Eichengreen (1992), "Is There a Conflict between EC Enlargement and European Monetary Unification?" NBER Working Paper 3950, Cambridge: National Bureau of Economic Research.

    (1993), "Shocking Aspects of European Monetary Integration," in Torres and Giavazzi, eds., *Adjustment and Growth in the European Monetary Union*, Cambridge: Cambridge University Press.

Bayoumi, T., M. Goldstein, and G. Woglom (1993), "Do Credit Markets Discipline Sovereign Borrowers?" Washington: International Monetary Fund (processed).

Bayoumi, T., and P. B. Kenen (1993), "How Useful Is an ERM-Wide Monetary Aggregate as an Intermediate Target for Europe?" *Review of International Economics* 1.

Bayoumi, T., and P. R. Masson (1994), "Fiscal Flows in the United States and Canada: Lessons for Monetary Union in Europe," CEPR Discussion Paper 1057, London: Centre for Economic Policy Research.

Begg, D., F. Giavazzi, L. Spaventa, and C. Wyplosz (1991), "European Monetary Union – The Macro Issues," in *Monitoring European Integration: The Making of Monetary Union*, London: Centre for Economic Policy Research.

Begg, D., and C. Wyplosz (1993), "The European Monetary System: Recent Intellectual History," in Giovannini, Guitian, and Portes, eds., *The Monetary Future of Europe*, London: Centre for Economic Policy Research.

Begg, I., and D. Mayes (1992), "Cohesion as a Precondition for Monetary Union in Europe," in Barrell, ed., *Economic Convergence and Monetary Union in Europe*, London: Sage for the Association for the Monetary Union of Europe and the National Institute of Economic and Social Research.

Bernanke, B. S. (1993), "Credit in the Macroeconomy," *Quarterly Review of the Federal Reserve Bank of New York* 18 (Spring).

Bini-Smaghi, L. (1993), "Discussion of Thygesen," in Torres and Giavazzi, eds., *Adjustment and Growth in the European Monetary Union*, Cambridge: Cambridge University Press.

Bini-Smaghi, L., T. Padoa-Schioppa, and F. Papadia (1994), *The Transition to EMU in the Maastricht Treaty*, Essays in International Finance 194, Princeton: International Finance Section, Princeton University.

Bini-Smaghi, L., and S. Vori (1992), "Rating the EC as an Optimal Currency Area," in O'Brien, ed., *Finance and the International Economy* 6, Oxford: Oxford University Press for the Amex Bank Review.

Black, S. W. (1991), "Transactions Costs and Vehicle Currencies," *Journal of International Money and Finance* 10.

Blanchard, O., and L. Katz (1992), "Regional Evolutions," *Brookings Papers on Economic Activity* 1.

Bofinger, P. (1993), "European Monetary Coordination by the EMS: Faultlines and Reform Proposals," paper prepared for a working group of the Association for the Monetary Union of Europe, Paris.

    (1994), "Is Europe an Optimum Currency Area?" CEPR Discussion Paper 915, London: Centre for Economic Policy Research.

Bovenberg, A. L., J. J. M. Kremers, and P. R. Masson (1991), "Economic and Monetary Union in Europe and Constraints on National Budgetary Policies," *IMF Staff Papers* 38.

Brittan, S. (1993), "How to Cope with the Slowdown," *Financial Times*, October 21.

Britton, A., and D. Mayes (1992), *Achieving Monetary Union in Europe*, London: Sage for the Association for the Monetary Union of Europe and the National Institute of Economic and Social Research.

Bryant, R. C., D. W. Henderson, G. Holtham, P. Hooper, and S. A. Symansky, eds. (1988), *Empirical Macroeconomics for Interdependent Economies*, Washington: The Brookings Institution.

Buiter, W. H., G. M. Corsetti, and P. A. Pesenti (1993), "International Monetary Co-operation and Financial Market Regulation: The Lessons of the 92–93 ERM Crisis" (processed).

Buiter, W. H., G. Corsetti, and N. Roubini (1993), "Excessive Deficits: Sense and Non-sense in the Treaty of Maastricht," *Economic Policy* 16.

Buiter, W. H., and K. M. Kletzer (1991), "Reflections on the Fiscal Implications of a Common Currency," in Giovannini and Mayer, eds., *European Financial Integration*, Cambridge: Cambridge University Press.

Burdekin, R. C. K., C. Wihlborg, and T. D. Willett (1992), "A Monetary Constitution Case for an Independent European Central Bank," *The World Economy* (March).

Burridge, M., and D. G. Mayes (1994), "The Implications for Firms and Industry of the Adoption of the ECU as the Single Currency in the EC," Economic Papers 106, Brussels: Commission of the European Communities.

Cameron, D. R. (1994), "British Exit, German Voice, French Loyalty: Defection, Domi-nation, and Cooperation in the 1992–93 ERM Crisis," New Haven: Yale University (processed).

Canzoneri, M. B., and B. T. Diba (1991), "Fiscal Deficits, Financial Integration, and a Central Bank for Europe," *Journal of the Japanese and International Econo-mies* 5.

Canzoneri, M. B., and C. A. Rogers (1990), "Is the European Community an Optimal Currency Area? Optimal Taxation Versus the Costs of Multiple Currencies," *Ameri-can Economic Review* 80.

Casella, A. (1992), "Participation in a Currency Union," *American Economic Review* 82.
    (1993), "Discussion of Krugman," in Torres and Giavazzi, eds., *Adjustment and Growth in the European Monetary Union*, Cambridge: Cambridge University Press.

Cassard, M., T. Lane, and P. R. Masson (1994), "ERM Money Supplies and the Transition to EMU," Washington: International Monetary Fund (processed).

Chiappori, P. A., C. Mayer, D. Neven, and X. Vives (1991), "European Monetary Union – The Micro Issues," in *Monitoring European Integration: The Making of Monetary Union*, London: Centre for Economic Policy Research.

Chowdhury, A. R. (1993), "Does Exchange Rate Volatility Depress Trade Flows? Evi-dence from Error-Correction Models," *Review of Economics & Statistics* 75.

Ciampi, C. A. (1989), "An Operational Framework for an Integrated Monetary Policy in Europe," paper annexed to the Delors Report (1989).

Cobham, D. (1995), "From the Causes of the European Monetary Crises of 1992–93 to Strategies for European Monetary Union," Department of Economics Discussion Paper 9501, St. Andrews, Fife: University of St. Andrews.

Cohen, B. J. (1993), "Beyond EMU: The Problem of Sustainability," *Economics & Politics* 5.

Cohen, D., and C. Wyplosz (1989), "The European Monetary Union: An Agnostic Evalua-tion," in Bryant et al., eds., *Macroeconomic Policies in an Interdependent World*, Washington: The Brookings Institution.

Collignon, S. M. (1992), "An Ecu Zone for Central and Eastern Europe: A Supportive Framework for Convergence," in Barrell, ed., *Economic Convergence and Monetary Union in Europe*, London: Sage for the Association for the Monetary Union of Europe and the National Institute of Economic and Social Research.

Collignon, S. M., et al. (1993), *The EMS in Transition*, London: Pinter for the Association for the Monetary Union of Europe.

Collins, S. M. (1988), "Inflation and the European Monetary System," in Giavazzi, Micossi, and Miller, eds., *The European Monetary System*, Cambridge: Cambridge University Press.

Commission of the European Communities (1977), *Report of the Study Group on the Role of Public Finances in European Integration*, Brussels: Commission of the European Communities.

(1990), "One Market, One Money," *European Economy* 44.

(1993), "Stable Money – Sound Finances: Report of an Independent Group of Economists," *European Economy* 53.

(1995), *Interim Report of the Independent Expert Group on the Preparation of the Changeover to the Single European Currency*, Brussels: European Commission.

Committee for the Study of Economic and Monetary Union (1989), *Report*, Luxembourg: Office for Official Publications of the European Communities [cited here as Delors Report (1989)].

Committee of Governors Ad Hoc Working Group on EC Payment Systems (1992a), *Payment Systems in EC Member States*.

(1992b), *Issues of Common Concern to EC Central Banks in the Field of Payment Systems*.

(1993), *Minimum Common Features for Domestic Payment Systems: Report of the Working Group on EC Payment Systems*.

Committee of Governors of the Central Banks of the Member States of the European Economic Community (1993a), *Annual Report 1992*.

(1993b), *Report on the Implications and Lessons to be Drawn from the Recent Exchange Rate Crisis*.

Cooper, R. N. (1968), *The Economics of Interdependence*, New York: McGraw-Hill for the Council on Foreign Relations.

(1992a), "The 'Eurofed' Needs Accountability," *Economic Insights*, Washington: Institute for International Economics.

(1992b), "Will an EC Currency Harm Outsiders?" *Orbis* (Fall).

Corden, W. M. (1972), *Monetary Integration*, Essays in International Finance 93, Princeton: International Finance Section, Princeton University.

(1991), "Exchange Rate Policy in Developing Countries," in de Melo and Sapir, eds., *Trade Theory and Economic Reform*, Oxford: Blackwell.

(1993), "European Monetary Union: The Intellectual Prehistory," in Giovannini, Guitian, and Portes, eds., *The Monetary Future of Europe*, London: Centre for Economic Policy Research.

Corsetti, C., and N. Roubini (1991), "Fiscal Deficits, Public Debt and Government Solvency: Evidence from OECD Countries," *Journal of the Japanese and International Economies* 5.

(1993), "The Design of Optimal Fiscal Rules for Europe after 1992," in Torres and Giavazzi, eds., *Adjustment and Growth in the European Monetary Union*, Cambridge: Cambridge University Press.

Crockett, A. (1991a), "The Role of Stage II," paper presented at the Estoril Conference on the Transition to Economic and Monetary Unification in Europe (processed).

(1991b), "Monetary Integration in Europe," in Frenkel and Goldstein, eds., *International Financial Policy: Essays in Honor of Jacques J. Polak*, Washington: International Monetary Fund.

Cukierman, A. (1991), "Policy Outcomes in Stage Two and in the EMS versus Outcomes in a Union," paper presented at the Milan Conference on Monetary Policy in Stage Two of EMU (processed).

Currie, D. (1992a), "European Monetary Union: Institutional Structure and Economic Performance," *Economic Journal* 102.

(1992b), "Hard-ERM, Hard ECU, and European Monetary Union," in Canzoneri, Grilli, and Masson, eds., *Establishing a Central Bank: Issues in Europe and Lessons from the US*, Cambridge: Cambridge University Press.

Cushman, D. O. (1983), "The Effects of Real Exchange Rate Risk on International Trade," *Journal of International Economics* 15.

Davenport, M. (1992), "Exchange Rate Policy for Eastern Europe and a Peg to the ECU," Economic Papers 90, Brussels: Commission of the European Communities.

De Grauwe, P. (1990), "The Cost of Disinflation and the European Monetary System," *Open Economies Review* 1.

(1991), "Is the European Monetary System a DM-Zone?" in Steinherr and Weiserbs, eds., *Evolution of the International and Regional Monetary Systems*, New York: St. Martins.

(1992a), *The Economics of Monetary Integration*, Oxford: Oxford University Press.

(1992b), "Fiscal Discipline in Monetary Unions," *International Economic Journal* 6.

(1993a), "The Political Economy of Monetary Union in Europe," CEPR Discussion Paper 842, London: Centre for Economic Policy Research.

(1993b), "Discussion of Krugman," in Torres and Giavazzi, eds., *Adjustment and Growth in the European Monetary Union*, Cambridge: Cambridge University Press.

(1994), "Towards EMU without the EMS," *Economic Policy* 18.

De Grauwe, P., and W. Vanhaverbeke (1993), "Is Europe an Optimum Currency Area? Evidence from Regional Data," in Masson and Taylor, eds., *Policy Issues in the Operation of Currency Unions*, Cambridge: Cambridge University Press.

De la Dehesa, G., and P. Krugman (1993), "Monetary Union, Regional Cohesion and Regional Shocks," in Giovannini, Guitian, and Portes, eds., *The Monetary Future of Europe*, London: Centre for Economic Policy Research.

Delors Report (1989); see Committee for the Study of Economic and Monetary Union.

Deutsche Bundesbank (1989), *The Deutsche Bundesbank: Its Monetary Policy Instruments and Functions*, Frankfurt: Deutsche Bundesbank.

(1992), "The Maastricht Decision on the European Economic and Monetary Union," *Monthly Report* (February).

Dobson, W. (1991), *Economic Policy Coordination: Requiem or Prologue?* Policy Analysis in International Economics 30, Washington: Institute for International Economics.

Dominguez, K. (1990), "Market Responses to Coordinated Central Bank Intervention," *Carnegie-Rochester Conference Series on Public Policy* 32.

Dooley, M. (1995), "A Retrospective on the Debt Crisis," in Kenen, ed., *Understanding Interdependence: The Macroeconomics of the Open Economy*, Princeton: Princeton University Press.

Dornbusch, R. (1990), "Two-Track EMU, Now!" in Pohl et al., *Britain and EMU*, London: Centre for Economic Performance.

Drazen, A. (1989), "Monetary Policy, Capital Controls and Seigniorage in an Open Economy," in de Cecco and Giovannini, eds., *A European Central Bank?* Cambridge: Cambridge University Press.

Driffill, J. (1988), "The Stability and Sustainability of the European Monetary System with Perfect Capital Markets," in Giavazzi, Micossi, and Miller, eds., *The European Monetary System*, Cambridge: Cambridge University Press.

Eaton, J., M. Gersovitz, and J. Stiglitz (1986), "The Pure Theory of Country Risk," *European Economic Review* 30.

Edison, H. J., and L. S. Kole (1994), "European Monetary Arrangements: Implications for the Dollar, Exchange Rate Variability and Credibility," International Finance Discussion Paper 468, Washington: Board of Governors of the Federal Reserve System.

Edwards, S. (1986), "The Pricing of Bonds and Bank Loans in International Markets," *European Economic Review* 30.

(1992), "Exchange Rates as Nominal Anchors," NBER Working Paper 4346, Cambridge: National Bureau of Economic Research.

Egebo, T., and A. S. Englander (1992), "Institutional Commitments and Policy Credibility: A Critical Survey and Empirical Evidence from the ERM," *OECD Economic Studies* 18.

Eichengreen, B. (1990), "One Money for Europe? Lessons from the U.S. Currency and Customs Union," *Economic Policy* 10.

(1991), "Costs and Benefits of European Monetary Unification," in Beregevoy, ed., *L'intérêt économique de l'union monétaire*, Paris: Ministry of Finance (in French).

(1992a), "Toward a European Central Bank," *Revista de Occidente* 138 (in Spanish).

(1992b), "Designing a Central Bank for Europe: A Cautionary Tale from the Early Years of the Federal Reserve System," in Canzoneri, Grilli, and Masson, eds., *Establishing a Central Bank: Issues in Europe and Lessons from the US*, Cambridge: Cambridge University Press.

(1992c), "Is Europe an Optimum Currency Area?" in Borner and Grubel, eds., *The European Community after 1992: The View from Outside*, London: Macmillan.

(1992d), *Should the Maastricht Treaty Be Saved?* Princeton Studies in International Finance 74, Princeton: International Finance Section, Princeton University.

(1993a), "European Monetary Unification," *Journal of Economic Literature* 31.

(1993b), "Labor Markets and European Monetary Unification," in Masson and Taylor, eds., *Policy Issues in the Design of Currency Unions*, Cambridge: Cambridge University Press.

(1993c), "The Crisis in the EMS and the Transition to EMU: An Interim Assessment," in Honkapohja, ed., *Economic Policy Issues in Financial Integration*, Helsinki: Hakapaino Oy.

(1994), *International Monetary Arrangements for the 21st Century*, Brookings Studies on Integrating National Economies, Washington: The Brookings Institution.

Eichengreen, B., and T. Bayoumi (1994), "The Political Economy of Fiscal Restrictions: Implications for Europe from the United States," *European Economic Review* 38.

Eichengreen, B., and J. Frieden (1993), "The Political Economy of European Monetary Unification," *Economics & Politics* 5.

Eichengreen, B., A. Rose, and C. Wyplosz (1994), "Is There a Safe Passage to EMU? Evidence on Capital Controls and a Proposal," CEPR Discussion Paper 1061, London: Centre for Economic Policy Research.

Eichengreen, B., J. Tobin, and C. Wyplosz (1995), "Two Cases for Sand in the Wheels of International Finance," *Economic Journal* 105.

Eichengreen, B., and C. Wyplosz (1993), "The Unstable EMS," *Brookings Papers on Economic Activity* 1.

Emminger, O. (1986), *D–Mark, Dollar, Nährungskrisen*, Stuttgart: Deutsche Verlags-Austalt.

Fase, M. M. G. (1993), "The Stability of the Demand for Money in the G7 and EC Countries," CEPS Working Document 81, Brussels: Centre for European Policy Studies.

Feldstein, M. (1993), "Does European Monetary Union Have a Future?" in Giovannini, Guitian, and Portes, eds., *The Monetary Future of Europe*, London: Centre for Economic Policy Research.

Fischer, S. (1987), "British Monetary Policy," in Dornbusch and Layard, eds., *The Performance of the British Economy*, Oxford: Oxford University Press.

Flood, R. P., and P. M. Garber (1984), "Gold Monetization and Gold Discipline," *Journal of Political Economy* 92.

Folkerts-Landau, D. (1991), "Systemic Financial Risk in Payment Systems," in *Determinants and Systemic Consequences of International Capital Flows*, Occasional Paper 77, Washington: International Monetary Fund.

Folkerts-Landau, D., and P. M. Garber (1992a), "The ECB: A Bank or a Monetary Policy Rule," in Canzoneri, Grilli, and Masson, eds., *Establishing a Central Bank: Issues in Europe and Lessons from the US*, Cambridge: Cambridge University Press.

(1992b), "The Private ECU: A Currency Floating on Gossamer Wings," NBER Working Paper 4017, Cambridge: National Bureau of Economic Research.

Frankel, J. A. (1988), *Obstacles to International Macroeconomic Policy Coordination*, Princeton Studies in International Finance 64, Princeton: International Finance Section, Princeton University.

(1993), "Discussion of Buiter, Corsetti, and Roubini," *Economic Policy* 16.

Frankel, J. A., S. Phillips, and M. Chinn (1993), "Financial and Currency Integration in the European Monetary System: The Statistical Record," in Torres and Giavazzi, eds., *Adjustment and Growth in the European Monetary Union*, Cambridge: Cambridge University Press.

Fratianni, M. (1993), "What Went Wrong with the EMS and European Monetary Union," Discussion Paper 101, Bloomington: Indiana Center for Global Business, Indiana University.

Fratianni, M., and J. von Hagen (1992), *The European Monetary System and European Monetary Union*, Boulder: Westview.

Fratianni, M., J. von Hagen, and C. Waller (1992), *The Maastricht Way to EMU*, Essays in International Finance 187, Princeton: International Finance Section, Princeton University.

Frenkel, J. A., and M. Goldstein (1991), "Monetary Policy in an Emerging European Economic and Monetary Union," *IMF Staff Papers* 38.

Froot, K. A., and K. Rogoff (1992), "The EMS, the EMU, and the Transition to a Common Currency," *NBER Macroeconomics Annual*, Cambridge: MIT Press.

Funabashi, Y. (1989), *Managing the Dollar from the Plaza to the Louvre*, Washington: Institute for International Economics.

Garber, P., and M. P. Taylor (1995), "Sand in the Wheels of Foreign Exchange Markets: A Skeptical Note," *Economic Journal* 105.

Gardner, E. H., and W. R. M. Perraudin (1993), "Asymmetry in the EMS," *IMF Staff Papers* 40.

Garrett, J. (1993), "The Politics of Maastricht," *Economics & Politics* 5.

Ghosh, A. R., and P. R. Masson (1994), *Economic Cooperation in an Uncertain World*, Oxford: Basil Blackwell.

Ghosh, A. R., and H. C. Wolf (1994), "How Many Monies? A Genetic Approach to Finding Optimum Currency Areas" (processed).

Giavazzi, F., and A. Giovannini (1988), "The Role of the Exchange-Rate Regime in a

Disinflation," in Giavazzi, Micossi, and Miller, eds., *The European Monetary System*, Cambridge: Cambridge University Press.

(1989), *Limiting Exchange Rate Flexibility*, Cambridge: MIT Press.

Giavazzi, F., and M. Pagano (1988), "The Advantage of Tying One's Hands: EMS Discipline and Central Bank Credibility," *European Economic Review* 32.

Giovannini, A. (1989), "National Tax Systems versus the European Capital Market," *Economic Policy* 9.

(1990a), "European Monetary Reform: Progress and Prospects," *Brookings Papers on Economic Activity* 2.

(1990b), *The Transition to European Monetary Union*, Essays in International Finance 178, Princeton: International Finance Section, Princeton University.

(1991), "The Currency Reform as the Last Stage of Economic and Monetary Union," CEPR Discussion Paper 591, London: Centre for Economic Policy Research.

(1993), "Central Banking in a Monetary Union: Reflections on the Proposed Statute of the European Central Bank," *Carnegie-Rochester Conference Series on Public Policy* 38.

Giovannini, A., and L. Spaventa (1991), "Fiscal Rules in the European Monetary Union: A No-Entry Clause," CEPR Discussion Paper 516, London: Centre for Economic Policy Research.

Goldstein, M., et al. (1993), *International Capital Markets, Part I: Exchange Rate Management and International Capital Flows*, Washington: International Monetary Fund.

Goldstein, M., and S. E. Haynes (1984), "A Critical Appraisal of McKinnon's World Money Supply Hypothesis," *American Economic Review* 74.

Goldstein, M., and G. Woglom (1992), "Market-Based Fiscal Discipline in Monetary Unions," in Canzoneri, Grilli, and Masson, eds., *Establishing a Central Bank: Issues in Europe and Lessons from the US*, Cambridge: Cambridge University Press.

Goodhart, C. A. E. (1992a), "The ESCB after Maastricht," in Goodhart, ed., *EMU and ESCB after Maastricht*, London: Financial Markets Group, London School of Economics and Political Science.

(1992b), "The External Dimensions of EMU," in Goodhart, ed., *EMU and ESCB after Maastricht*, London: Financial Markets Group, London School of Economics and Political Science.

(1992c) "National Fiscal Policy within EMU: The Fiscal Implications of Maastricht," London: London School of Economics and Political Science (processed).

(1995), "The Political Economy of Monetary Union," in Kenen, ed., *Understanding Interdependence: The Macroeconomics of the Open Economy*, Princeton: Princeton University Press.

Goodhart, C. A. E., and S. Smith (1993), "Stabilization," in "The Economics of Community Public Finance," *European Economy: Reports and Studies* 5.

Gotur, P. (1985), "Effects of Exchange Rate Volatility on Trade: Some Further Evidence," *IMF Staff Papers* 32.

Greenspan, A. (1993), "No Single Regulator for Banks," *Washington Post*, December 15.

Grilli, V. (1989), "Seigniorage in Europe," in de Cecco and Giovannini, eds., *A European Central Bank?* London: Cambridge University Press.

Grilli, V., D. Masciandaro, and G. Tabellini (1991), "Political and Monetary Institutions and Public Financial Policies in the Industrial Countries," *Economic Policy* 13.

Gros, D. (1987), "The Effectiveness of Capital Controls: Implications for Monetary Autonomy in the Presence of Incomplete Market Separation," *IMF Staff Papers* 34.

(1991), "Reserve Requirements and EMU in Stage Two," paper presented at the Milan Conference on Monetary Policy in Stage Two of EMU (processed).

Gros, D., and E. Jones (1994), "Fiscal Stabilisers in the US Monetary Union," CEPS Working Document 83, Brussels: Centre for European Policy Studies.

Gros, D., and N. Thygesen (1992), *European Monetary Integration*, New York: St. Martin's.

Group of Ten (1993), *International Capital Movements and Foreign Exchange Markets: Report to the Ministers and Governors by the Group of Ten Deputies.*

Guttentag, J. M., and J. R. Herring (1986), *Disaster Myopia in International Banking*, Essays in International Finance 164, Princeton: International Finance Section, Princeton University.

Haldane, A. G. (1991), "The Exchange Rate Mechanism of the European Monetary System," *Bank of England Quarterly Bulletin* (February).

Henning, C. R. (1994), *Currencies and Politics in the United States, Germany, and Japan*, Washington: Institute for International Economics.

Hoffmeyer, E. (1993), "Preparatory Steps toward the Economic and Monetary Union: Statement at the European Currency Conference" (processed).

Hughes Hallett, A. J. (1992), "Discussion of Currie," in Canzoneri, Grilli, and Masson, eds., *Establishing a Central Bank: Issues in Europe and Lessons from the US*, Cambridge: Cambridge University Press.

Hughes Hallett, A. J., and Y. Ma (1994), "Transatlantic Policy Coordination with Sticky Labour Markets: The Reality of the Real Side" (processed).

Hughes Hallett, A. J., and D. Vines (1991), "On the Possible Costs of European Monetary Union," Discussion Paper 2, Glasgow: International Centre for Macroeconomic Modeling at the University of Strathclyde.

Huhne, C. (1991), "Opting Out Will Never Be an Option," *Independent on Sunday*, December 15.

Ingram, J. C. (1959), "State and Regional Payments Mechanisms," *Quarterly Journal of Economics* 73.

(1973), *The Case for European Monetary Integration*, Essays in International Finance 98, Princeton: International Finance Section, Princeton University.

International Monetary Fund (IMF) (1984), *Exchange Rate Volatility and World Trade*, Occasional Paper 28, Washington: International Monetary Fund.

(1993), *World Economic Outlook: October 1993*, Washington: International Monetary Fund.

Italianer, A. (1993), "Mastering Maastricht: EMU Issues and How They Were Settled," in Gretschmann, ed., *Economic and Monetary Union: Implications for National Policy-Makers*, Amsterdam: European Institute of Public Administration.

Italianer, A., and J. Pisani-Ferry (1994), "The Regional-Stabilization Properties of Fiscal Arrangements," in Mortensen, ed., *Improving Economic and Social Cohesion in the European Community*, London: Macmillan.

Italianer, A., and M. Vanheukelen (1993), "Proposals for Community Stabilization Mechanisms: Some Historical Applications," in "The Economics of Community Public Finance," *European Economy: Reports and Studies* 5.

Jacquet, P. (1993), "The Politics of EMU: A Selective Overview," in Giovannini, Guitian, and Portes, eds., *The Monetary Future of Europe*, London: Centre for Economic Policy Research.

Johnson, K. H. (1994), "International Dimensions of European Monetary Union: Implications for the Dollar," International Finance Discussion Paper 496, Washington: Board of Governors of the Federal Reserve System.

Kenen, P. B. (1969), "The Theory of Optimum Currency Areas: An Eclectic View," in Mundell and Swoboda, eds., *Monetary Problems of the International Economy*, Chicago: University of Chicago Press.

(1981), "The Analytics of a Substitution Account," Banca Nazionale del Lavoro, *Quarterly Review* (December).

(1983), *The Role of the Dollar as an International Currency*, Occasional Paper 13, New York: Group of Thirty.

(1988a), "Reflections on the EMS Experience," in Giavazzi, Micossi, and Miller, eds., *The European Monetary System*, Cambridge: Cambridge University Press.

(1988b), *Managing Exchange Rates*, London: Royal Institute of International Affairs.

(1989), *Exchange Rates and Policy Coordination*, Ann Arbor: University of Michigan Press.

(1991), "Exchange Rate Arrangements, Seigniorage, and the Provision of Public Goods," in Frenkel and Goldstein, eds., *International Financial Policy: Essays in Honor of Jacques J. Polak*, Washington: International Monetary Fund.

(1992a), "Speaking Up for Emu," *Financial Times*, July 28.

(1992b), *EMU after Maastricht*, Washington: Group of Thirty.

(1992c), "Third World Debt," in Newman et al., eds., *The New Palgrave Dictionary of Money and Finance*, London: Macmillan.

(1993a), "EMU, Exchange Rates, and the International Monetary System," *Recherches Economiques de Louvain* 59.

(1993b), "EMU Reconsidered," paper presented at the Washington Conference on European Economic and Political Integration sponsored by the Department of State (processed).

(1994a), "Floating Exchange Rates Reconsidered: The Influence of New Ideas, Priorities, and Problems," in Kenen, Papadia, and Saccomanni, eds., *The International Monetary System*, Cambridge: Cambridge University Press.

(1994b), "Monetary Arrangements: Comment," in Henning, Hochreiter, and Hufbauer, eds., *Reviving the European Union*, Washington: Institute for International Economics.

(1995), "Capital Controls, the EMS, and EMU," *Economic Journal* 105.

Kenen, P. B., and D. Rodrik (1986), "Measuring and Analyzing the Effects of Short-Term Volatility in Real Exchange Rates," *Review of Economics & Statistics* 68.

Kennedy, E. (1991), *The Bundesbank: Germany's Central Bank in the International Monetary System*, London: Royal Institute of International Affairs.

Kneeshaw, J. T., and P. Van den Bergh (1989), *Changes in Central Bank Money Market Operating Procedures in the 1980s*, BIS Economic Papers 23, Basle: Bank for International Settlements.

(1990), "Economic and Monetary Integration and the Aggregate Demand for Money in the EMS," *IMF Staff Papers* 37.

Kremers, J. M., and T. D. Lane (1990), "Economic and Monetary Integration and the Aggregate Demand for Money in the EMS," *IMF Staff Papers* 37.

(1992), "The Demand for Money in Europe: Reply to Barr," *IMF Staff Papers* 39.

Krugman, P. (1980), "Vehicle Currencies and the Structure of International Exchange," *Journal of Money, Credit and Banking* 12.

(1984), "The International Role of the Dollar: Theory and Prospect," in Bilson and Marston, eds., *Exchange Rate Theory and Practice*, Chicago: University of Chicago Press.

(1993), "Lessons of Massachusetts for EMU," in Torres and Giavazzi, eds., *Adjustment and Growth in the European Monetary Union*, Cambridge: Cambridge University Press.

Kumar, V., and J. Whitt (1992), "Exchange Rate Variability and International Trade," Federal Reserve Bank of Atlanta, *Economic Review* 77.

Lamfalussy, A. (1989), "Macro-Coordination of Fiscal Policies in an Economic and Monetary Union in Europe," paper annexed to the Delors Report (1989).

Lane, T. D. (1993), "Market Discipline," *IMF Staff Papers* 40.

Langfeldt, E. (1992), "European Monetary Union: Design and Implementation," in Barrell, ed., *Economic Convergence and Monetary Union in Europe*, London: Sage for the Association for the Monetary Union of Europe and the National Institute of Economic and Social Research.

Lastra, R. M. (1992), "The Independence of the European System of Central Banks," *Harvard International Law Journal* 33.

Leahy, M. P. (1994), "The Dollar as an Official Reserve Currency under EMU," International Finance Discussion Paper 474, Washington: Board of Governors of the Federal Reserve System.

Levine, P., and J. Pearlman (1994), "Labour Market Structure, Conservative Bankers, and the Feasibility of Monetary Union," CEPR Discussion Paper 903, London: Centre for Economic Policy Research.

Ludlow, P. (1982), *The Making of the EMS*, London: Butterworth.

(1993), "Beyond Maastricht: Recasting the European Political and Economic System," CEPS Working Document 79, Brussels: Centre for European Policy Studies.

MacDougall, D. (1992), "Economic and Monetary Union and the European Community Budget," *National Institute Economic Review*.

McKinnon, R. I. (1982), "Currency Substitution and Instability in the World Dollar Standard," *American Economic Review* 72.

(1984), *An International Standard for Monetary Stabilization*, Policy Analyses in International Economics 8, Washington: Institute for International Economics.

McNamara, K. R. (1994), "Economic and Monetary Union in Europe: Do Domestic Politics Matter? Does Hegemony?" Princeton: Princeton University (processed).

Mancera, M. (1991), "Characteristics and Implications of Different Types of Currency Areas," in *Policy Implications of Trade and Currency Zones*, Kansas City: Federal Reserve Bank of Kansas City.

Martin, L. L. (1993), "International and Domestic Institutions in the EMU Process," *Economics & Politics* 5.

Martin, P. (1992), "Choosing Central Bankers in Europe," Geneva: Graduate Institute of International Studies (processed).

Masson, P. R., and J. Melitz (1990), "Fiscal Policy Independence in a European Monetary Union," *Open Economies Review* 2.

Masson, P. R., and S. Symansky (1992), "Evaluating the EMS and EMU Using Stochastic Simulations," in Barrell and Whitley, eds., *Macroeconomic Policy Coordination in Europe: The ERM and Monetary Union*, London: Sage.

Masson, P. R., and M. P. Taylor (1992), "Issues in the Operations of Monetary Unions and Common Currency Areas," in Goldstein et al., *Policy Issues in the Evolving International Monetary System*, Washington: International Monetary Fund, Occasional Paper 96.

Mastropasqua, C., S. Micossi, and R. Rinaldi (1988), "Intervention, Sterilization and Monetary Policy in European Monetary System Countries, 1979–87," in Giavazzi, Micossi, and Miller, eds., *The European Monetary System*, Cambridge: Cambridge University Press.

Melitz, J. (1993), "Reflections on the Emergence of a Single Market for Bank Reserves in a European Monetary Union," CEPR Discussion Paper 818, London: Centre for Economic Policy Research.

206   References

(1994), "French Monetary Policy and Recent Speculative Attacks on the Franc," in Cobham, ed., *The 1992–93 Upheavals in the European Monetary System*, Manchester: Manchester University Press.

Minford, P. (1993), "Discussion of Bayoumi and Eichengreen," in Torres and Giavazzi, eds., *Adjustment and Growth in the European Monetary Union*, Cambridge: Cambridge University Press.

Mishkin, F. (1993), "Comment on Monticelli and Viñals," in Giovannini, Guitian, and Portes, eds., *The Monetary Future of Europe*, London: Centre for Economic Policy Research.

Monetary Committee of the European Community (1993), *Report on the Lessons to be Drawn from the Disturbances on the Foreign Exchange Markets*.

Monticelli, C., and M. O. Strauss-Kahn (1992), "European Integration and the Demand for Broad Money," Basle: Economic Unit of the Committee of Governors of the EEC Central Banks (processed).

Monticelli, C., and J. Viñals (1993), "European Monetary Policy in Stage Three: What Are the Issues?" in Giovannini, Guitian, and Portes, eds., *The Monetary Future of Europe*, London: Centre for Economic Policy Research.

Muehring, K. (1992), "Currency Chaos: The Inside Story," *Institutional Investor*, October 12.

Mundell, R. A. (1961), "A Theory of Optimum Currency Areas," *American Economic Review* 51.

(1993), "EMU and the International Monetary System," in Giovannini, Guitian, and Portes, eds., *The Monetary Future of Europe*, London: Centre for Economic Policy Research.

Neumann, M. J. M. (1991), "Central Bank Independence as a Prerequisite of Price Stability," in "The Economics of EMU," *European Economy*, Special Edition 1.

Nölling, W. (1993), *Monetary Policy in Europe after Maastricht*, London: Macmillan.

Norman, P. (1992), "The Day Germany Planted a Currency Time Bomb," *Financial Times*, December 12–13.

Obstfeld, M. (1986), "Rational and Self-Fulfilling Balance-of-Payments Crises," *American Economic Review*, 76.

(1994), "The Logic of Currency Crises," NBER Working Paper 4640, Cambridge: National Bureau of Economic Research.

Padoa-Schioppa, T. (1988), "The European Monetary System: A Long-Term View," in Giavazzi, Micossi, and Miller, eds., *The European Monetary System*, Cambridge: Cambridge University Press.

(1994), "Introduction" to *Europe on the Road to Monetary Union*, Oxford: Oxford University Press.

Padoa-Schioppa, T., and F. Saccomanni (1992), "Agenda for Stage Two: Preparing the Monetary Platform," CEPR Occasional Paper 7, London: Centre for Economic Policy Research.

Papadia, F., and F. Saccomanni (1994), "From the Werner Plan to the Maastricht Treaty: Europe's Stubborn Quest for Monetary Union," in Steinherr, ed., *Thirty Years of European Monetary Integration: From the Werner Plan to EMU*, London: Longman.

Pisani-Ferry, J. (1992), "After the Monetary Turmoil," *Economic Insights*, Washington: Institute for International Economics.

Pisani-Ferry, J., A. Italianer, and R. Lescure (1993), "Stabilization Properties of Budgetary Systems: A Simulation Exercise," in "The Economics of Community Public Finance," *European Economy: Reports and Studies* 5.

Pisani-Ferry, J., et al. (1993), *A French Perspective on EMU*, Paris: Commissariat Général du Plan.

Portes, R. (1993), "EMS and EMU after the Fall," *The World Economy* 16.

Revenga, A. (1993), "Credibility and Inflation Persistence in the European Monetary System," Working Paper 9321, Madrid: Banco de España.

Rey, J. J. (1993), "Comment on Monticelli and Viñals," in Giovannini, Guitian, and Portes, eds., *The Monetary Future of Europe*, London: Centre for Economic Policy Research.

Rieke, W. (1994), "Monetary Arrangements: Comment," in Henning, Hochreiter, and Hufbauer, eds., *Reviving the European Union*, Washington: Institute for International Economics.

Rogoff, K. (1991), "NAChos and ECUs: On the Relative Merits of a North American Currency Union versus a European Currency Union," paper presented at a meeting of the Federal Reserve Board and Academic Consultants (processed).

Rose, A. K., and L. E. O. Svensson (1993), "European Exchange Rate Credibility Before the Fall," NBER Working Paper 4495, Cambridge: National Bureau of Economic Research.

Russo, M., and G. Tullio (1988), "Monetary Policy Coordination within the European Monetary System: Is There a Rule?" in Giavazzi, Micossi, and Miller, eds., *The European Monetary System*, Cambridge: Cambridge University Press.

Sala-i-Martin, X., and J. Sachs (1992), "Fiscal Federalism and Optimum Currency Areas: Evidence for Europe from the United States," in Canzoneri, Grilli, and Masson, eds., *Establishing a Central Bank: Issues in Europe and Lessons from the US*, Cambridge: Cambridge University Press.

Sarcinelli, M. (1992) "The European Central Bank: A Full-Fledged Scheme or Just a Fledgling," Banca Nazionale del Lavoro, *Quarterly Review* 181.

Sardelis, C. (1993), "Targeting a European Monetary Aggregate: Review and Current Issues," Economic Papers 102, Brussels: Commission of the European Communities.

Schulmann, H. (1993), "Comment on Begg and Wyplosz," in Giovannini, Guitian, and Portes, eds., *The Monetary Future of Europe*, London: Centre for Economic Policy Research.

Spaventa, L. (1993), "Comment on Mundell," in Giovannini, Guitian, and Portes, eds., *The Monetary Future of Europe*, London: Centre for Economic Policy Research.

Spinelli, F. (1983), "Currency Substitution, Flexible Exchange Rates, and the Case for International Monetary Cooperation: Discussion of a Recent Proposal," *IMF Staff Papers* 30.

Strauss-Kahn, M. O. (1992), "A Framework to Assess Monetary Policy Instruments and Procedures in EC Countries," Basle: Economic Unit of the Committee of Governors of the EEC Central Banks (processed).

Svensson, L. E. O. (1992), "Assessing Target Zone Credibility: Mean Reversion and Devaluation Expectations in the EMS 1973–1992," *European Economic Review* 36.

(1993), "Fixed Exchange Rates as a Means to Price Stability: What Have We Learned?" NBER Working Paper 4504; Cambridge: National Bureau of Economic Research.

Swoboda, A. K. (1991), *The Road to European Monetary Union: Lessons from the Bretton Woods Regime*, The 1991 Per Jacobsson Lecture, Washington: The Per Jacobsson Foundation, International Monetary Fund.

Thursby, J. G., and M. C. Thursby (1987), "Bilateral Trade Flows, the Linder Hypothesis, and Exchange Risk," *Review of Economics & Statistics* 69.

Thygesen, N. (1989), "A European Central Banking System – Some Analytical and Operational Considerations," paper annexed to the Delors Report (1989).

(1993a), "EMU: A Solid Framework from Maastricht," in Giovannini, Guitian, and Portes, eds., *The Monetary Future of Europe*, London: Centre for Economic Policy Research.

208   **References**

(1993b), "Economic and Monetary Union: Critical Notes on the Maastricht Treaty Revisions," in Torres and Giavazzi, eds., *Adjustment and Growth in the European Monetary Union*, Cambridge: Cambridge University Press.

(1994), "Monetary Arrangements," in Henning, Hochreiter, and Hufbauer, eds., *Reviving the European Union*, Washington: Institute for International Economics.

Turner, P., and J. Van't dack (1993), *Measuring International Price and Cost Competitiveness*, BIS Economic Papers 39, Basle, Bank for International Settlements.

Ungerer, H., O. Evans, T. Mayer, and P. Young (1986), *The European Monetary System: Recent Developments*, Occasional Paper 48, Washington: International Monetary Fund.

Ungerer, H., J. J. Hauvonen, A. Lopez-Claros, and T. Mayer (1990), *The European Monetary System: Developments and Prospects*, Occasional Paper 73, Washington: International Monetary Fund.

United Kingdom (U.K.) Treasury (1989), *An Evolutionary Approach to Economic and Monetary Union*, London: Her Majesty's Stationery Office.

(1991), *Economic and Monetary Union – Beyond Stage I: Possible Treaty Provisions and Statute for a European Monetary Fund*.

van der Ploeg, F. (1991a), "Macroeconomic Policy Coordination Issues during the Various Phases of Economic and Monetary Integration in Europe," in "The Economics of EMU," *European Economy*, Special Edition 1.

(1991b), "Budgetary Aspects of Economic and Monetary Integration in Europe," CEPR Discussion Paper 492, London: Centre for Economic Policy Research.

Viñals, J. (1994), "Building a Monetary Union in Europe: Is It Worthwhile, Where Do We Stand, and Where Are We Going?" Working Paper 9412, Madrid: Banco de España.

von Hagen, J. (1992), "Fiscal Arrangements in a Monetary Union: Evidence from the U.S.," in de Boissieu and Fair, eds., *Fiscal Policy, Taxes, and the Financial System in an Increasingly Integrated Europe*, Deventer: Kluwer.

von Hagen, J., and M. Fratianni (1993), "The Transition to European Monetary Union and the European Monetary Institute," *Economics & Politics* 5.

von Hagen, J., and M. J. M. Neumann (1994), "Real Exchange Rates within and between Currency Areas: How Far Away Is EMU?" *Review of Economics & Statistics* 76.

von Hagen, J., and R. Suppel (1994), "Central Bank Constitutions for Monetary Unions," CEPR Discussion Paper 919, London: Centre for Economic Policy Research.

Weber, A. A. (1991a), "EMU and Asymmetries and Adjustment Problems in the EMS," in "The Economics of EMU," *European Economy*, Special Edition 1.

(1991b), "Reputation and Credibility in the European Monetary System," *Economic Policy* 12.

(1993), "Discussion of Corsetti and Roubini," in Torres and Giavazzi, eds., *Adjustment and Growth in the European Monetary Union*, Cambridge: Cambridge University Press.

Williamson, J. (1992a), "External Implications of EMU," in Barrell, ed., *Economic Convergence and Monetary Union in Europe*, London: Sage for the Association for the Monetary Union of Europe and the National Institute of Economic and Social Research.

(1992b), "How to Reform the ERM," *Economic Insights*, Washington: Institute for International Economics.

(1993) "The Rise and Fall of Political Support for EMU," in Giovannini, Guitian, and Portes, eds., *The Monetary Future of Europe*, London: Centre for Economic Policy Research.

Williamson, J., and C. R. Henning (1994), "Managing the Monetary System," in Kenen, ed., *Managing the World Economy: Fifty Years after Bretton Woods*, Washington: Institute for International Economics.

Wyplosz, C. (1989), "Asymmetry in the EMS: Intentional or Systemic?" *European Economic Review* 33.

(1991), "Monetary Union and Fiscal Policy Discipline," in "The Economics of EMU," *European Economy*, Special Edition 1.

Index

Author index

Subject index